Yale Historical Publications
Lewis P. Curtis, Editor

History of Art: 20
George A. Kubler, Editor

When the materials are all prepared and ready, the
    architects shall appear.
I swear to you the architects shall appear without fail,
I swear to you they will understand you and justify you,
The greatest among them shall be he who best knows you,
    and encloses all and is faithful to all,
He and the rest shall not forget you, they shall perceive
    that you are not an iota less than they,
You shall be fully glorified in them.

Whitman, *Leaves of Grass*, 1855.

THE SHINGLE STYLE

and

THE STICK STYLE

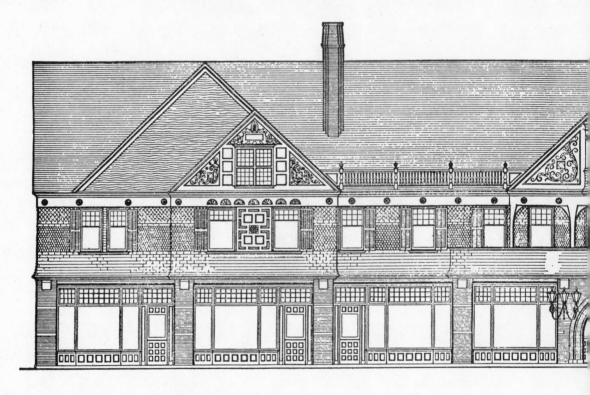

REVISED EDITION

BY VINCENT J. SCULLY, JR.

Architectural Theory and Design
from Downing to the Origins of Wright

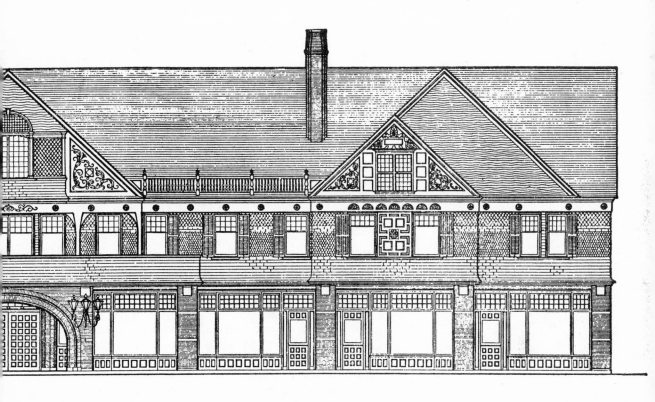

NEW HAVEN AND LONDON, YALE UNIVERSITY PRESS

To my parents and my wife

Contents

Illustrations

Preface to the Revised Edition

This edition of *The Shingle Style* unites, for the first time since they were written, Parts I and II of my doctoral dissertation, *The Cottage Style,* of 1949. Part I was separated from the rest, considerably cut, and published as an article in the *Art Bulletin* of June, 1953. I am grateful to that distinguished publication for permitting its reprinting here. So republished, it reunites the Stick Style, with which it deals, with the Shingle Style, which grew out of it.

I have made a few corrections and additions in footnotes and captions, and have tried to bring the Bibliographical Note up to date. The text has been left as it was written: youthful and earnest, for which no apologies can be made. It was, in any event, the first study that tried to take the written statements of nineteenth-century architects at face value and to reconsider their work in the light of their intentions. Since no work of art is a simple sum of its creator's objectives, there is always some danger of falling into the "intentional fallacy" through such an approach. But that fallacy can be avoided by a close visual analysis of the works of art themselves, so that intentions and results are tested against each other and a more complete knowledge of the form and meaning of each work can be gained. The character of the creative process as a whole can also be approached in this way, but such was not the major intention here, where the focus was obsessively close upon the houses of the Stick and Shingle styles themselves.

No American living in 1970 can look back upon those houses without some nostalgia, disappointment, or even sorrow. They promised a great deal for American life which has not been fulfilled, despite their many distinguished descendants three generations ago and today. Some of their architects, too, felt nostalgia for times gone by and sadness for promises unfulfilled, and they made a creative force out of those emotions. Perhaps this generation will do the same. Clearly enough, the stick and shingle houses, like the colonial work which in part inspired them, were the product of an America which, despite its civil strife, was infinitely smaller and less psychologically beset than that of the present day. Regarded purely as architecture, those houses were surely even better than I thought they were when I wrote about them, and they have proved to be even more important in a historical sense and as the inspiration for new architecture themselves. The work of Robert Venturi, for example, began to build directly upon their example in 1960, exactly as that of Frank Lloyd Wright had done in 1889 (Figs. 155, 162, 163). They were the freest and, on the whole, among the most generous forms that the United States has yet produced, and they created that kind of architectural environment. In their own way they were also the gentlest forms: the most relaxed and spiritually open and, in the Shingle Style especially, the most wholly wedded to the landscape.

Generous and gentle: they are not words which we can easily apply to ourselves in these years of blood and madness. There was evil in the nineteenth century too. All the more reason to value these houses and their architects, long dead, whose purposes were humane.

New Haven, Connecticut
1970   V.J.S.

Preface

Although this book is concerned with only one phase in the development of American domestic architecture—the wooden, suburban building of the period 1872 to about 1889—the objectives of the study are larger than these limits in time and program might seem at first to indicate.

The primary objective is to illuminate the main course of theory and design which developed by the late 19th century into a unique American achievement in architecture, one which has since been acclaimed by the whole world.[1] The synthesis making that achievement possible would seem to have taken place in wooden domestic architecture between the above dates. The tightness of the time sequence in this development is itself significant. One approaches, in these years and in this program, a critical moment during which the past bore fruit and from which much later growth evolved. The philosophical and formal basis for Frank Lloyd Wright's work, for example, was in large measure laid down during this period, as were also the bases for the colonial revival and 20th-century eclecticism.

Elsewhere I have briefly indicated some of the main characteristics of this development.[2] Here I shall attempt to present the material with full documentation and in detail. My concern is with a process of growth in architectural thought and design and with the buildings, projects, and writings of architects themselves as these formed part of the process. I shall be less concerned with the biographies of individual architects and with their clients,

1. As in Bruno Zevi, *Towards an Organic Architecture*, London, 1949. Wishing to direct European architecture along a new path, Zevi, an Italian architect, calls to his support the American development, with which he is apparently familiar principally through the comments of Siegfried Giedion, *Space, Time and Architecture* (Cambridge, 1943), Pt. 5, "American Development," pp. 258–348.

2. Antoinette F. Downing and Vincent J. Scully, Jr., *The Architectural Heritage of Newport Rhode Island* (Cambridge, Mass., 1952), "The Shingle Style," pp. 141–63; pls. 186–230. See also my "American Villas. Inventiveness in the American Suburb from Downing to Wright," *Architectural Review, 115* (March, 1954), 168–79.

except as these seem to clarify the development itself in significant ways.

Nevertheless, a secondary objective of the study is to present, in their historical context and as part of a general movement, some works by important American architects who are too little known at the present time: Robert Swain Peabody, of Boston; William Ralph Emerson, of Boston; John Calvin Stevens, of Portland, Maine; Arthur Little, of Boston; Wilson Eyre, of Philadelphia; Bruce Price, of New York; and the firm of McKim, Mead, and White before 1887. No claim can be made here that definitive attention has been given any one of these men; all deserve further study.

Finally, this book deals with one generation's search for expression and for order in American architecture, with its typically 19th century quest for a usable past and for types, and, lastly, with its momentary transcendence of the types and its eventual but not total reversion to them. The problem involves a single but revealing aspect of the modern world's search for itself.

In somewhat longer form this work was presented in 1949 as a dissertation for the degree of Doctor of Philosophy in Yale University. I wish to express my appreciation to George Heard Hamilton, under whose direction the dissertation was written, and to Lewis Curtis, Sumner McK. Crosby, and George Kubler, who read the manuscript and assisted in revising it. My gratitude also goes to Carroll L. V. Meeks, Theodore Sizer, and the late John Marshall Phillips, who assisted in various ways.

I am especially indebted to Henry-Russell Hitchcock, Jr., of Smith College, who gave me free access to his architecture files and whose previous scholarship in 19th- and 20th-century American architecture forms a substratum for this book. I am also obligated to William King Covell, James McNeely, Wayne Andrews, and to all those who have allowed me to reproduce photographs for publication. Further acknowledgment is made in the captions.

My thanks are due Mrs. Charles Wakeman and Folke Nyberg for assistance with the illustrations, to Robert Branner for editorial help, and to Miss Ruth Marriner for typing. The index was made by David Horne. To my wife who has, since 1948 when this work was begun, checked references, taken photographs, criticized the text, and otherwise assisted in numberless ways, goes much more appreciation than can easily be acknowledged here. My gratitude also goes to the members of the Yale Press who took part in producing this book, and with whom I enjoyed the most pleasant and instructive of associations. I am especially grateful for the Morse fellowship which gave me necessary time for travel and research during 1951–52, and to the Morse Fund which was of assistance in publication.

V. J. S.

New Haven, Connecticut
1954

Introduction. Romantic Rationalism and the Expression of Structure in Wood:

Downing, Wheeler, Gardner, and the "Stick Style" 1840-1876[1]

By the later nineteenth century, American domestic architecture had clearly begun to demonstrate positive characteristics of originality and invention. In order to understand the character of this architecture, now acclaimed by critics in all countries, it is most important that we familiarize ourselves with the theoretical and formal tradition out of which it grew. This Introduction is therefore concerned with the rural and suburban architecture of the mid-century. To understand it, and moreover really to see it, we must look into the opinions of the theorists of the time, and examine their proposals for a new domestic architecture as they really intended to present them. In this way, we may hope to acquire an understanding of this architecture as it was intended to be, and a vision of it as it was intended to be seen.

Since this is our aim, an article which appeared in the new *American Architect and Building News,* in 1876, can be of great assistance to us.[2] Entitled

1. In a somewhat longer version this Introduction formed Part I of "The Cottage Style," my doctoral dissertation presented in Yale University, June 1949. It is reprinted here, with kind permission, from *Art Bulletin, 35* (June 1953), 121.

2. Roos characterizes the *American Architect and Building News* as "our first architectural magazine" (Frank J. Roos, Jr., *Writings on Early American Architecture,* Columbus,

"American Architecture—Past," it reveals a reaction against the mid-century, and it demonstrates what the new forces of change in the later seventies believed the mid-century to be. After discussing Colonial and Greek Revival architecture quite sympathetically, but mentioning no names of individual architects, it continues:

> But after a while the Gothic revival which had set in abroad made itself felt here. . . . It upset all our good habits of work; and while it took away from unskillful men the safeguard of a definite rule of procedure, at the first it supplied them with no principles of guidance . . . every man's mother wit was his own guide. Here was a great community, growing fast, quite unsupplied with buildings to suit its needs, and calling for an immense amount of work; a large, enterprising body of mechanics, altogether unused to design, but having plenty of confidence in themselves, and believed by a good part of the community to be as capable of design as anybody; and there was no trained and organized body of architects to fix the standard of taste. . . . Not one but a dozen new styles were given us for imitation. Since nobody understood them, nobody could prove that another did not. . . . Mr. Downing and a host of incapable persons published books full of bad designs; and enterprising carpenters and masons, or amateurs who could or could not handle a pencil, with these books on hand, felt themselves as good as architects. . . . Of course, under these circumstances, any general discipline was impossible, and style went to the bad . . . the common building of the country lost almost at once its character of decent refinement, and flowered into indescribable vulgarity. . . .[3]

This early and violently unfavorable reaction to mid-century building is extremely interesting in view of later developments. What concerns us at present is the general way in which this work is characterized, namely, as an architecture of carpenters, working at top speed to fill a nationwide need for

---

1943, p. 7). This statement is misleading, since architectural magazines of various kinds had existed earlier, notably *Sloan's,* which ran for a few years in the late sixties, and the *American Builder,* which began publication in 1869 and continued throughout the rest of the century. However, the *American Architect* was the first magazine planned specifically to appeal to architects as professional men rather than to vernacular builders, and which was able to maintain a continuous existence. Its appearance marked that new dominance of the architectural magazine over the architectural Pattern Book which was very important in the developments of the later seventies and eighties. Its first editor was William Rotch Ware, a graduate of the Ecole des Beaux-Arts.

3. "American Architecture—Past," *American Architect, I* (July 29, 1876), 242.

fast building and using as inspiration "books full of bad designs."[4] The name mentioned as most important in this development—and the only American name mentioned in the entire article—is that of Andrew Jackson Downing. Moreover, as one moves backward in time through the books published in the early seventies, the sixties, and the fifties, one finds that Downing's name is constantly invoked by each of the authors. Each of them feels himself to be continuing, expanding, or redefining Downing's objectives and ideas.[5] It would therefore seem logical to concern ourselves first of all with Downing himself and, through him, with those "enterprising carpenters" who, with Downing's and his successors' "books on hand, felt themselves as good as architects," and through whose work "style went to the bad."

It shall be my intention to show that through a study of the texts and published designs of Downing and of the other House Pattern Books of the mid-century, it is possible to acquire a real understanding of and sympathy for the aspirations of American domestic architecture during this period, especially that built of wood. In aspiration, for example, this architecture is not regional, but truly national, and may even be considered to exhibit the major characteristics of a fully developing architectural style. If there is not here the "royal progress" of Gothic art in the twelfth century, there appear in retrospect to have been at least many of the same characteristics of structural development and organic growth. Above all, it will be seen that the various "styles" supposedly involved eclectically do not affect the basic logic of the main development, which is a free and independent one, and that these "styles" are indeed usually used as a kind of pretext for, or rationalization of, independent formal invention.

A study of the bibliography of nineteenth century domestic architecture reveals immediately one very important fact—the disappearance in the mid-century of the older Builders' Guides in favor of the new House Pattern

4. It may be interesting to note some of the article's reasons for believing that the situation had improved somewhat by 1876. It says, "foreign study became more common and influential. . . . The profession began to work together; a distincter demarcation was established between building and architecture" (*ibid.*, p. 244). It will be observed that already, in 1876, some of the characteristics both of academic thought and of the class-conscious architect were becoming apparent here.

5. For example: "The prevailing taste in country dwellings, before Mr. Downing's time, was defective enough . . . and we revere the memory of Downing, and of others like him, who were instrumental in bringing in a better taste in such matters" (Charles Evertson Woodward, *Woodward's Country Homes* . . . , New York, 1865, pp. 17–18). "The admirable publications of the much lamented Downing gave a new and lasting impulse to the architecture of our country residences" (William Henry Cleaveland, William Backus, and Samuel D. Backus, *Village and Farm Cottages* . . . , New York, 1856, Preface, p. iv).

Books. As Hitchcock has stated: "Down into the 1830's books of the Builders'
Guide type predominated, but from the mid-forties on, House Pattern Books
began to appear in greater quantity and soon superseded the Builders' Guides
almost completely."[6] Hitchcock notes the main difference between the two
types as follows: in the Builders' Guides, "the graphic material consists chiefly
of plates of the orders, together with other plates showing elements of detail
both structural and ornamental," with possibly a few plans and elevations of
houses included; but ". . . books in which plans and designs for houses form
the bulk of the graphic material may properly be called 'House Pattern Books'
as distinguished from Builders' Guides." The Builders' Guides were, actually,
the chief vehicle for the Greek Revival in domestic work, and their main
purpose was to teach carpenters how to handle the classical details.[7] Owen
Biddle's book of 1805[8] and Asher Benjamin's of 1806,[9] although neither of
them yet offered the Greek orders "correctly" in the tradition of Chambers,
set the tone for those which followed. These chiefly contain plates of classical
details, explanations of simple systems of geometrical measurement in order
to cut moldings, and the like. Benjamin's most popular work, *The Practical
House Carpenter*,[10] which was issued seventeen times between 1830 and
1857, contains no plans or complete elevations, and concentrates solely upon
details, all classical. Benjamin's *Builder's Guide*,[11] a similar work, was first
published in 1839 and last issued sometime shortly after 1858. It is important
to note that these books, having been for some time exceedingly popular, went
out of favor in the late fifties. Minard Lafever's publications also follow the
same curve of popularity and eventual disappearance. His *Modern Builder's*

6. Henry-Russell Hitchcock, *American Architectural Books: A List of Books, Portfolios,
and Pamphlets on Architecture and Related Subjects Published in America before 1895*,
3rd ed., Minneapolis, 1946, p. iii.

7. See Talbot Hamlin, "The Greek Revival in America and Some of Its Critics," *Art
Bulletin, 24* (1942), 244ff., figs. 10–20.

8. Owen Biddle, *The Young Carpenter's Assistant; or, A system of architecture, adapted
to the style of building in the United States*, Philadelphia, 1805. The last issue of this book
appeared in 1858.

9. Asher Benjamin, *The American Builder's Companion; or, A new system of architecture
particularly adapted to the present style of building in the United States of America*, Boston,
1806. Last issue 1827. This was the first to offer Greek orders. For data on other books cited,
see Hitchcock, *op.cit.*

10. Asher Benjamin, *The Practical House Carpenter*, etc., Boston, 1830. Last issue
1857 (n.d.).

11. Asher Benjamin, *The Builder's Guide, illustrated by sixty-six engravings, which
exhibit the orders of architecture*, Boston, 1839.

Guide,[12] published in 1833, went through seven printings and disappeared after 1855; and his *Beauties of Modern Architecture*,[13] 1835, also had its last printing in 1855. His last work, *The Architectural Instructor*, 1856, now significantly enough teeming with complete designs for "cottages, villas, and mansions," nevertheless seemed to pin its hopes for sale upon the fact that it contained "a history of architecture from the earliest ages."[14] Even so it had, so far as is known, only one printing.

All of these Greek Revival books (except the very latest of Lafever's) are concerned with the details of the architectural envelope rather than with the totality of the architecture itself. A skin-deep architecture of wood, delicately and abstractly adjusting to its own properties the forms of stone, the Greek Revival concealed behind its elegant and enigmatic surface the realities of its inherited wooden frame, with its use of post and beam, mortice and tenon.[15] Heralded by its protagonists and acclaimed by Hamlin as peculiarly "American," it was surely no more so than the Palladian architecture of the eighteenth century.[16] Both transposed into wood forms which were widespread internationally in masonry, and the Greek Revival (romantic-classic) house in wood was an indication of enthusiasm for the rigid clarity presumably demonstrated by antique prototypes. In Greek Revival architecture, site, planning, materials, and construction were essentially secondary, or were at least dominated by the abstract cube and its placement in space. It was an architecture which was applied from without; it did not grow from within or depend upon peculiarly American conditions. In this it was similar to eighteenth century colonial architecture, and in this it continued and indeed concluded the long development of Renaissance design.

It was what we may call the "romantic rationalism" of the 1840's which eventually, by the fifties, brought the Greek Revival to an end in America.

---

12. Minard Lafever, *Modern Builder's Guide,* New York, 1833. It is interesting to note that the 1846 edition added "a plan and elevation of a country residence" (Hitchcock, *op.cit.,* p. 58).

13. Minard Lafever, *Beauties of Modern Architecture,* New York, 1835.

14. Minard Lafever, *The Architectural Instructor,* New York, 1856.

15. Only Benjamin's *Practical House Carpenter* contains a complete framing plan and elevation, pls. 55 and 56. In his Preface Benjamin acknowledges his indebtedness to Nicholson's English publications for his structure. See Peter Nicholson, *The Carpenter's New Guide,* London, 1792. American editions ran from 1818 to 1867, with a "thoroughly revised" edition appearing in 1854 (Hitchcock, *op.cit.,* p. 69).

16. Talbot Hamlin, *Greek Revival Architecture in America,* New York, 1944; and see also his useful article cited above, note 7. For a discussion of Hamlin's methods and point of view, see C. L. V. Meeks' review in *Art Bulletin, 26* (1944), 283.

The man most responsible for this shift in architectural practice, and one who may be credited with starting American domestic architecture along a new path, is Andrew Jackson Downing, 1815–1852.[17] Downing was an enormously influential writer on domestic building, who came to his architectural interests through his own profession of landscape gardening, as Loudon had done in England in the preceding decades.[18] In 1841 appeared his *Treatise on the Theory and Practice of Landscape Gardening . . . with Remarks on Rural Architecture;* in 1842 *Cottage Residences;* in 1850 *The Architecture of Country Houses;* while from 1846 to 1852 he edited a periodical, the *Horticulturist,* a group of his editorials from which were published posthumously in 1853 under the title of *Rural Essays.*[19] Downing represents, consequently, the same turning-away from the newly developing industrial scene as do the painters of the Hudson River School.[20] Like them, his yearning for the country was a consciously romantic reaction, and like the country toward which they moved

17. Hamlin, "The Greek Revival in America," *op.cit.* Hamlin, unsympathetic to Downing, nevertheless states: "The chief attack from the side of the romanticists came from that extraordinary genius—one too much forgotten today—Andrew Jackson Downing" *(ibid.,* p. 250). Hamlin separates the realists and the romanticists of the forties into two separate groups, consigning Downing to the romantic or "Gothicist" school. As we shall see, this is not entirely correct. Downing is both a rationalist and a romantic, as were all the great so-called "romantic" critics of the nineteenth century, such as Pugin, Ruskin, Viollet-le-Duc.

18. Loudon's *Encyclopaedia of Cottage, Farm and Villa Architecture and Furniture,* London, 1835, was one of the English late Regency books which had considerable effect upon Downing in the first stages of his development. [In 1970: The influence and general importance of Loudon should be emphasized rather more than I did here. He is clearly Downing's primary source and a fundamental figure in the international "picturesque-eclectic" movement. Cf. G. L. Hersey, "J. C. Loudon and Architectural Associationism," *Architectural Review, 144* (August 1968), 89; and Carroll L. V. Meeks, "Picturesque Eclecticism," *Art Bulletin, 32* (1950), 226.]

19. Andrew Jackson Downing: *A Treatise on the Theory and Practice of Landscape Gardening Adapted to North America . . . With remarks on rural architecture . . . ,* New York and London, 1841 (sixteen issues of eight editions to 1879); *Cottage Residences; or, A series of designs for rural cottages and cottage villas, and their gardens and grounds, adapted to North America,* New York and London, 1842 (thirteen issues to 1887); *The Architecture of Country Houses, including designs for cottages, farm houses and villas, with remarks on interiors, furniture, and the best modes of warming and ventilating,* New York, 1850 (nine issues to 1866); and *Rural Essays,* New York, 1853 (seven issues to 1881). To this list should also be added: George Wightwick, *Hints to Young Architects . . . with additional notes and hints to persons about building in this country by A. J. Downing,* 1st Amer. ed., New York, 1847.

20. Cf. Frederick Arnold Sweet, *The Hudson River School and the Early American Landscape Tradition,* Chicago (Art Institute), New York (Whitney Museum), 1945.

at this period, Downing's country also was essentially suburban. The influence of the English picturesque suburban movement, as best represented in John Nash's Park Villages of 1826–1827, now for the first time began to make itself felt in America.[21]

Downing is important to us because he decisively established the principles of asymmetrical, picturesque design in America and thereby laid the foundation for a whole new sequence of experiments in planning and spatial organization. Moreover, in his own development he eventually advanced beyond the purely picturesque, absorbed the ethical principles of Pugin and the *Ecclesiologist,* and transposed these into the specifically American idiom of construction in wood. In sum, he performed the difficult feat of creating and widely disseminating a new architectural sensibility and method in America, and one which was eventually to flower into grand and original achievements. Consequently, it is eminently worthwhile to study his works in some detail— to see how he grew and what he grew into—in order to understand the basis for the larger architectural development which was to follow.

In his *Landscape Gardening* of 1841 Downing arrives at the subject of what he calls "rural architecture" through his interest in the rural scene as a whole. "*Architectural beauty* must be considered conjointly with the *beauty of the landscape* . . . ," and country houses, ". . . if properly designed and constructed . . . will even serve to impress a character on the surrounding landscape." As "the leading principles which should be our guide in landscape or Rural Architecture," he states that architecture must be considered "1st, as a useful art, in *Fitness for the End in View;* 2nd, as an art of design, in *Expression of Purpose;* 3rd, as an art of taste, in *Expression of Some Particular Architectural Style.*" It is significant that the remarks on "fitness" and "expression of purpose" which then follow are extremely meager, and mention only in passing convenience and good site-planning under "fitness" and porches and chimneys as domestic features under "expression of purpose."[22] These having been disposed of—and the contrast between this superficial treatment and the much greater emphasis given to these matters in *Cottage Residences,* only a year later, was to be striking—Downing then launches into a discussion of the many different styles which he feels are available for the rural architect. On the whole he is anti-Greek, but his main characteristic in this section is what may appear to contemporary readers as a rather thoughtless eclecticism. Neverthe-

---

21. Cf. John Summerson, *John Nash, Architect to King George IV,* London, 1935. Also, for Park Villages, part of Nash's development at Regent's Park and indeed his last architectural work: John Summerson, *Georgian London,* New York, 1946, pp. 167–68.

22. *Landscape Gardening,* 2nd ed., 1844, pp. 341, 343–48.

less, it is controlled by a perfectly coherent preference for the irregular over the regular, the loose over the controlled. So far, he is still the landscape gardener, not as yet clear in his architectural thinking and echoing only partially assimilated ideas from English late Regency sources.[23] All he is really sure of at this point is that he loves the country, admires the picturesque, and in general is on the side of variety, experiment, and freedom rather than of restraint. He states: "A blind partiality for any one style in building is detrimental to the progress of improvement, both in taste and comfort. The variety of means, habits, and local feelings, will naturally cause many widely different tastes to arise among us; and it is only by means of a number of distinct styles, that this diversity of tastes can be accommodated."[24]

By 1842, however, when *Cottage Residences* appeared, Downing had passed beyond his first tentative and derivative stage. He now shifted his emphasis from "styles" to matters of more practical consideration and, when he felt himself compelled to discuss the question of style, attempted somewhat more realistically to grapple with the question.

In *Cottage Residences*, which remained his most popular architectural work, Downing also first stated at length the nature of his architectural aesthetic. Again, as he writes in his Preface, his intention is to further the building of rural homes which will "harmonize with our lovely rural landscapes," and which at the same time will exhibit a "pure moral tendency . . . a domestic feeling, that . . . purifies the heart." He says: "All Beauty is an outward expression of inward good . . . ," and one can feel that the ethical, romantic-rationalist revolution of A. W. N. Pugin had, by this time, undoubtedly begun to affect Downing's thinking.[25] Downing emphasizes three principles

---

23. Downing appends a bibliographical note which indicates his sources: "Note.—To readers who desire to cultivate a taste for rural architecture, we take pleasure in recommending the following productions of the English press. Loudon's *Encyclopedia of Cottage, Farm, and Villa Architecture,* a volume replete with information on every branch of the subject; Robinson's *Rural Architecture,* and *Designs for Ornamental Villas;* Lugar's *Villa Architecture;* Goodwin's *Rural Architecture;* Hunt's *Picturesque Domestic Architecture,* and *Examples of Tudor Architecture;* Pugin's *Examples of Gothic Architecture,* etc. [this, of course, is the elder Pugin]. The most successful American architects in this branch of art, with whom we are acquainted, are Alexander J. Davis, Esq., of New York, and John Notman, Esq., of Philadelphia" *(ibid.,* p. 387). (In *Cottage Residences,* Downing reproduces one design each by Notman, Design IX, and Davis, Design X.) For an account of that English movement toward the picturesque which was further developed and disseminated by such books as those listed above, see Donald Pilcher, *The Regency Style, 1800 to 1830,* London, 1948, especially ch. 11, "The Landscape Garden and Its Influence."

24. Downing, *Landscape Gardening,* p. 381.

25. *Cottage Residences,* p. iii. In *Landscape Gardening,* 1841, Downing said that a home might be enjoyed without "the loss of moral rectitude," Preface, p. ix. It will be noted that

which govern architectural beauty: "the Principle of Fitness or Usefulness . . . the Principle of Expression of Purpose . . . the Principle of the Expression of Style." He defines them as follows: "Fitness being the *beauty of utility;* Expression of Purpose, the *beauty of propriety;* and Expression of Style, the *beauty of form and sentiment,* which is the highest in the scale."

First, under "fitness," comes the ordering of the plan. The "convenient arrangement of the rooms" is the most important aspect of planning. Care must be taken to orient properly for "aspect" and "view." The size of family and the type of social intercourse must be taken into consideration, and the "ideal of domestic accommodation" is ". . . Each department of the house being complete in itself, and intruding itself but little on the attention of family or guests when not required to be visible. . . ."[26] The ordering of interior space, therefore, comes entirely under the heading of "fitness" for Downing, and that space is thought of not as a total volume, but as a series of rooms, each developed according to its particular function. This is a rational and utilitarian attitude toward planning, striving for maximum economy and efficiency in domestic arrangement, but very little concerned with the aesthetic possibilities of interior space as a whole. Nevertheless, its very rationality and freedom from concern with the academic discipline of axes or symmetry gives to this planning a flexibility which enables it to adapt itself to all kinds of functional requirements without hardening into a rigid and lifeless pattern. This vitality of plan remains an important factor in the mid-century, as Giedion has indicated.[27]

A further aspect of this desire for efficiency and one which also remains peculiarly American is Downing's advocacy of mechanical contrivances, sanitary conveniences, and labor-saving gadgets. A "bathing room," as well as a

---

these moral preoccupations connected with architecture, usually associated with Ruskin, are here pre-Ruskinian, *Modern Painters* appearing only in 1842, and the *Seven Lamps of Architecture* not appearing until 1849. The ideas of the younger Pugin were certainly available, although not specifically mentioned by Downing at this point. Cf. Augustus Welby Northmore Pugin: *Contrasts,* 1836, 2nd ed., 1841; and *True Principles of Christian or Pointed Architecture,* 1841.

26. *Cottage Residences,* pp. 10–12. The desire for differentiated rooms was despised by Thoreau, who also attacked Downing for his theories on color and who himself preferred houses of one great room where many kinds of living might take place. Cf. Henry David Thoreau, *Walden, or, Life in the Woods,* Boston, 1854; Signet ed., New York, 1942, pp. 36–37, 164–65.

27. Siegfried Giedion, *Space, Time and Architecture,* Cambridge, 1943, Part V, "American Development," pp. 258–348. Giedion's discussion of this whole period is valuable. However, he confuses what is really post-centennial planning with the planning of the earlier period. The differences between the two are important.

toilet, should be included in every house, says Downing (although he rarely indicates space for one in his plans), "though the expense may yet for some time prevent their general introduction in small cottages." Since domestics are comparatively rare in America, then all the more use should be made of "domestic labor-saving apparatus to lessen the amount of service required, or to render its performance easy," and Downing recommends "the rising cupboard or dumb waiter, the speaking tube, and the rotary pump."[28]

Under "fitness," Downing includes materials and construction. Wood, he feels at this point in his development, is the least desirable material, and "should never be employed when it is in the power of the builder to use any other." Furthermore, ". . . In point of taste, a house built of wood strikes us the least agreeably, as our pleasure in beholding a beautiful form is marred by the idea of the frailness of the material composing the form."[29] However, and this is the important point here: "When we are necessarily restricted to the employment of a certain material, both fitness and good taste require that there should be a correspondence between the material used and the style adopted for the building."[30]

So much for "fitness." Expression of purpose is simply "truthfulness," which can increase our pleasure in a building by revealing it for exactly what it is. A house should look like a house, a church like a church, a barn like a barn. "A blind passion for a particular style of building may also tend to destroy expression of purpose. It would certainly be difficult for a stranger in some of our towns, where a taste for Grecian temples prevails, to distinguish with accuracy between a church, a bank, and a hall of justice." The features which Downing feels give domestic quality to a house are peculiarly significant. He states that large windows indicate "large and spacious apartments within" and that, altogether, "the most prominent features conveying expression of purpose in dwelling houses are, the chimneys, the windows, and the porch, veranda, or piazza, and for this reason, whenever it is desired to raise the character of a cottage or villa above mediocrity, attention should first be bestowed on these portions of the building." It will be noted here that the features discussed by Downing are, with the exception of the chimneys, the

---

28. *Cottage Residences*, pp. 13, 14.

29. *Ibid.*, p. 16. This is anti-Greek Revival, in being a stricture against the imitation of stone forms in wood. In his prejudices against wood, Downing at this point is actually behind parts of the English aesthetic development. Hunt, Lugar, etc., since the twenties and thirties, had been pushing enthusiastically for the use of wood, an especially striking phenomenon in view of the fact that wood was not at this time a cheap or readily available building material in England. See note 23 above.

30. *Ibid.*, p. 18.

voids in the architectural whole, the windows and the verandas. They are spatial elements and those created by wooden members. He goes on: ". . . a broad shady veranda suggests ideas of comfort and is suggestive of purpose, for the same reason bay or oriel windows, balconies, and terraces increase their interest, not only by their beauty of form, but by their denoting more forcibly those elegant enjoyments which belong to the habitation of man in a cultivated and refined state of society."[31] Two points are important here: first, Downing's preoccupation with forms which are picturesque and varied and at the same time voids in the composition; and secondly, the associative values of cultivation, refinement, or whatever, which are read into the forms.

Downing's basically picturesque, or pictorial, vision is well illustrated in his discussion of color which immediately follows and which he includes under this same heading of "truthfulness." The use of white paint had been for some two generations in America the usual method of emphasizing abstract perfection of form in wooden buildings at the expense of expression of the material. Downing is against white. He states that it is "entirely unsuitable and in bad taste. . . . The glaring nature of this colour, when seen in contrast with the soft green of foliage, renders it extremely unpleasant to an eye attuned to harmony of colouring, and nothing but its very great prevalence in the United States could render even men of some taste so heedless of its bad effect. No painter of landscapes, that has possessed a name, was ever guilty of displaying in his pictures a glaring white house, but, on the contrary, the buildings produced by the great masters have uniformly a mellow softened shade of colour, in exquisite keeping with the surrounding objects." And Downing reproduces a chart of "shades of gray . . . and . . . drab or fawn color, which will be found pleasing and harmonious in any section of the country."[32] Downing's objection to white paint at this point, consequently, is a purely pictorial rejection of it, not especially because it hides a material, but because it clashes rather than harmonizes with the landscape.

Downing by this time has developed in *Cottage Residences* what might be considered a complete disquisition upon the nature of architecture. He has considered program, plan, structure, interior space, and visual effects in general, and has proposed an architecture in close harmony with its surroundings, based upon utility, structure, and the picturesque. He could in effect stop there, but he does not. Instead he states that all this is not architecture, but only building, ". . . only a useful, not a *fine art.*" What is necessary now is the

---

31. *Ibid.,* pp. 19, 20, 21, 22.

32. *Ibid.,* pp. 22–23, 24. Downing absorbed much of this from Uvedale Price, *Essays on the Picturesque,* London, 1798, which appeared in a second edition in 1842.

"Principle of the Expression of Style." This consists of two things: first, "beauty of form," and secondly, ". . . the sentiment associated with certain modes of building long prevalent in any age or country." In describing these qualities Downing becomes rather vague and at the same time self-consciously doctrinaire. In discussing "unity," one of the principles of composition governing "beauty of form," he states: "These rules of Unity are not infrequently violated by architects, but always at the expense of the beauty and perfection of their works, as no artist is superior to principles."[33] This tone carries over into his definitions of "uniformity" and "symmetry." "Uniformity in building is the repetition of the same forms in the different portions or sides of the building. . . . Hence, those persons who have the least taste and imagination, will be found to prefer a plain square or cube, above all others, for a house, as being the first principle of beauty which they are able to discover in architecture."[34] With "symmetry," as he defines it, however, Downing feels more at home, and here he seizes the kernel of the picturesque method of design. He states: "As Uniformity is the balance of two regular parts, so the principle of Symmetry may be defined as the balance of two irregular parts."[35] Symmetry to Downing, therefore, is an occult balance of forces rather than the static opposition of masses around a central axis, an essentially picturesque and free vision of form. Moreover, this definition by Downing is extremely important, since it establishes as a basic principle of design the value of what we would call "asymmetrical" composition, one of the primary characteristics not only of the mid-century domestic style, but of the rest of the original nineteenth century domestic development as a whole. It denotes the destruction of Renaissance sensibility and the foundation of something new. It further establishes Downing as a part of that picturesque revolution which had been going on in England since the middle of the eighteenth century.

The "principles of Harmony, Variety, etc." are connected with the above and need not be discussed "in our present limits," says Downing, evidently very glad to be finished with this abstract aesthetic speculation,[36] and he concludes his discussion with those subjects which are closest to his heart, the

33. *Ibid.,* pp. 25, 26. He then cites as an authority Sir Joshua Reynolds.

34. *Ibid.,* p. 27. Downing's note here reveals his two real preoccupations, the practical and the picturesque. "As besides this, a square or parallelogram is the most economical form in which a house can be built, and as a small house does not easily admit irregularity, we have adopted it in designing the greater number of cottages which follow, but we have endeavoured to raise them above mere uniformity, by adding such characteristic ornaments as give also some variety to the composition." See also note 23 above.

35. *Ibid.,* p. 28.

36. *Ibid.,* p. 29.

nature of domestic architecture and the picturesque. "The different styles of architecture . . . have . . . had their origin in some lofty enthusiasm of the age . . . generally in . . . religion." Therefore, "All domestic architecture, in a given style, should be a subdued expression or manifestation of that style, adjusted to the humbler requirements of the building and the more quiet purposes of domestic life. Hence it would evidently be absurd to copy a cathedral, in building a dwelling in the Gothic style, or a temple in a cottage of the Grecian mode."[37] We should note how this tempers eclecticism, since it rejects the characteristic monumental versions of the chief styles as unsuitable for domestic—or at least rural domestic—use. Although Downing still feels that many styles are available for imitation—including the "Roman" and "Italian" (not the Grecian), the "Swiss," the "Flemish," and especially the later English domestic Gothic, particularly "Tudor"—nevertheless, "In adopting any style for imitation, our preference should be guided not only by the intrinsic beauty which we see in a particular style, but by its appropriateness to our uses. This will generally be indicated by the climate, the site, or situation, and the wants of the family who are to inhabit it."[38] Here is a rational attitude toward building which is combined with a very real desire for picturesque variety, to which a number of formal stylistic languages from the past, much "adapted" (as later generations would put it), are required to contribute. In a way peculiar to the nineteenth century, having in a sense thrown off the immediate past and headed pell-mell toward the future, Downing manufacturers for himself "Gothic" and "Italian" precedents which are really mirrors of his own preoccupations and his own necessities.

> For domestic architecture we would strongly recommend those simple modifications of architectural styles, where the beauty grows out of *the enrichment of some useful or elegant features of the house, as the windows or verandas,* rather than those where some strongly marked features, of little domestic beauty, overpower the rest of the building. The Rural Gothic style, characterized mainly *by pointed gables,* and the Italian, *by projecting roofs, balconies and terraces,* are much the most beautiful modes for our country residences. *Their outlines are highly picturesque and harmonious with nature. Their forms are convenient, their accessories elegant, and they are highly expressive of the refined and unostentatious enjoyments of the country.* We have pointed out in another work the objections that may fairly be urged against the false taste so

37. *Ibid.,* pp. 29–30.
38. *Ibid.,* p. 31.

lately prevalent among us, in building our country homes in the form of Greek temples, sacrificing thereby *the beauty of variety, much convenience, and all the comfort of low and shady* verandas, to the ambitious display of a portico of stately columns; and we are happy to see that the fashion is on the decline. Let us hope speedily to see in its place a correct taste, springing up in every part of the country, which shall render our cottage homes beautiful, not by borrowing the features or enrichments of a temple or palace, but by seeking beautiful and appropriate forms, characteristic of domestic life, and indicative of home comforts.[39]

Although Downing may recommend "an old English villa" for the "sentiment" or "the associations" connected with it, recalling the past "with a kind of golden glow, in which the shadowy lines of poetry and reality seem strangely interwoven and blended," nevertheless, "A great deal of the charm of architectural style, in all cases, will arise from the happy union between the locality or site, and the style chosen. . . ."[40] So Downing concludes. He reveals himself in sum as a blend of the rationalist—or realist—and the romantic, in his architectural thinking combining utility and the picturesque. Moreover, he labors under a kind of semantic necessity in which variety of form and freedom from stylistic restriction becomes confused with variety of "styles." Yet his most apparent characteristic seems to be his concern for efficient planning, simple and straightforward construction, and "expression of purpose." These, coupled with his romantic love for the picturesque, would seem to be the most important elements in him, while his discussion of "styles" becomes a kind of pretext for the advancement of forms which in actuality evolve from the main stream of his logic. We shall see that structure, which becomes even more important, as well as utility and the picturesque, remain the principal threads in Downing and in the whole mid-century rural and suburban domestic style which may be said to grow from him.[41]

39. *Ibid.,* pp. 32–33. The italics are mine. There is so far nothing new or peculiarly American in these preferences of Downing's at this period, as already noted. Similar preferences are stated by J. B. Papworth, *Rural Residences,* London, 1818, or by Francis Goodwin, *Domestic Architecture,* London, 1834.

40. *Cottage Residences,* pp. 33, 34.

41. The latent tendencies toward a "functional" approach which exist in Downing at this time may call to modern minds the much more precisely stated doctrines of functionalism advanced in the eighteen-forties by Horatio Greenough. The latter has lately received considerable attention as a precursor of twentieth century aesthetic doctrines. The recent book by James Marston Fitch, *American Building and the Forces Which Shape It,* Boston, 1948, devotes considerable space to Greenough, as does John A. Kouwenhoven, *Made in America,* New York, 1948. Unfortunately, both these writers have little sympathy

In *Cottage Residences* Downing includes designs for ten houses and for the complete landscaping of their grounds. Certain characteristics of the architecture are immediately apparent. The first is that most of the plans are simple, comparatively efficient, very economical of space, but by no means spatially exciting. The ground floor plan is usually a central hall with rooms opening from it on either side. In general, this hall is no larger than necessary to allow circulation. It is conceived as a place to pass through, not as a spatial feature. A staircase rises to as small a hall as possible on the second floor, around which the bedrooms are simply grouped. The whole complex is as regular as possible and is usually enclosed within a rectangle. Downing's Plans I and V (Fig. 1) are typical of this mode, with Plan V indicating another of the planning characteristics of the larger houses, namely, that the kitchens are often in the basement. Design V, with its elliptical dining room, is also an example of the more or less Adamesque use of circular, elliptical, and octagonal shapes which had been current in America for some time, although these, as in Design V, rarely as yet reveal themselves upon the exterior. As in Design VI (Fig. 2), rooms are sometimes thrown together, separated only by partial partitions or by sliding doors. This again had been a common practice since late colonial days. Rooms are generally high, one spatial aspect always insisted upon during the mid-century. Usually eleven feet or more in height, they remain basically isolated volumes of space of pronouncedly vertical proportions.

Two of the designs in *Cottage Residences* were submitted by Downing's favorite rural architects, John Notman of Philadelphia and Alexander Jackson Davis of New York.[42] "Significantly, their designs were much grander than those which were to exert the profoundest effects upon later developments.

---

for the architecture of the mid-century, and they seize upon Greenough as a kind of light shining in an aesthetic wilderness. This is an obvious overstatement, and it does not give proper weight to the fact that Greenough had small influence on the architectural development of his time.

42. The house designed by Davis was built *(Cottage Residences,* Design IX, p. 164, and Design X, p. 171: "Residence of J. Rathbone, Esq., of Albany"). For Davis' Gothic villas, see Edna Donnell, "A. J. Davis and the Gothic Revival," *Metropolitan Museum Studies,* 1936, Part VI; and, further, Roger Hale Newton, *Town and Davis, Pioneers in American Revivalistic Architecture, 1812–1890,* New York, 1942, although this book contains no plans. Since Davis was Downing's renderer, it has been suggested, notably by Wayne Andrews ("Alexander Jackson Davis," *Architectural Review,* May 1951, p. 307), that Davis was the actual initiator of most of Downing's published designs, including those for small cottages. In my view, however, Donnell's study firmly establishes Downing's independence and creativeness in this relationship.

Notman's plan is of a Palladian regularity, while Davis', also quite regular, produces a very dramatic crossing of axes around a central hall. Neither is quite typical, however, of the general run of plan types used by Downing. Both give much more importance to a monumental central hall than is usual, and the Davis plan in particular is much more elaborate. Another design which is somewhat more pretentious is No. VIII (p. 151), an imposing and solid "Italian villa"—a type introduced in America by Downing, but common in English publications since John Nash's "Cronkhill," of 1802. It is interesting to note that Henry Austin used this design out of Downing, with some modifications, for one of his villas.[43]

More significant for Downing's own personal development and the future development of the mid-century is Downing's Design VI, an Italian villa built of wood, with vertical siding and overhanging eaves supported by brackets (Fig. 2). This villa, says Downing, will be pleasing to discriminating persons, because "It is highly irregular . . . ," with great "picturesqueness and variety. . . ." But the important statement here is this: "We have supposed this villa to be built of wood, the bracketed construction giving it a character of lightness. . . ." Here, for the first time, Downing states his awareness of positive aesthetic qualities in wooden frame structures. This is important, because a feeling for the wood frame vertically sheathed as a light, thin skeleton of sticks was to become a basic factor in the development of the mid-century domestic style. Indeed, a sense of the exposed wooden member and its expressive possibilities had already made its appearance in English publications (Fig. 3).[44]

43. Norton House, New Haven, ca. 1849. C. L. V. Meeks, "Henry Austin and the Italian Villa," *Art Bulletin, 30* (1948), 145ff., figs. 9, 10, and 11.

44. *Cottage Residences,* p. 124. It is important that this bracketed villa of Downing's seems to bear a certain relationship to a project which appeared in S. H. Brooks, *Designs for Cottage and Villa Architecture,* London, n.d., pl. XLVI (Fig. 3, herewith): "A Perspective View of a Cottage in the Swiss Style." Although this book lists no date of publication, the latest date on any of its plates is 1839, which would make it probable that the book itself was published in that year. The design mentioned has a high, asymmetrical massing similar to that of Downing's Design VI, and its roof, extremely projected, is supported by tremendous wooden brackets. The whole is of exposed wood frame construction filled in with brick, and its exposed studs remind one of the vertical battens developed by Davis and later to become of extreme importance in Downing's development. Most interestingly—although not yet of importance so far as Downing's development is concerned—is the fact that its heavy studs rise in places uninterruptedly from the sill past the plate of the second floor. This was also one of the characteristics of the "balloon frame" construction which was developing in Chicago during the eighteen-thirties. At any rate, the Brooks Swiss Cot-

The development of Downing's Design v, "A Cottage Villa in the Bracketed Mode" (Fig. 1), is even more striking in this respect. Downing says:

> This bracketed mode of building, so simple in construction and so striking in effect, will be found highly suitable to North America. . . . (The coolness and dryness of the upper story, afforded by the almost veranda-like roof, will render this a delightful feature in all parts of our country where the summers are hot, and the sun very bright, during the long days of the season.) Indeed, we think a very ingenious architect might produce an American *Cottage Style,* by carefully studying the capabilities of this mode, so abounding in picturesqueness, and so easily executed.[45]

Downing proposes a new style, the cottage style, where utility and the picturesque are most important and where the aesthetic character of wooden structure is recognized.[46] He goes on concerning the "bracketed mode": "It is admirably adapted to two kinds of construction which must, for some time, be the most prevalent in the United States—wood, and brick covered by cement."[47] In the first illustration opposite page 99 in *Cottage Residences* (Fig. 1), Downing shows this house built in masonry, a simple block, very crisp and linear in feeling and capped by a gabled roof which projects widely and is supported on brackets. We recall that Downing had so far, in the abstract, favored masonry over wood. However, he continues: "Its comparative lightness of character renders it well suited for wood,"[48] and opposite page 105 he illustrates an alternative design of the house in wood (Fig. 4). The comparison between the two designs is striking. The wooden house is sided vertically and therefore appears much more vertical in its proportions than the masonry version, although the proportions are actually the same. Secondly, it looks much lighter and expresses itself immediately as a light frame structure of which the most important component is the underlying vertical stud.

---

tage expresses itself much more as skeleton construction, if of a heavy timber type, than anything which was to appear in America for some time, although such expression was eventually to become much more important and wide-spread here than in England.

45. *Cottage Residences,* p. 99.

46. Coolidge, in *Mill and Mansion,* points out the dominance in Lowell during the late forties and fifties of what he calls the "Bracketed Style" (pp. 85–90, 247, 248; pls. 66, 70, 71, 72, 73). We shall see, however, that the nature of this style which develops through Downing does not reside only in the bracket.

47. *Cottage Residences,* pp. 99–100. Note that he has no inherent interest in the expression of masonry material, but assumes as much as Nash a pseudo-ashlar of painted cement.

48. *Ibid.,* p. 100.

The masonry design has projecting stone lintels over the windows, while the windows of the wooden house are set in panels framed by vertical strips which are continuous from the foundation to the top of the upper windows and which are crossed by flat horizontals above and below each window. The feeling is again of the vertical stud crossed by the horizontal plates of the frame, with the windows fitted into the interstices between studs. This vertically connects aesthetically with the preference for high rooms. The vertical stud, the comparatively narrow but high windows between the studs, and the high room spaces behind create a coherent synthesis of aesthetic and structural expression. Upon the exterior, the whole becomes light planar skins of wall, beautifully scaled to wood and expressive of the structure as wooden frame sided by thin boards. Moreover, through the vertical shadows cast by the battens one feels the vertical stud inside. In the sharpness of all the shadows one also feels complementary activity of the contemporary reproductive process of line engraving, which itself could only most naturally produce a sensitivity for the decisively articulated, the thin and the skeletal. Consequently, although Downing may claim to prefer masonry, the fact remains that his wooden house is all wood in scale and feeling, while his stone house, its mass eaten into by the light gabled roof and all its outlines linear and precise, is not particularly expressive of the solemn pressures of masonry courses. Whatever he may say, in reality he feels for wood and the skeleton of the wood frame in a way he does not for brick or stone, and this feeling for the wooden frame was to become more and more conscious as the mid-century approached.

It is significant of the increasing acceptance of this feeling that when Downing reproduced his Design v in the second edition of *Landscape Gardening,* which appeared in 1844, it was the wooden rather than the masonry version which he chose for reproduction, accompanied by a text in which he mentions that it "partakes somewhat of Italian and Swiss features."[49] And he concludes: "We hope to see this Bracketed Style becoming every day more common in the United States, and especially in our farm and country houses, when wood is the material employed in their construction."[50]

49. When he first proposed this "Bracketed Style" in *Cottage Residences,* he had not mentioned "Italian" or "Swiss." "Italian" certainly related to the Italian villas, such as Design vi, where he first felt for wood. "Swiss," a European cottage style, is then related in his mind with the similar type of wooden expression which he now desires. It is possible, of course, that the original idea came from Brooks' Swiss cottage. But the process shows Downing's loose relationship to the "styles." They remain on the whole, as here, only convenient designations for cottage types.

50. *Landscape Gardening,* etc., 2nd ed., New York, 1844, pp. 363–64, and fig. 48, "The Bracketed Mode."

More important, therefore, than utility or the picturesque—although intimately related to them—and vastly more material than a parade of styles, is this awareness of the structural fact of wood in America stated by Downing. Much more than brick, in most sections of the country, wood had always been the most available and easily handled material, and the tradition of its use was in the finger-tips not only of the carpenter-mechanic, but also of the average amateur builder. This new aesthetic sensitivity to the expression of light wood structure, stated by Downing, in a sense stripped the skin off the Greek Revival and brought the frame to light as the skeleton of a new and organically wooden style.

In Downing's ". . . additional notes" to Wightwick's *Hints to Young Architects . . .* of 1847, his sense of the nature of wood and wooden techniques as of critical importance has considerably deepened. Although intellectually he still prefers stone as more permanent, he nevertheless states emphatically that the architect should use the material most easily obtained, and continues:

A large part of the United States is still in this condition with regard to *wood,* which, especially in the newer States, is still so abundant as to be much the cheapest building material. When it is necessary to build of wood, our advice is always to choose a style which is rather light, than heavy—in other words one in which the style and material are in keeping with each other. It is in false taste to erect a wooden building in a massive and heavy style, which originated in the use of stone, as it would be senseless to build a mock fortification, intended to stand a real siege, whose walls and battlements are of thin pine boards.[51]

All of Downing's "notes" in the *Hints* are extremely practical and to the point, and he states his aesthetic creed with ease and assurance. A light frame house, echoing its site and, if possible, bold and irregular in outline, emerges as a kind of type. It should be observed again that in the sample specifications for the guidance of young architects which Downing includes, it is still a mortice and tenon system of wood frame construction which Downing is describing. In this frame the posts (or studs) and beams are fairly thick in section, the tenon or dowel of one fitting into the mortice or socket of the other, so that the whole frame takes on a rigidity which can be stabilized laterally by a very small amount of diagonal knee-bracing. There is no indication at this point that Downing had ever heard of the new balloon frame, by this time already in wide use in the West. This is important, because it shows the growth in him of an aesthetic which partook of the same feeling for

51. George Wightwick, *op. cit.* (see note 19, above, pp. xxii-xxiii).

wooden skeleton construction which, in a structural sense, produced the balloon frame. The two developments, the aesthetic and the structural one, are therefore parallel at this time and apparently not in touch with each other. When they finally converged, they were to complement and reinforce each other. However, they already had a curious relationship. Downing's and Davis' verticality of expression through vertical boarding, stripping, and battens was analogous to the new balloon frame's continuous verticality of the structural stud (Fig. 11). The technological innovation of the West and the aesthetic innovation of the East here followed exactly parallel courses so far as basic formal sensitivities were concerned.[52]

Consequently, in Downing's *Country Houses* of 1850 we can best direct our interest toward the cottages and farmhouses rather than toward the larger villas or "country houses." It was certainly the smaller houses which those "enterprising carpenters" copied at first, and it was through them that the characteristic forms of the early seventies developed. More than this, they became the real vernacular architecture not only of the mid-century, but beyond. Also, with this in mind, we need spend less time with Downing's reiteration of his aesthetic in *Country Houses,* except to observe that he has turned his order of discussion around and placed his emphasis at the end, with the structural and the practical. His discussion of "beauty," however, is important as emphasizing the nature of picturesque vision. He states that there are two kinds of beauty: absolute and relative. Absolute beauty is beauty of form governed by the universal and "abstract ideas" of "Proportion, Symmetry, Variety, Harmony, and Unity." Relative beauty "expresses peculiar moral, social, or intellectual ideas, and is usually termed 'beauty of expression.'" Here Downing of course again tangles with the styles, all of which express different values which may be desirable, but he gets through this rapidly and moves on to the picturesque. "The Picturesque is seen in ideas of beauty manifested with something of rudeness, violence, or difficulty . . . the idea of power exerted rather than the idea of beauty which it involves." The picturesque for Downing is not only a romantic love for the wild but also a method of combining absolute and relative beauty: "As regularity and proportion are fundamental ideas of absolute beauty, the Picturesque will be

52. Giedion and Field have both discussed the development of the balloon frame, but felt no analogous or complementary development in mid-century architectural expression. They both tend to regard as more important—as do Kouwenhoven and Fitch—the more eighteenth century and Greek Revival "plain wall," arriving thereby at a critical position not far from that of the eclectic apologists. Cf. Giedion, *op.cit.,* pp. 269–77; Walker Field, "A Reexamination into the Invention of the Balloon Frame," *Journal of the American Society of Architectural Historians,* 11 (October 1942), 3.

found always to depend upon the opposite conditions of matter—irregularity, and a partial want of proportion and symmetry. Thus, the purest Greek architecture, or the finest examples of Palladio, are at once highly symmetrical and beautiful; the varied Italian villa, or the ruder Swiss chalet, highly irregular and picturesque."[53]

Secondly, Downing allies the picturesque to the "True" in architecture, which includes all the items of fitness and expression of purpose discussed in *Cottage Residences*. His emphasis on "truth" at this time is very important, because it places him—on his own terms and in relation to American conditions—in the main stream of the new moral, and at the same time basically rational and socially conscious, phase of the Gothic Revival, first stated by the younger Pugin and developed in their own peculiar ways by Ruskin and the Camden Society.[54] Downing states that there should be "the *general truth* that the building is intended for a dwelling house; . . . the *local truth* that it is intended for a town or country house: . . . the *specific truth* that it is intended for a certain kind of country house—as a cottage, farm-house, or villa." It is worth noting that in connection with "local truth," which is adjacent to site and to country planning, Downing says that country houses ought to "spread out," but that building economy tends to pull them together and force them up vertically, an interesting comment in view of the general verticality of mid-century architecture. He goes on in discussing cottages to state that they should not imitate the great styles; when they do, they violate "truthfulness." It is wrong for cottages "to imitate as closely as cheap and flimsy materials and a few hundred dollars will permit, the style and elaborate ornament of the villa, with its expenditure of thousands." The cottage now is clearly emerging as non-stylistic building, the potential carrier of basic techniques and immediate tradition. Significantly, Downing attacks both the Grecian "temple cottage" and the Gothic "cocked hat" cottage. Truthfulness and simplicity must rule in cottage building, and to this end Downing attacks unnecessary ornament and advocates instead the planting of vines.[55]

The final and most significant statement, which marks the real integration of the wooden cottage style, is made in the chapter, "Materials and Modes of

53. *The Architecture of Country Houses*, pp. 10, 20, 28–29. It is worthy of note that, concerning symmetry, Downing cites Ruskin. "The author of 'Modern Painters' conceives it to be the symbol of abstract justice" (p. 14). This is the first time he mentions Ruskin.

54. The tie here may be direct, through Gervase Wheeler, an Englishman who came to America in the forties and brought much of the new critical vocabulary with him. For Pugin, the Camden Society, and Ruskin, see Kenneth Clark, *The Gothic Revival*, New York, 1929.

55. *Country Houses*, pp. 31, 33–34, 40–41, 42–48.

Construction." Downing states that there are two methods of siding the frame in wood construction, the horizontal and the vertical. "In the *horizontal boarding,* the weather is kept out of the joint by the upper board overlapping the under one; in the *vertical boarding,* it is kept out by a narrow strip, called a *batten,* about two inches wide, which is nailed over the joint formed by the meeting of the two boards."[56] He goes on:

> We greatly prefer the vertical to the horizontal boarding, not only because it is more durable, but because it has an expression of strength and truthfulness which the other has not. The main timbers which enter into the frame of a wooden house and support the structure, are vertical, and hence the vertical boarding properly signifies to the eye a wooden house; . . . It is as incorrect, so far as regards truthfulness of construction, to show horizontal lines on the weather-boarding of a wooden house, as it would be to mark vertical lines on the outside of a brick or stuccoed wall.[57]

In the very simple Design I (Downing's fig. 6, opp. page 73; my Fig. 5), all the characteristics of this original domestic style are clearly shown. The siding is vertical, with battens; the roof is a light and projecting plane, supported by its rafters, which are left visible, and the whole casts a deep shadow. The building has a light, match-box look in which the feeling of the wall is entirely that of a thin skin of wooden boards. The quality of it as wood, scaled to wood, is also connected in Downing's mind with the idea of the picturesque, ". . . the picturesqueness of wood clearly expressed by using it *boldly* (not neatly and carefully) . . ." This, plus the "bold shadows thrown by the projecting roof . . . the rafter brackets and window hoods . . ."—all of which are also essentially possibilities of wooden construction—give the cottage its "picturesque" and "domestic" character.[58] Consequently, the concepts of utility, wood structure, and the picturesque all come together, mingle, and produce a style.

One point should be made very clearly at this time, namely, that Downing was by no means necessarily the inventor of the elements which are fused

56. *Ibid.,* p. 50, and fig. 1, p. 51.

57. *Ibid.,* pp. 51–52. From his reference to "timbers" it would appear that Downing was still talking about the mortice and tenon, not the balloon, frame. Yet for visual relationships, in regard to techniques of framing, the elevation of the balloon frame (Fig. 11) should again be noted.

58. *Ibid.,* p. 73. This new "boldness" is important; it is part of that new, partially picturesque, desire for the expression of materials which was so important in the original developments of the mid-century.

here to create a style, although it is definitely he who presents this type of building as a particular mode. Downing, for instance, apparently did not invent the batten, so important as a schematic expression of the studs inside, nor does he claim to have done so. Actually, it was Davis who was probably the first to propose the use of battens with vertical siding. In his own *Rural Residences*, 1837, he had included three projects so sided: a dramatic "Village School," a "Gatehouse in the Rustic Cottage Style" and, most important of all, a "Farmer's House" with vertically battened siding and brackets as well.[59] Whence the battens derived can only remain a matter of conjecture. Probably they had been a carpenter's way of siding small structures since time immemorial. In Japan they had certainly been used with vertical siding for centuries, as had overhanging roofs and exposed rafters.[60] If the vertically boarded and battened wall does indeed derive in some fashion from Japan, it would represent the first American assimilation of Japanese sensitivity to skeletal structure in wooden architecture, which was later, in the seventies and eighties, to exert a profound influence. At any rate, as Downing came to an appreciation of the positive aesthetic qualities of wood frame structure only after some hesitation, so in his use of vertical board and battens he apparently followed Davis. Nevertheless, when he did come to them, he in a sense made them his own. It was Downing who fixed his main attention upon the cottage style, assembled its formal elements, established its positive aesthetic basis, propagandized for it, and thereby carried it on for future development.

Downing's Design II illustrates even more clearly the nature of this style (Fig. 6).[61] More irregular than Design I, this quality, says Downing, makes it "more picturesque," and "the bay window, the rustic trellises covered with vines, and the bracketed vine-canopy" give it "more *feeling*." The vertical battens rising from the foundation to the exposed rafters of the overhanging

59. Alexander Jackson Davis, *Rural Residences . . .* , New York, 1837. This book seems to have always been very rare and personal. It was never republished, and Hitchcock doubts if it was ever completely issued (Hitchcock, *American Architectural Books*, pp. 29–30). Loudon's *Encyclopaedia,* London, 1835, which we know was extensively used by Davis (see Edna Donnell, "A J. Davis and the Gothic Revival," passim), included small areas of vertical siding with a suggestion of battens as picturesque features. However, nowhere before Davis, that I can discover, was a clearly vertically battened wall used as the siding for a whole structure in America. The expression is similar to that which Brooks achieved by actually exposing his vertical studs. Cf. Brooks, *op.cit.,* pl. 1.

60. For vertical board and batten walls in Japan, see Edward Sylvester Morse, *Japanese Homes and Their Surroundings . . . [with] illustrations by the author,* Boston, *1886* [5], figs. 34–38, 246.

61. *Country Houses,* pp. 78–79, figs. 9 and 10.

roof visually project upon the surface of the sheathing the vertical studs behind. Indeed, the feeling is not so much of a thin skin of sheathing as it is of a plastic skeleton which is skinless. The battens truly "skeletonize" the wall, and the bones and tendons of the structure exert their actual presence. There is little feeling of this wall as enclosing a unified volume within. Nor is there any feeling of a really three-dimensional flow of masses. The feeling is all for the wall as light, articulated panels. In effect, the whole character of the building makes itself felt in the section of the wall, and its peculiar lightness and gentleness of scale arise from this fact.

Design xi[62] further illustrates another aspect of that expression of thinness of wall and expression of the frame (Fig. 7). Here the exterior is shingled in a way which is in striking contrast to the way shingles would be used in the eighties. This cottage is called "Swiss," a kind of generic identification by type, and again its skeleton expression recalls a design by S. H. Brooks (Fig. 8).[63] Downing's illustration is an elevation of his house partially shingled. "This is a frame house, doubly covered on the outside of the frame, i.e. with rough but jointed inch boards, so as to form a plane surface, and then with an external coating of shingles cut in an ornamented pattern."[64] Actually, both boards and shingles are contained within strict vertical panels framed by wood strips which rise from foundation to rafters and again indicate the timber skeleton within. Unlike the shingles of the eighties which flow around corners, these are sharply cut off from any surface continuity by this sense of the skeleton frame which obtrudes. Again the visual effect is of a skinless architecture with all its nerves and tendons exposed. It is an architecture of sticks, expressing the structural fact of the members of its frame. This quality of the stick is even more apparent in those shadowy voids which Downing loved, the piazza and the veranda. Downing's fig. 45, a "Bracketed Veranda from the inside," is a drawing seen from within one of these verandas looking out upon a romantic shore complete with castle and ships.[65] Each of the clearly exposed structural members is a stick, the posts with their brackets supporting a beam lintel which is notched to receive the rafters which carry the light and projecting roof.

A picturesque desire to be close to nature, coupled with a feeling for

---

62. *Ibid.*, p. 123, figs. 46–51. This house was actually built.

63. "Design in the Swiss Style of Architecture," S. H. Brooks, *Designs for Cottage and Villa Architecture*, London, n.d., pl. XLIV, p. 66. Similar in both is the way in which the wall panels are framed by a wooden skeleton. In the Brooks design, however, the walls are masonry rather than shingles.

64. *Country Houses*, p. 127.

65. *Ibid.*, p. 122.

skeleton construction, produces here in the stick style of Downing and Davis the prototypes of all the American living porches which were to be built in the nineteenth century, and whose importance was profound in habituating Americans to indoor-outdoor living. The interior space now really begins to extend itself to the outside. A small, anonymous house which was built in Newport, Rhode Island, in 1846 can illustrate the typical board and batten house and the nature of its veranda (Fig. 9). Houses of this type were built all over the United States in the forties and fifties, and especially in California, where, at the present time, much of the suburban work of Wurster, Esherick, Belluschi, Dailey, and others consciously attempts to recreate their qualities and to develop further the tradition which they initiated.[66]

In view of all this, it is most significant that Downing, the instigator of the whole tradition, concludes his discussion of this mode of building by calling it an "American Style," and by repeating once more his reasons for naming it so: "If we call this style American, it is only because we foresee that our climate and the cheapness of wood as a building material, in most parts of the country, will, for a long time yet, lead us to adopt this as the most pleasing manner of building rural edifices of an economical character."[67]

The immediate future in the early fifties did indeed lie with the wooden cottage—or stick style, as I should like to call it—and the nature of its development can be seen nowhere more clearly than in the theory and building of the Englishman, Gervase Wheeler, who came to America in the forties. Downing himself used one of Wheeler's designs as Design xxv in *Country Houses*— "A Plain Timber Cottage Villa," built in Brunswick, Maine (Fig. 10).[68] Downing quoted Wheeler as follows:

66. A revealing comment upon the nation-wide character of this type in the fifties and upon the relation to it of the present "Bay Region" architects is to be found in the article, "House at Atherton, California," Wurster, Bernardi and Emmons, Architects, *Progressive Architecture*, October, 1948, pp. 72–76. The article states: "In the design of this country house for Grace and Kenneth Mortsolf, the architects used standard wood framing— much as has been done for the past one hundred years in these parts. The lines of the house are even similar to things built in the mining towns back in the fifties" (p. 75). The house exhibits vertical siding with battens, a light projecting roof, and a large window under the gable which is framed by a vine—all of these characteristics belonging also to Downing's Design II (Figs. 9 and 10). The house might almost have been built by Downing, except for the white paint, of which he would never have approved.

67. *Country Houses*, "A Bracketed Farm-house in the American Style," p. 163, figs. 70, 71.

68. *Ibid.*, pp. 298–304. This house was actually built. It should be noted that the plan, fig. 121, also makes use of a generous hall, although without a fireplace. Wheeler's design for this Brunswick house was used—with very few alterations, the most important one being a decrease in the size of the hall—by William Brown, of Lowell, Mass., in a house

In this country, and especially in some districts, wood must for many years be relied upon as the material for building. It is the existence of this necessity which has, in fact, given birth to the style of erection which may be considered as almost national; for nowhere else in Europe will be found the class of houses that abounds (and more especially in the New England States) in every part of the Union. . . . And whilst this material seems, from causes apparent to everyone, to be thus imperatively demanded, it becomes the duty of the architect to meet the emergencies of the case, and, like a true artist, to endeavour to abstract beauty from the elements given to him,—beauty, too, the result, as all true architectural beauty must be, of *fitness* and harmony.

Of Design xxv itself, Wheeler states:

This is essentially *real*. Its character is given by simplicity and fitness of construction. . . . The construction itself, though simple, is somewhat peculiar. It is *framed,* but in such a manner as that on the exterior the construction shows, and gives additional richness and character to the composition.

At the corners are heavy posts, roughly dressed and champfered, and into them are mortised horizontal ties, immediately under the springing of the roof; these, with the posts, and the studs, and framing of the roof, showing externally.[69]

The word "real" is vitally important here. Its use in connection with architecture stems directly from the first issue of the *Ecclesiologist,* critical organ of the Cambridge Camden Society, founded in 1839 "to promote the study of Ecclesiastical Architecture and Antiquities." The *Ecclesiologist* was first published in 1841. Its crusade for architecturally more "ecclesiastical" churches was based upon a standard of architectural morality, or reality, as in this sense: "But if ornamental appendages are bad when anything real is given up for their sake, much more are they so when they are imitations of that which they are not. Stucco, and paint, and composition, and graining are not out of place in the theatre or the ball-room; but in God's House everything

---

he built for Benjamin Butman at Worcester, Mass., in 1853. See William Brown, *The Carpenter's Assistant,* 5th ed., Boston, 1853, figs. 11, 13, pp. 42–44. The movement in the mid-century then is generally toward smaller halls. Although the living hall may occasionally be found, it is recessive at this period, in contrast to later developments which would see the expansion of the living hall as the spatial core of the house.

69. *Country Houses,* pp. 298–302.

should be *real*."[70] This is an attack upon the concept of "taste" on grounds of morality and structural logic. "Composition" must fall before the demands of "reality." The best expression of this in England is perhaps to be seen in the work of William Butterfield, the favorite of the *Ecclesiologist,* whose purposely harsh All Saints' Church, Margaret Street, London, 1850–1859, is the perfect Camdenian church.[71] Consequently, this whole attack upon established "taste" and emphasis upon a new architectural "reality" was of extreme importance in the growth of a new architecture, but Wheeler, in touch with the American Downing as well as the English *Ecclesiologist,* did more than this. He transposed the ethical word "real" so as to apply it to the effects to be drawn from the skeletal framing. By so doing, he infused it into the very bones of architectural design as something to be experienced and expressed. He was attempting to do for architecture what Whitman was soon to attempt to do for the experience of life in America, and it was in this double, rather poignant, meaning that "reality" was later to become the central word of Sullivan's and Wright's architectural philosophy.

In accordance with this position, Wheeler in Design XXV was presenting a wooden structure of which the skeleton was actually exposed, following an aesthetic of fitness and reality with wood. Wheeler may therefore be said to emphasize Downing's ideas of fitness and expression of purpose, to reinforce them with a peculiarly Camdenian reality, and to carry on and develop further the new wooden style.[72]

Wheeler's most important book of designs was his first, *Rural Homes,* published in 1851 and issued nine times through 1868.[73] Significantly, Ruskin, already quoted by Downing, is now invoked in Wheeler's Preface like a guardian angel. ". . . I have mentally headed every page with a sentence suggested

70. *Ecclesiologist,* 1, No. 1, 1841. See also Kenneth Clark, *The Gothic Revival,* New York, 1929, ch. VIII, "Ecclesiology," pp. 192–227.

71. See John Summerson, "William Butterfield," *Architectural Review, 98* (December 1945), 166.

72. Upjohn's designs for wooden churches published at this time are much like Wheeler's designs in their expression of the posts and plates of the frame. Cf. Richard Upjohn, *Upjohn's Rural Architecture,* New York, 1852; also Everard M. Upjohn, *Richard Upjohn, Architect and Churchman,* New York, 1939, figs. 68, 69. See also Upjohn's Berwick Academy, South Berwick, Maine, 1852–53, *ibid.,* fig. 88. Upjohn's wooden churches from the mid-forties on were of the vertically boarded and battened type (*ibid.,* figs. 40, 41, 42).

73. Gervase Wheeler, *Rural Homes; or, Sketches of houses suited to American country life, with original plans, designs,* etc. New York, 1851 (9 issues through 1868). Wheeler's second book, *Homes for the People in Suburb and Country,* etc., New York, 1855, is somewhat less interesting, although it had six issues, also through 1868. It quotes Solon Robinson's description of the balloon frame, but adds nothing new.

as matin and evensong to every architect and amateur—Mr. Ruskin's great
maxim, 'Until *common sense* finds its way into architecture, *there can be but
little hope for it.*'[74] Following this practical maxim, Wheeler discusses convenience and relation to site much as did Downing and then, like Downing,
presents a series of house designs followed by a discussion of warming and
ventilation, furniture, etc. He ends with a very moving description of the
American village as he would like to see it planned and built, wherein he
speaks continually of gardens, space, and shadowy verandas, so that the whole
seems to emerge as a loosely grouped series of airy pavilions, built with those
light and weathering sticks of which we have already spoken, gentle and
delicate in scale among the trees.[75] Again, it is the suburban evocation of
agrarian values which forms, as with Downing, Wheeler's sociological program. One recalls again John Nash's Park Villages of 1826–1827. Yet, for all
the poetry of his feeling concerning the village, Wheeler had that same core of
structural rationalism beneath his love for the picturesque. Of wood he says:
"Let timber, and timber only, be evident in every part of your building," and
if one must have a smooth surface, which Wheeler deplored, then trust "to
your verandas, projections of roofs, window caps, sills and other features, to
cast shadows and reflexes enough to break the monotony of a level surface of
tint, which you will find by these natural causes more varied than if lined off
into blocks with white paint and a rule stick." Again, as with Downing, structural sensitivity goes hand in hand with picturesque vision. Wheeler's relation to the Gothic is, like Downing's, at the cottage level, a basic awareness of
a connection in method and structural expression between the structurally
organic building of the Middle Ages and his own rational and picturesque
desires. He says of what he calls "Gothic styles": "But the great principle upon
which all were based, and in which all agreed, was *reality:* every form of

74. It must be noted that Ruskin's *The Seven Lamps of Architecture,* first published in
London in 1849, appeared in an unauthorized edition in New York in the same year. It
then went through twenty-five issues up to 1894. *The Stones of Venice* was issued twenty-
four times in America between 1851 and 1894. These statistics reveal Ruskin as by far the
most popular writer upon architecture—and upon aesthetics as a whole—in America
throughout this entire period. Cf. Hitchcock, *American Architectural Books,* 3d rev. ed.,
1946, pp. 85–92. Principles of *truth* and *reality,* based upon a new aesthetic morality and
spiced by Ruskin's peculiarly picturesque vision, may therefore be truly said to have
formed the basic approach to architecture of a vast body of the reading public throughout
the third quarter of the nineteenth century and for some time afterward.

75. *Rural Homes,* ch. XVI, pp. 263–98. The sense is of a quiet agrarian life, with a scale
which is more comprehensible to man than that of the industrialized city. It is not without importance as showing the vitality of this tradition in America that Frank Lloyd
Wright's Broadacre City of 1931 strives to create a similar psychological landscape for life.

even the simplest moulding; every line and portion of the building was contrived exactly to answer the purpose for which it was intended; and in this
we will gladly follow the mighty artist-minds of old whilst we scorn the petty
trickery of servilely copying a bit here and there of their immortal works, and
leaving unnoticed the inborn principle which made each bit of detail beautiful."[76]

This creative relationship between mediaeval forms and new invention in
the nineteenth century has never been understood by such classicistically
minded critics as Talbot Hamlin. He, for instance, insisting always upon the
"lath-and-plaster" vaults of Upjohn's Trinity Church, assigns to the Greek
Revival "the integration of *structure* forms with *use* forms and *appearance*
forms," and to the Gothic Revival, "complete separation of effect and construction."[77] This judgment would appear to be faulty not only insofar as
the significant developments of the later seventies are concerned, but also, as
the reader must now be aware, in relation to the whole development of an
original domestic style in the 1850's as well.[78]

The Olmstead House, by Wheeler, built in 1849, and discussed on pages
72–77 of *Rural Homes*, is an excellent example of this creative relationship to
mediaeval building (Fig. 12). Wheeler says of it, at the very end of his description, "Its style is Gothic—so far at least as the high roofs, the pointed arches
of the tracery in front and the character of the labels over the windows—
determine any distinctive style." The general appearance of the building is
similar to that with which we are already familiar, with high, overhanging
planes of roof, exposed posts and bracing. Wheeler is at pains to explain the
"tracery" which supports the overhang of the front gable and the exposed
framing which ties the side gable together.

> It will be seen that the peculiar feature about the house is the extreme
> projection of the roof. In fact, the veranda is shaded by the main roof
> itself, the latter being supported by framing of a very simple and effective

76. *Ibid.*, pp. 29, 31–32.

77. Hamlin, "The Greek Revival in America," pp. 254–56.

78. The influence of Viollet-le-Duc in the seventies and early eighties was profound.
The influence of Ruskin has already been noted. Frank Lloyd Wright's reading in the
eighties, for example, revolved around Ruskin's *Stones of Venice* and Viollet-le-Duc's
Dictionnaire Raisonné. He also admired Hugo's strictures against the Renaissance, so
abominated by Hamlin, and there is also the fact that his mother, hoping from his earliest
childhood that he would become an architect, hung pictures of the great cathedrals in his
room. Cf. Hamlin, "The Greek Revival in America," p. 257. Henry-Russell Hitchcock,
In the Nature of Materials: The Buildings of Frank Lloyd Wright, New York, 1941; Frank
Lloyd Wright, *An Autobiography,* 2nd ed., New York, 1943, p. 75.

character on the end. . . . The sharp gable over the side is framed so that the construction shows externally—this being no sham, but the actual framing of the roof within, the chamber ceilings of that part of the house being lathed upon the curved beams that support the roof. The sides of the house are planked, and their joints covered with battens. . . .[79]

This exposing of the stick work of trusses would also remain a basic component of the mid-century domestic style and was to reach its most elaborate development in the last phases of that style in the mid-seventies. Wheeler, consequently, reinforced with a new and more incisive logic the practical and aesthetic principles of Downing's cottage style. With him the formation of the principles behind the first phase of the mid-century cottage style may be said to be complete, and the Pattern Books with their line engravings established as its carriers.

There is, consequently, little need to discuss all the ramifications of this style to 1875. A decided reaction against it was exemplified during the early fifties by massive Italian villa types, eventually with curvilinear and plastically sculptural roofs. From a variation of these developed the "Second Empire" mansarded houses in both masonry and wood, which continued the reaction on into the late fifties and the sixties.[80] These also tended to dominate sensitivities to the character of wood for a while, and to substitute an attempt at weight and solidity for the more natural stick-line articulations of the cottage mode.[81] By the early seventies, however, this reaction toward the heavy and the sculptural had in general run its course, and the stick style emerged before 1876 as the main carrier of the American vernacular in wood. During the period 1850–1876 it followed a course of development already plainly charted by Downing and Wheeler. All the elements of the frame moved toward their

79. *Rural Homes,* pp. 73, 77.

80. I have discussed this process in some detail in the section entitled, "Nineteenth-Century Resort Architecture," in *The Architectural Heritage of Newport, Rhode Island,* Cambridge, Mass., 1952, esp. pp. 124–27, 129–32.

81. An early indication of this anti-wood reaction may be seen in Calvert Vaux, who dedicated his book to Mrs. Downing and to the memory of Downing himself (who drowned in a steamboat accident on the Hudson in 1852). In reference to wood construction, Vaux stated, ". . . it is not desirable to make it especially prominent, as if it was something to be especially proud of" (Calvert Vaux, *Villas and Cottages,* New York, 1857, p. 70). Another reaction against wood of a somewhat different order was that of Orson Squire Fowler with his "Octagon Form and Gravel Wall." These concrete octagons tended to disappear by the time of the Civil War, however. Cf. Orson Squire Fowler, *A Home for All; or, The gravel wall and octagon mode of building,* New York, 1848 (8 issues to ca. 1857). See also *Art Bulletin, 28* (June 1948), which contains articles by Walter Creese and Clay Lancaster on Fowler and his octagons.

own expression, and the sense of a basketry of wooden members became the dominant factor in design. Also, as with Downing, architectural forms from other cultures and times were brought into the development, but did not dominate it or destroy its originality. Instead they were absorbed by it and used to reinforce its own direction. This was the case with the Swiss chalet, in the fifties, when such a popular Pattern Book writer as Henry William Cleaveland, who felt himself to be continuing the work of Downing, discussed one of his designs (Fig. 13) in the following terms:

> Its principle feature is the verandah or gallery, covered by the projecting roof, and supported by the open framework. This is at once bold and simple, suggestive of summer enjoyment and of winter protection.
>
> In its main characteristics this house resembles the Swiss cottage. Circumstances similar to those which make this style proper on the Alpine slopes often exist among us, and it is for some such position that the design is intended. It would suit well the southern slope of some steep and rugged hill. . . .[82]

One of the best and most typical of these stick style chalets was the Willoughby House, built in 1854, on Hallidon Hill in Newport by Leopold Eidlitz, architect (Fig. 14).[83] Downing's desire for deep verandas and for expression of wood and Wheeler's desire for "reality" in wood frame construction all reach further expression in this boldly wooden structure set on the side of its hill, with its jagged shadows complemented by the serried structure of the pines which were planted around it. European traditions of wooden craftsmanship merge here with the general American development, and the Willoughby House was itself reproduced in a Pattern Book.[84]

By the sixties a feeling for mediaeval half-timber work, already implied in the feeling for wood and Gothic of Downing and Wheeler, produced such a building as the J. N. A. Griswold House in Newport, R.I., built in 1862 by Richard Morris Hunt (Fig. 15). This is one of the best of the stick style houses which Hunt built in America after his return from the Beaux-Arts in the fifties.

82. Henry William Cleaveland, William Backus, and Samuel D. Backus, *Village and Farm Cottages: The requirements of American village homes considered and suggested; with designs for such houses of moderate cost,* New York, 1856 (4 issues to 1869), pp. 91–92.

83. Leopold Eidlitz, 1823–1908, was born in Prague and educated at the Polytechnic in Vienna. He came to America in 1843, and entered the office of Richard Upjohn. He was the builder of many excellent chalets, including one for himself overlooking the Hudson. Cf. Montgomery Schuyler, "A Great American Architect: Leopold Eidlitz," *Architectural Record,* XXIV, 1908, pp. 164–79, 277–92, 366–78.

84. John Bullock, *The American Cottage Builder: A series of designs, plans, and specifications from $200 to $20,000. For homes for the people . . . ,* New York, 1854.

Later, as a "Vanderbilt architect" of the early nineties, Hunt was to profess a nostalgic admiration for these earlier and less pretentious houses and to wish that they might not be forgotten.[85] Though the Griswold House evokes mediaeval half-timber—and indeed is very similar to the European rustic types which were being built during the early fifties in the Bois de Boulogne and elsewhere by Hunt's colleagues at the Ecole—it can nevertheless be seen that the house has by no means a mediaeval look. It is not dominated by a desire for antiquarian correctness, but is instead a creative amalgamation of picturesque intentions and use of the wooden frame, enhanced by a feeling for the hard rather than for the fuzzy line, like the hard-line engravings of the Pattern Books themselves. Like Wheeler, Hunt is here "essentially real," and the multiplication of expressed posts, plates, and diagonal braces continues the dominant skeletal logic of the developing stick style. Here the skeleton becomes a total basketry of sticks, and the house is a woven fabric, penetrated by the veranda voids of space which the structural members themselves define.[86]

Indeed, this increased sensitivity toward visual sticks and their multiple relationships is exactly in accord with the development which the balloon frame itself had undergone by the early sixties. Bell, in his *Carpentry Made Easy,* of 1858, the first book on the balloon frame to appear, had made no mention of diagonal bracing for this frame and had drawn his structural details in straight elevation (Fig. 11), so that the continuous vertical studs with the windows between bore a close resemblance to the vertically boarded and battened walls of Davis and Downing.[87] But Woodward, in his *Country Homes,* of 1865, developed his balloon frame drawings in isometric, discussed diagonal bracing, lathing, and sheathing in some detail, and consequently multiplied visually the relationships between vertical, horizontal, and diagonal members.[88] Each thin wooden member of the balloon frame—by this

85. When Hunt returned to America from the Ecole des Beaux-Arts in Paris in 1855, the psychological atmosphere was not yet prepared here for the grandiose monumentality which was later to become his main aspiration. When Schuyler wrote Hunt's professional biography in 1895, he was apparently somewhat appalled at Hunt's later palazzi and stressed Hunt's earlier, more vernacular works as much as possible. Cf. Montgomery Schuyler, "The Works of Richard Morris Hunt," *Architectural Record,* 5 (1895), 97.

86. An even earlier example of emphasis on the stick, using some diagonal elements in wall panels, can be found in Richard Upjohn's Hamilton Hoppin House, Middletown, R.I., 1856–57. Cf. Upjohn, *Upjohn,* fig. 77.

87. William E. Bell, *Carpentry Made Easy; or, The science and art of framing on a new and improved system. With specific instructions for building balloon frames . . . ,* Philadelphia, 1858 (9 issues to 1894, 2nd ed. from 1875), pp. 47–54; pls. 4, 5, 6.

88. George Evertson Woodward, 1829–1905, *Woodward's Country Homes . . . ,* New York, 1865 (8 editions to sometime after 1870; last two n.d.), pp. 151–66; figs. 107, 113, 120. Woodward also constantly refers to Downing (*ibid.,* pp. 17–18).

time 2″ x 4″ or sometimes even 2″ x 3″ in section—attains structural integrity only through the opposed tensions of a variety of other members. Studs rise, plates are nailed to them at second-floor level, joists are laid upon the plates against the studs and are nailed into both. Diagonal ribbing and lathing are used for lateral stability, and one senses a constantly increasing preoccupation on the builder's part with the organic relationship of all the members of the working skeleton, including a multitude of diagonals. Moreover, in his *National Architect*, of 1868, Woodward was the first of the Pattern Book writers to illustrate houses which made use of schematized panels of diagonal bracing as part of the exterior expression of the skeleton.[89] In general, therefore, this increased preoccupation with the articulation of all framing systems caused the wall itself to become a totally articulated wooden frame (Fig. 16).

This sensitivity to the wooden frame, in part remotely inspired by half-timber, in part by the balloon frame and other light framing methods, worked toward a single result in the houses of the later sixties. This was the conscious multiplication of sticks and the further complication of their relationships. Moreover, the houses of the basic cottage mode itself tended to become larger. Impelled both by a larger industrial prosperity and by technical virtuosity, they really did balloon out into space. An excellent example of this is the Bassett House, New Haven, 1868 (Fig. 17), built by Bassett as the first house of a real estate development.[90] Here the diagonal sticks take over the architectural fabric and reach out to envelop exterior space in an interwoven web of wooden members. Here is what might be called a baroque manipulation of the stick. This development reached its high point by the early seventies, and such a structure as the New Jersey State Building, designed by Carl Pfeiffer for the Philadelphia Centennial of 1876 (Fig. 18), displays the apogee of skeletal expression—all stick and no wall, with boldly expressed energies in its tensile relationships.[91] There are many similar designs by the young ar-

89. George Evertson Woodward, *Woodward's National Architect; Containing 1000 original designs, plans and details . . .* , New York, 1868 (5 issues in various forms to 1877), Design 6, pl. 23.

90. Arnold Dana, *Pictorial New Haven, Old and New* (New Haven Historical Society, No. 75), p. 41. This house coincides in time with the publication of Charles Locke Eastlake, *Hints on Household Taste,* London, 1868. However, the first American edition of this work did not appear until 1872, and, in general, there is little reason to suspect any important relationship between Eastlake's rather watered-down Gothic revival *Sachlichkeit,* derived from Pugin and Ruskin, and the later phases of the stick style in America. They belong to the same general architectural movement, but Eastlake's actual influence was mainly in furniture design, and the epithet "Eastlake" applied to the houses of the early seventies—an epithet coined by the Eclectic Apologists of the early twentieth century—cannot be regarded as a very satisfactory stylistic designation.

91. *American Architect and Building News, 1 (1876),* 109.

chitects of the early seventies, published in the *Architectural Sketch Book* and elsewhere during this period.[92] In many ways, the houses built by Greene and Greene in Pasadena at the end of the nineteenth century and early in the twentieth pick up once more this late moment in the stick style and, somewhat as in the porch of the Bassett House, fully express the possible articulations of the members of a frame. Again, the more recent houses of Harwell Harris, who has been involved for some time in a close investigation of the work of Greene and Greene, show an increased emphasis on the stick.

While many buildings illustrate the wildest phase of the stick in the mid-seventies, the Sturtevant House, Middletown, R.I., 1872, by Dudley Newton (Figs. 21, 22, 23), can illustrate very satisfactorily all the qualities of the completely developed stick style.[93] Here the plan shows a continuation of the romantic-rationalist sensitivities of the forties. It is asymmetrical and irregular; the Renaissance cube has given way to spatial reflex and movement. Downing's desire for picturesque variety is now the basis of the design. The entrance is enfolded by the house, and the whole is surrounded by the deep voids of a veranda. The rooms within are still separate one from another, like Downing's rooms, but the relationships between them are flowing and easy. The kitchen is close to the dining room, and the utilitarian, labor-saving intention, inspired by the possibility of few servants, which Downing had possessed and which goes back to Jefferson, is very apparent here and is, in the nineteenth century, most peculiarly American. A flexible wooden frame creates these spaces, and the skeleton is constantly felt in the vertical and horizontal stripping which articulates the plane of the wall and within which the windows are set. The windows and the glass doors, especially those opening upon the veranda, are tall and narrow, so that one feels them not as holes cut in a wall but as voids between the insistent vertical members of the frame.

92. The *Architectural Sketch Books* were published in New York and Boston in the early seventies and were the vehicle of expression for the new architectural generation during the depression years. Many of the most interesting designs of the fully developed stick style were republished in *Examples of Architecture,* Boston, 1880.

93. I do not assign the Sturtevant (originally Jacob Cram) House to Dudley Newton without some qualms. Newton was a local Newport architect, and the Sturtevant family states positively that he was the architect of the house. Because of its quality, however, one may speculate as to whether Newton might not have been acting as Clerk of the Works for some out-of-town firm, such as the Boston architects, Peabody and Stearns (Robert Swain Peabody and John Goddard Stearns, whose work became of great importance in the late seventies and early eighties). Various published sketches by Peabody and Stearns bear some relationship in feeling to the Sturtevant House, as does also their Nathan Matthews House, Newport, 1871–72. See *Architectural Sketch Book* (Boston), 111, No. 2, August 1875.

The roofs are high and jaggedly interpenetrative, and their trusses are exposed in diagonal stick work which casts further shadows upon the already skeletonized wall. The posts, plates, and diagonal braces of the veranda create fully that pavilion of space which the porches of Downing and Davis had initiated in America, and they show, even more than the iron façades of the period, how skeleton design had by this time reached a phase of complete virtuosity. Moreover, in the double plates of the porch framing, increasing as they do the sense of tensile activity in the frame and creating a kind of "openwork fascia" between them, there is a hint of the influence of Japanese framing and sense of space, which appears here as an enrichment of the American feeling for the frame. These elements, too, were later to play an important part in the American development as a whole.[94]

Similar strength in the early seventies was in such a man as Eugene Clarence Gardner, of Springfield, Mass., whose thinking demonstrates the best aspects of the developed stick style.[95] Gardner, whose own designs in wood are pure stick style (Fig. 19),[96] continued without break the tradition of Downing. Moreover, expanding the possibilities for free invention opened up by Downing when he broke the grip of the grand styles, Gardner himself never speaks of "style." He is a free man where thought about design is concerned. Like Downing and Wheeler, Gardner desired a suburban orientation for domestic architecture. He also disliked and feared the city. "Trout Streams are Better than City Sewers" is the title of one of his chapters, and he wished for a city of "magnificent distances," where one feels that he is not recalling Haussman's Paris, but rather is evoking that insistently Jeffersonian agrarian dream out of which Broadacre City was to grow. Like Downing, but with a more masculine gusto, Gardner insists upon the variety which is necessary to life. Each client must have a different house, of which the form will grow from the specific needs of that particular client. Most of Gardner's plans are like those

94. There was a Japanese building of wood at the Philadelphia Centennial of 1876, and this was discussed in *American Architect, 1* (1876), 136. Another important article on Japanese framing and open planning appeared in the same year *(ibid.,* pp. 26–27). For later important use of the "openwork fascia" and of interwoven spatial areas, see McKim, Mead, and White's Casino at Newport and White's dining room at "Kingscote," both of 1880–81 (Downing and Scully, *Architectural Heritage of Newport,* pls. 198, 200).

95. Eugene Clarence Gardner, *Homes and How to Make Them,* Boston, 1874 (3 issues to 1878), and *Illustrated Homes: A series of papers describing real houses and real people,* Boston, 1875.

96. "The Poet's Abiding Place," *Illustrated Homes,* p. 220. This is similar in feeling to Richardson's house at Arrochar, Staten Island, 1868, which can be characterized as "stick style."

of the Sturtevant House, free, varied, both utilitarian and plastic, but with
the entrance hall still only a circulation area and each volume of room separate from each other room, even though the rooms may open widely into
each other through sliding doors.[97]

By 1876, therefore, the stick style had developed into an interwoven basketry of sticks, and this feeling for the interweaving of building elements
was to develop later into that sense of the interweaving of spatial areas so
important in the achievements of the early eighties.[98] At the same time, this
way of building had formed a broad basis for new, original, and non-eclectic
growth. Born out of the alliance of picturesque variety with structural and
utilitarian "reality," it offered by 1876 a solid platform for further invention
in the domestic field; and by 1876 it was undoubtedly time that something
new should occur. The Pattern Books which had carried the original development since Downing had, by the early seventies, with the exception of
Gardner, lost much of their force and a good deal of their quality. The designs
in Bicknell's books of the period, for instance, while straight stick style, are
not good stick style. Although still imbued with the sense of the structural
skeleton (Fig. 20), they nevertheless tend to be coarse and rather awkward.[99]
They are generally pretentious and unsure of themselves, high-shouldered
agrarian cousins, twitching with nervous overcompensation in the urbanized
Eastern world of the early seventies. The cause of this is certainly apparent, for
the Jeffersonian-Jacksonian America which had produced the democratic
development of the Pattern Books was only a memory in the East by 1876.
The Civil War, the intoxication of industrialism, money, and power, had
changed the fiber of the country in a way which Thoreau earlier had feared.
A new and complicated urban culture was destroying the simpler, more
agrarian way of life. The roots of the old agrarianism had been largely torn
up and, with them, much in the way of individual initiative and pioneer
pride. However, a longing for these roots, or for their memory, was to continue to be one of the most positive factors in American society and in the
later phases of the domestic development itself.

97. The designs in *Illustrated Homes* illustrate all these characteristics, as well as the
typical expression of stick style of the houses as a whole. In plan, Gardner also occasionally
makes use of plain rectangles and even squares, as in "The Poet's Abiding Place."

98. The so-called traditional American "plain wall," hailed by Giedion and his followers, cannot therefore be considered of importance in the mid-century development and
its later effects. Cf. Giedion, *Space, Time and Architecture*, pp. 269–77. See note 52.

99. Basically a vulgarization of the material in *Woodward's National Architect*. There
are many Bicknell publications. Most typical is Amos Jackson Bicknell, *Detail, Cottage
and Constructive Architecture*, New York, 1873 (7 eds. to 1886), e.g. pl. 64.

Although a young generation of architects had now to cope with new and more difficult problems, still one of their primary sources of strength was to remain their romantic-rationalist background, rooted in the stick style of the mid-century. This had been, since Downing's time, always upon the side of originality, invention, and new growth. As even the hostile *American Architect and Building News* admitted in 1876, it was "... enterprising, inventive even, full of vivacity ... and ... it has life in it."[100] The longing for originality and invention which the stick style builders had developed by the early seventies was stated forcefully, if rather hysterically, by the vernacular builders' magazine, the *American Builder*. It insisted: "Nothing so cramps invention as the trammels of tradition. The cold hand of the dead clasping about our throats will yet choke utterance. What we want is, not to further rivet upon us the chains of the past, but to rise up to the possibilities of our own times and country."[101]

Yet the gift of the mid-century to the future was summed up more ably, and with a larger sense of the issues involved, by E. C. Gardner in 1875. For him all ways were open, and each man bore the responsibility of his freedom: "The noblest use of a good thing is as a foundation upon which something better may be builded.... the time has passed when any man or company of men can speak with authority. The duty of each to work out his own salvation has changed all the old plans of progress. To provoke original thought and inquiry is better than to give dogmatic instruction."[102]

Freedom and experiment in theory and in design were, consequently, the rich gifts of mid-century America to the architectural development which was to follow. The romantic-rationalists and their Pattern Books had carried domestic design through its first difficult phase of adjustment to nineteenth century conditions. More complex social aspirations, new structural and spatial expressions, and more sophisticated disciplines were now to arise. Yet the development here called the stick style influenced the approach to architectural form of the development which was to follow. It had begun to explore the possibilities of an architecture based upon the dynamics of interwoven members, rather than upon the statics of cubical masses, a line of investigation which was to prove exceedingly fruitful.

100. "American Architecture—Present," pp. 250–52.

101. *American Builder*, 8 (February 1873), 30. This monthly began publication in March 1868 and continued in various forms until May 1895. In the early seventies it was the spokesman for the rather materialistic utilitarianism of the vernacular builder and extremely hostile to the professional pretensions of the registered architect.

102. *Illustrated Homes,* pp. 286–87.

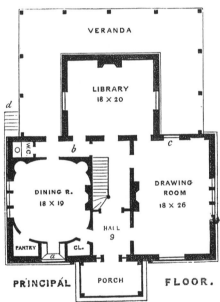

VERANDA

LIBRARY
18 × 20

d

W.C.

b

c

DINING R.
18 × 19

DRAWING
ROOM
18 × 26

HALL
9

PANTRY   CL.

a

PRINCIPAL   PORCH   FLOOR.

1. "A Cottage Villa in the Bracketed Mode," Design v
from Downing's *Cottage Residences*

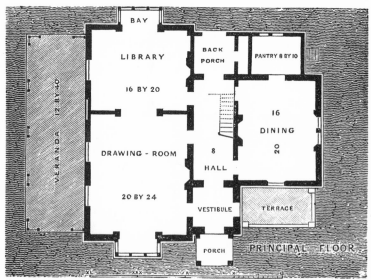

2. "A Villa in the Italian Style, Bracketed," Design VI
from Downing's *Cottage Residences*

3. "A Perspective View of a Cottage in the Swiss Style," Plate XLVI
from S. H. Brooks' *Designs for Cottage and Villa Architecture*

4. "A Cottage Villa in the Bracketed Mode," wooden version
of Design V from Downing's *Cottage Residences*

5. "A Laborer's Cottage," Design 1 from Downing's *Country Houses*

6. "Small Bracketed Cottage," Design 11 from Downing's *Country Houses*

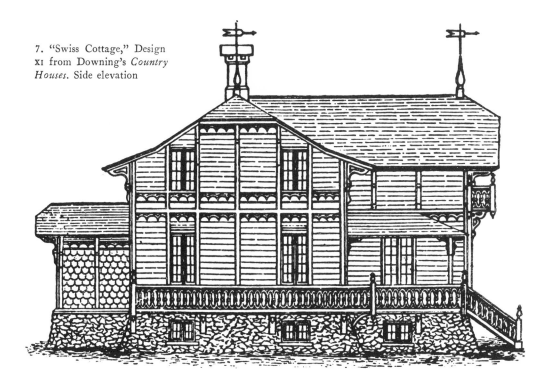

7. "Swiss Cottage," Design
XI from Downing's *Country
Houses*. Side elevation

8. "Design in the Swiss
Style of Architecture,"
Plate XLIX from Brooks'
*Designs for Cottage and
Villa Architecture*

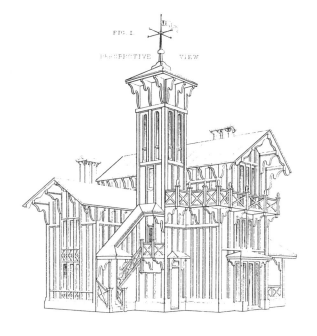

9. Board and batten house, Newport, R. I.,
ca. 1846 (King Covell)

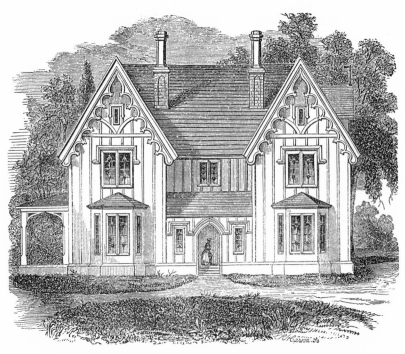

10. "A Plain Timber Cottage Villa," Brunswick, Maine, by Gervase Wheeler.
Design xxv from Downing's *Country Houses*. Front elevation

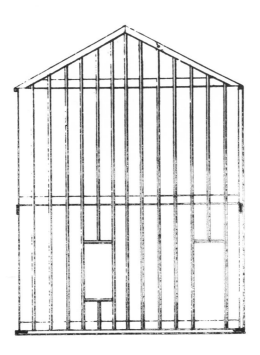

11. Balloon frame, Plate VI from
Bell's *Carpentry Made Easy*

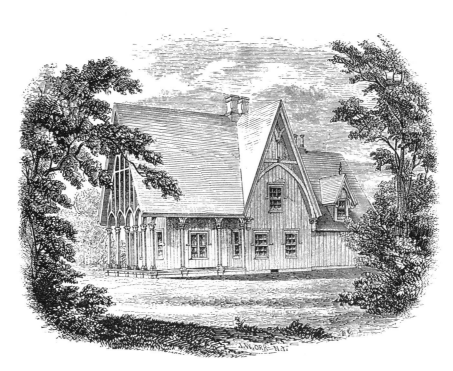

12. Olmstead House, near Hartford, Conn., by Gervase Wheeler,
from Wheeler's *Rural Homes*

13. Design XIII from Cleaveland's *Village and Farm Cottages*

14. Willoughby House, Hallidon Hill, Newport, R. I., by Leopold Eidlitz, 1854
(King Covell)

15. J. N. A. Griswold House, Newport, R. I., by Richard Morris Hunt, 1862
(King Covell)

16. Design VI from Woodward's *National Architect*

17. Bassett House, 484-486 Newhall Street, New Haven, Conn., 1869-1870

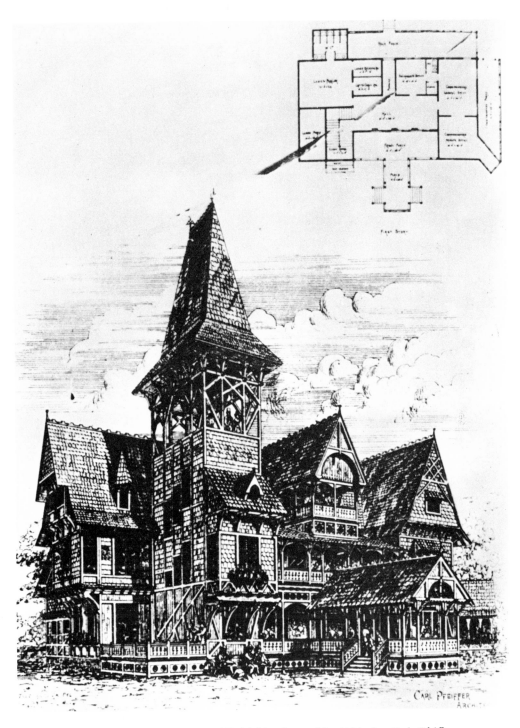

18. New Jersey Building, Philadelphia Centennial, 1876, by Carl Pfeiffer,
from *American Architect*

19. "The Poet's Abiding Place," from Gardner's *Illustrated Homes*

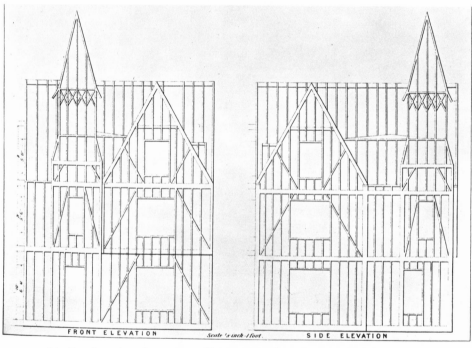

FRONT ELEVATION   *Scale ⅛ inch-1 foot*   SIDE ELEVATION

20. Framing plans for cottage, Plate LXXXIV from Bicknell's *Detail, Cottage
and Constructive Architecture*

21. Sturtevant (Jacob Cram) House, Middletown, R. I., by Dudley Newton, 1872. Exterior (King Covell)

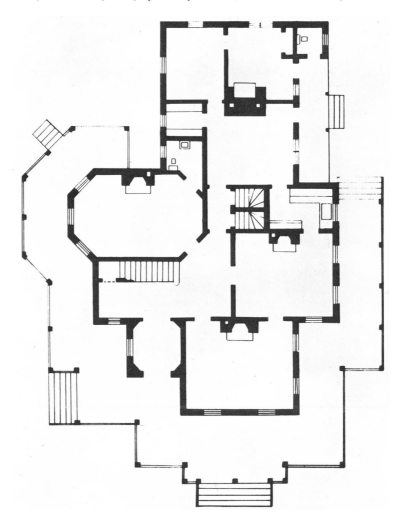

22. Sturtevant House. Plan

23. Sturtevant House. Detail of veranda (King Covell)

1. The Stick Style Reviewed.
H. H. Richardson and English
"Queen Anne," 1869–76

Many cultures have developed important architectural expression by apply-
ing techniques of wood construction to the erection of homes. The delicately woven pavilions of Japan and the heavy-roofed mountain houses of
southern Germany, Switzerland, and northern Italy come immediately to
mind.[1] Throughout northern Germany, Poland, Russia, and Scandinavia
long traditions of building with wood have produced characteristic and impressive forms.[2] These are the timber countries, and America itself has always
been a land of timber. Yet until the middle of the 19th century the United
States cannot be considered to have produced a uniquely American expression of timber form and domestic program. Continuing in the 17th century
a late medieval English tradition of space organization and building in wood,
the American houses of the period can easily be distinguished from their
English prototypes but cannot be considered American in any fundamental
sense.[3] Moreover, throughout the 18th and early 19th centuries American
building in wood turned further away from peculiarly wooden forms and
sought, from the English architectural books and later the American Build-

1. As illustrated in E. S. Morse, *Japanese Homes and Their Surroundings*, Boston,
1886; H. Stolper, *Bauen in Holz*, Stuttgart, 1933; P. Howald, *Das Gürbetal und sein
Bauenhaus*, Bern, n.d. (Berner Heimatbücher, No. 17); Christian Rubi, *Das Simmen-
thaler Bauenhaus*, Bern, n.d. (Berner Heimatbücher, Nos. 35–6).

2. As illustrated, e.g., in L. Dietrichson and H. Munthe, *Die Holzbaukunst Norwegens*,
Berlin, 1893; J. Meyer, *Fortids Kunst i Norges, Bygder*, Oslo, 1926; G. Näsström, *Svensk
Funktionalism* (Stockholm, 1930), ch. 1; and Roman Piotrowski, *Architektura Polska*,
Warsaw, 1952 (Do Polowy, No. 19).

3. Hugh Morrison, *Early American Architecture* (New York, 1952), ch. 3, pp. 49–98.

ers' Guides, to reproduce in wood the refined elegance and the cubical clarity of the stone, brick, and stucco forms of European provincial baroque and romantic classicism.[4] Again, the American houses can usually be distinguished from their European prototypes by linear precision and the thinness through which the wooden sheathing and details proclaim themselves. In all these developments the framing skeleton of the structure itself remained covered over. The skin of the house contained and defined its form; its expression was essentially cubical and closed.

Yet by the 1840's American domestic architecture in wood began to develop along lines of structural expression, picturesque massing, and free formal invention. Andrew Jackson Downing with his pattern books,[5] and the pattern book writers who followed him, buried the older, more abstract, and less supple Greek revival under a shower of ridicule and abuse. They absorbed the ethical romanticism of the English Gothic revival and applied its principles to American wooden-framed structures. Asymmetrical and free in plan, varied in massing, the wooden houses disseminated by the pattern books of the midcentury were distinguished most of all by the articulation of their thin wooden members and by the skeletal qualities derived from their frames. From the vertically boarded and battened cottages of the 40's and 50's to the involved basketry of the houses of the early 70's, primary emphasis was always given to structural and visual multiplication of the framing sticks. For Downing, Wheeler, and their followers the "truth" and the "reality" of the building resided in such expression. For these reasons I have attempted elsewhere to apply the name "stick style" to the development in wooden domestic architecture between 1840 and 1876.[6]

The architects of the stick style, though they participated in the whole

4. *Ibid.*, chs. 13, 14, pp. 381–472; T. Hamlin, *Greek Revival Architecture in America* (London, 1944), *passim*.

5. Andrew Jackson Downing, *A Treatise on the Theory and Practice of Landscape Gardening Adapted to North America . . . with remarks on rural architecture . . . ,* New York and London, 1841 (16 issues of 8 editions to 1879); *Cottage Residences; or, a series of designs for rural cottages and cottage villas, and their gardens and grounds, adapted to North America,* New York and London, 1842 (13 issues to 1887); *The Architecture of Country Houses, including designs for cottages, farm houses and villas, with remarks on interiors, furniture, and the best modes of warming and ventilating,* New York, 1850 (9 issues to 1866); and *Rural Essays,* New York, 1853 (7 issues to 1881). To this list should be added George Wightwick, *Hints to Young Architects . . . with additional notes and hints to persons about building in this country by A. J. Downing,* 1st American ed. New York, 1847.

6. See my "Romantic Rationalism and the Expression of Structure in Wood. Downing, Wheeler, Gardner, and the 'Stick Style,' 1840–1876," *Art Bulletin, 35* (1953), 121–42. See also my chapter "The Stick Style" in Downing and Scully, pp. 117–40; pls. 157–85.

suburban picturesque movement which had been going on in England since the mid-18th century, were also concerned with American conditions. As pattern book architects they were interested in cheap, small houses for everyone. Thus, one of their cultural bases was egalitarian, democratic, and Jacksonian. Again, their orientation toward the country, or failing that toward the suburb, could be traced back in America to the idealistic agrarianism which had played so large a part in Thomas Jefferson's philosophy.[7] Finally, their compelling concern with utility, labor-saving devices, and material expediency had long been part of the American attitude toward life. Such utilitarianism had been an important element in Jefferson's thought as well.

Democratic, agrarian, utilitarian, and preoccupied with American framing techniques, the builders of the stick style broke with the grand styles of the past and absorbed influences from the comparable wooden styles of Switzerland and Japan. Most of all, they brought the long and complex development of Renaissance design to a close and opened the field to new invention along 19th-century American lines. Eugene Clarence Gardner, one of the last of the important pattern book authors, stated in 1875:

> The noblest use of a good thing is as a foundation upon which something better may be builded. . . . the time has passed when any man or company of men can speak with authority. The duty of each to work out his own salvation has changed all the old plans of progress. To provoke original thought and inquiry is better than to give dogmatic instruction.[8]

Thus, by the 70's all paths seemed open to the future, and America was provided with a vernacular base of design which, as a hostile critic admitted in 1876, was "enterprising, inventive even, full of vivacity . . . and . . . it has life in it." [9]

The 1870's, however, brought profound and sweeping changes in American architecture. During this decade a new generation of architects came into its own. For the first time since the pattern books of the 40's had initiated an anonymous builders' development the professional architect began to exert a dominant influence upon the main stream of American domestic design. From among the architects of the 70's one pathfinding artistic personality

7. Cf. Alfred Whitney Griswold, *Farming and Democracy* (New York, 1948), ch. 2, "The Jeffersonian Ideal," pp. 8–46.

8. Eugene Clarence Gardner, *Illustrated Homes: a series of papers describing real houses and real people* (Boston, 1875), pp. 286–7.

9. "American Architecture—Present," editorial in the first professionally oriented architectural periodical, *American Architect and Building News, 1* (1876), 250–2.

emerged, to whose influence the other architects of the period were all in one way or another subjected. This was Henry Hobson Richardson. As early as 1869–71 Richardson began to experiment with a new kind of open interior space, based upon a concept of the living hall, which was closely related to the so-called "Queen Anne" planning being developed at the same time in England by Richard Norman Shaw. By 1874 Richardson, in his Watts Sherman House at Newport, a partial Americanization of Shaw's Queen Anne, had made his main contribution to the domestic development of the 70's. Thereafter, for the rest of the decade and until Richardson's return to domestic design in the early 80's, the field of experiment was open to the new generation as a whole. Upon these architects influences other than Richardson's and Shaw's Queen Anne were at work. American colonial architecture —partly brought into focus, as was the Queen Anne, by exhibitions at the Philadelphia Centennial of 1876—began to have a powerful effect and to supplement the Queen Anne itself. Other sources of inspiration and direction also began to be explored; Japanese architecture, for instance, had an important influence.

This was a self-conscious generation, tormented, as the men of the mid-century had seldom been, by a sense of history, of memory, and of cultural loss. Vaguely disturbed by the materialism of American culture as they found it, conscious of a spiritual mission to improve it, at the same time proud of themselves as a professional class, these architects pursued an erratic course among the new problems which confronted them. Eventually assimilating the new influences in their own creative way, they nevertheless developed certain academic attitudes and habits of design that were later to corrupt the very synthesis they accomplished. Consequently, it is necessary to consider in some detail the writings and theory of the architects and critics of the period. In these there took shape the patterns of thought and design which were of decisive importance for the future of American domestic architecture and American culture as a whole.

In his domestic work in wood in the late 60's Henry Hobson Richardson had become what might be called an architect of the stick style in its later phases. This fact can be clearly seen in the house he built for himself at Arrochar on Staten Island in 1868 (Fig. 1).[10] Its massing is high and angular, and its roof is a typical late stick-style variation of the Second Empire mansard. Its walls are skeletally articulated, and the clapboards are contained within the usual indications of the major members of the structural frame. The house is typical of its period. It shows Richardson's direct link with the

10. This house was never published in its period. It was rediscovered by Wayne Andrews and photographed by him.

stick style, but it is almost purely Richardsonian in the grave dignity it extracts from its wooden elements. The plan contained none of the innovations which were about to become important.[11]

These innovations appear in the work of Richardson between 1869 and 1871 in his Codman project (Fig. 2). (The Dorsheimer plan, found among Richardson's archives by Hitchcock and published by him as possibly belonging to the Dorsheimer House, Buffalo, 1868, cannot bear any relation to that house and is no longer believed by Hitchcock himself to be so related.)[12] In the Codman project a small entry opens into a large hall. At the far end a fireplace inglenook and a staircase face the door. A drawing room opens off the hall to the left and a dining room to the right. Except for the service areas behind the dining room, the three units of hall, drawing room, and dining room form the only spatial divisions of the ground floor. The great hall creates one large volume, from which the subsidiary volumes branch clearly. Both the space division and the functions are thus simplified. The hall with its fireplace serves not only as a horizontal and vertical circulation area but also as an open and informal main living area. The specific functions of secluded living and dining are assigned to specialized spaces. The hall thus becomes the living core of the house and expresses that function in an expansion of space and in a combination of essential architectural and functional elements: entrance, fireplace, and stairs.[13]

11. There is no living hall, nor does the exterior give any more expression of a unified interior volume than do the other stick style structures of the period.

12. Henry-Russell Hitchcock, *The Architecture of H. H. Richardson and His Times* (New York, 1936), fig. 16 and pp. 83–4. William Edward Dorsheimer, 1832–88, was a prominent Democratic politician in New York during this period. From 1867 to 1871 he was federal district attorney for the northern district of the state, when the Buffalo house was built. From 1874 to 1878 he was lieutenant-governor of the state, with his headquarters, naturally, in Albany. It is probable that during this period an Albany house was projected but never built because of Dorsheimer's fall from political favor and consequent removal from Albany because of a disagreement with Tilden. He was, however, elected to Congress in 1882. *Dictionary of American Biography, 5,* 387–8.

Parisian town house types of the midcentury very closely resemble this Dorsheimer plan. As an example of the type, the Maison Imbert des Mottelettes, Rue d'Amsterdam, by Mortier, makes use of an axial passage between two shops to a central courtyard, very similar to the Dorsheimer arrangement of an axial corridor with a room on either side which opens into a central living hall. Victor Calliat, *Parallèle des maisons de Paris construites depuis 1830 jusqu'à nos jours* (Paris, 1857; 2d ed. 1864), pl. 116.

13. The use for which such a hall was intended and to which it was put has been stated by no one more succinctly than by Henry James in his novel *The Other House* (written originally as a play, *The Promise*), 2 vols. New York, 1896; new ed. London, 1947. James writes (p. 6) of his heroine, "ushered into the hall, it struck her first as empty. . . . Bright, large and high, richly decorated and freely used, full of 'corners'

Such a hall was new at this moment in American planning. Some of the houses of the 40's and 50's had provided a large central hall, but this had generally remained a kind of dramatized vestibule. Usually its function had been merely circulatory, as in a house by Alexander Jackson Davis, published by Downing.[14] Another, smaller Davis house made use of a room with fireplace off the entrance and labeled "hall," but this opened into the living room only and contained no staircase; thus it by no means formed the spatial core of the house.[15] Actually, most domestic planning of the midcentury in America tended to play down the hall except as a circulation area, though often ample and occasionally impressive with its staircase.[16] It is true that the pattern book writers, Calvert Vaux in the 50's and Henry Hudson Holly in the 60's, included among their many plans some that made use of living halls, but these had by no means dominated their plan-types and do not seem to have greatly affected American planning as a whole.[17] Though the living hall as such had consequently been at least available as a plan since the 40's, it had tended to remain a recessive feature. More significantly, the domestic planning of the late 60's and early 70's in general, as evidenced in the last phases of the stick style, was inclined to be even less concerned than in its earlier phases with the hall as anything but a utilitarian passageway. It was narrowed down, its stairs directed upward as steeply as possible, and its potentialities as a spatial feature were generally, if not always, ignored.[18]

Thus the great hall of the Codman project can be called the first of a new line of domestic planning in America, and its origins are probably

---

and communications, it evidently played equally the part of a place of reunion and of a place of transit. . . . The shaded summer sun was in it now, and the odour of many flowers."

14. Downing, *Country Houses*, design 31, p. 338, fig. 161.

15. L. B. Brown House, Rahway, New Jersey. *Ibid.*, design 23, p. 292, figs. 125–6.

16. Austin's and Upjohn's Italian villa halls are excellent examples of this. Cf. C. L. V. Meeks, "Henry Austin and the Italian Villa," *Art Bulletin*, 30 (1948), 145–9. See also Everard Upjohn, *Richard Upjohn, Architect and Churchman*, New York, 1939.

17. Calvert Vaux, *Villas and Cottages*, New York, 1857. Henry Hudson Holly, *Holly's Country Seats*, New York, 1863. See also Gervase Wheeler's "A Plain Timber Cottage Villa," published as design 25 in Downing's *Country Houses*, 1850. This house had a large hall, but without fireplace. When the design was adapted by another builder and pattern book writer, the hall, significantly, was reduced in size. Cf. William Brown, *The Carpenter's Assistant* (5th ed. Boston, 1853), pp. 42–4, figs. 11, 13.

18. The Sturtevant House at Newport (Downing and Scully, pl. 179) and E. C. Gardner's projects are examples, as are also those in the Boston and New York Architectural Sketch Books of the early 70's.

not difficult to discover. The French influences, so strong in the mysterious Dorsheimer plan, are less apparent here. Though midcentury Parisian examples of houses containing a large hall with fireplace and stairs exist and were published, they were extremely rare and actually closer in conception to the monumental vestibule than to the living hall.[19] English examples were more numerous, and much more similar in function both as circulation area and as living hall. It is impossible to say whether Richardson saw and was impressed by any typical medieval halls of this type during his summer tour through England on his way to the École des Beaux-Arts in 1859.[20] Nor need he, in 1869, have been familiar with the buildings of Philip Webb, Nesfield, or Norman Shaw, since their work had not been published at that time.[21] Still, in the late 60's two English sources might easily have given Richardson the idea for the living hall. The first, Kerr's *The English Gentleman's House, or, how to plan English residences,* was published in 1864, with a second edition in 1865.[22] Kerr's book contains several examples of midcentury houses that use a living hall with fireplace and stairs. The most important and most skillfully designed was undoubtedly Hinderton, Cheshire, by Alfred Waterhouse, dated 1859.[23] Hinderton contained a small but pivotal hall (Fig. 3). It included both a large fireplace and a staircase. Library, dining rooms, and drawing rooms opened off the hall, which thus became not an extra room but the spatial center of the house. The early date is interesting, since it reveals that Shaw was by no means the first architect to bring the medieval hall to 19th-century English house planning.

Kerr's book presents the living hall as an important and peculiarly Elizabethan feature in English planning of the late 50's and early 60's.[24] In his historical sketch of English house development he emphasizes the changing nature of the hall under the pressure of Italian Renaissance influence. Plans

19. As in the house in the Rue de Courcelles by Victor Lenoir, illustrated by Calliat, pl. 41. Here the hall, labeled "galerie," contains a fireplace, and an antechamber in which the staircase rises. It is the only such example in Calliat.

20. Hitchcock, *Richardson,* pp. 24–5.

21. No reproductions of Shaw's drawings were published until 1871, nor was Webb, with the exception of one city house, published during the period.

22. Robert Kerr, *The English Gentleman's House, or, how to plan English residences,* London, 1864; 2d ed. 1865. Kerr was professor of architecture at the Royal Academy and after a youth reported to have been architecturally wild was settling down into an academic cast of mind.

23. *Ibid.* (1865), pl. 29.

24. *Ibid.,* pl. 35. Kerr's own predilection was for the Renaissance. He himself had few medieval sympathies.

of Wolterton Manor, Oxburgh Hall in Norfolk, and Hengrave Hall in Suffolk are reproduced as typical of medieval practice.[25] These contained fireplaces and were communal living spaces, but they included no staircases. Hatfield and Longleat are reproduced as typically Elizabethan, using fireplaces, window bays, stairs, and galleries.[26] The stairs, according to Kerr, began to appear under Renaissance influence when more rooms were added for privacy. In such a scheme the hall becomes both living and circulation center, as in the Codman House. Kerr clearly states this concept of the dual nature of the developed Elizabethan hall: "The combined Hall and Staircase . . . assume very much the character of a Gothic Hall, with its Entry and Screen; its main area, however, being occupied by a stately Staircase." [27] This belief in the semi-Renaissance character of the living and circulation hall in England in the 1860's may also be important in the "Queen Anne" attitude of Norman Shaw. Halls with stairs seem to have become associated with that 16th-century—and in the vernacular 17th- and early 18th-century—period in English domestic architecture, which was half medieval and half Renaissance. Indeed, a better name for Shaw's early houses might be Elizabethan rather than Queen Anne. The term "Queen Anne" is undoubtedly a misnomer when applied to this whole development, but it was used from the very beginning and has the advantage of pointing up the direction the movement took from a late medievalism toward an eventual 18th-century classicism. In a strange way the development called Queen Anne re-created the whole process of the English Renaissance itself.

Not only Kerr's book, which Richardson certainly knew, but also the British architectural magazine *Builder*, to which Richardson subscribed, published several examples of living-hall plans in the late 60's.[28] These became more numerous between 1866 and 1868. In 1866 only one such plan appeared and that in Kerr's rather tight and academic manner.[29] In 1867 again only one appeared, very like the one of 1866, enclosed within a rectangular plan academically composed, but using stairs and fireplace as its significant components.[30] In 1868, however, four such plans were published,

25. *Ibid.*, pls. 6–8.

26. *Ibid.*, pls. 9, 40.

27. *Ibid.*, p. 444.

28. Hitchcock, *Richardson*, p. 73. The relation of the Western R. R. Offices, Springfield, Mass., 1867–69, to Gilbert Scott's Foreign Office, *Builder*, July 14, 1866, certainly reveals a connection.

29. Leigh Park, near Portsmouth, by R. W. Drew, *Builder*, March 17, 1866.

30. A frightful building: "Normanhurst," Battle, Sussex, by Habershorn, Brock, and Webb (not Philip). *Builder*, June 8, 1877. One senses that these people read Kerr too

none of them outstanding but as a group capable of suggesting to a perceptive young architect that a large hall with fireplace and stairs offered possibilities for a new kind of spacious planning.[31]

Of all these plans Richardson's for the Codman House is undoubtedly the best (Fig. 2). Although the hall is somewhat awkward in shape, it nevertheless opens out the space of the house more emphatically than do the halls in the English plans, and the subsidiary spaces, as already pointed out, are kept to a minimum. Outside, the Codman House still conformed in general to that sense of the skeletal stick that was typical of its period. But the diamond-paned windows bring to the surface a sense of the interior volume of space that is foreign to the stick style: instead of appearing as neutral voids between the studs of the skeleton, the windows, with their many leaded panes begin to give a sense of continuity to the surface. It is just this sense of the surface enclosing a volume which is new here and in sharp contrast to the purely skeleton energy of the midcentury stick style.

These, then, were the Richardsonian innovations in domestic design in America: a new sense of open interior space and a new feeling for the surface as enclosing that space. In the nature of structural expression, at least as far as wood is concerned, there was the beginning of a shift in emphasis from the skeleton itself to the surfacing material. This can be seen in Richardson's house for F. W. Andrews, Newport, 1872 (Fig. 4). It also was part of the movement toward a continuity of surface, expressive of interior volumes, which Richardson first displayed in the leaded windows of the Codman project.

The Andrews House [32] exhibits the same kind of plan as the Codman project but more loosely developed (Fig. 5). The subsidiary rooms seem really to cluster about the hall, to depend upon it for cohesion, and to modify it by their smaller and different shapes.[33] The plan of the Andrews House, then, although it may be traced to English influence, nevertheless opened up the interior space more fully than did comparable English plans. Richard-

carefully. Certainly their hall becomes as much like a *cortile* as possible, as it does in Kerr's own designs.

31. One of these, Ascot-Heath House, Berkshire, is by Kerr himself. *Builder,* Dec. 19, 1868. It bears much more of a resemblance to the Dorsheimer project than to the Codman House.

32. Hitchcock, *Richardson,* pls. 35, 36.

33. We know the Andrews House only from drawings; it was built but later burned, and no photographs have as yet been discovered. Thus it is impossible to state definitely that there was an actual flow of space between the rooms and the hall. Nevertheless, the wide openings to be seen in the plan would indicate at least a close visual relationship.

son's use of clapboards on its ground floor and shingles on the upper floors must probably by this time be attributed to the influence of Norman Shaw's Queen Anne. While the over-all impression of the exterior of the Andrews House is of the stick style, high, angular, and skeletal, the diamond windows of the otherwise purely stick-style Codman project, which tended to create a continuity of surface, have here been reinforced by the warm texture of shingles, which also serve to emphasize the surface as opposed to the skeleton. This important change in the treatment of surface, striking as it does directly at the heart of the stick style and transforming it, can be traced only to Shaw's published work, which began to appear in the English architectural magazines in 1871.

In March of that year *Building News* published the impressive full-page photolithographs of Leyes Wood, Sussex (Fig. 6), which Shaw had built in 1868.[34] The new photolithographic process, just put into use by *Building News* but not by the *Builder,* reproduced Shaw's marvelously textural rendering technique with a richness of light and shade that line engraving could never have captured. Just as the formal sensitivity that produced the stick style of the midcentury owed much to the sharp delineation of line engravings, so in the early 70's the pictorial lushness of photolithographic reproduction was intimately related to the architectural movement toward textured, flowing, and painterly surfaces.[35] Elegant and assured, Shaw's renderings of

34. *Building News,* Mar. 31, 1871. This was the first Shaw work published anywhere.

35. This point is not without significance. The whole angular, sharp, jagged nature of the stick style in America and of "Victorian Gothic" as a whole is so similar to the hard line technique of the wood engravings of the architectural reproductions in the books of the period that there must be considered to be an aesthetic affinity between them. Each obviously affects, modifies, and partly forms the other, and sets up a whole system of vision in hard lines. Conversely, the widespread introduction of photolithography in the early 70's, which made possible a painterly and extremely textural reproduction of architectural rendering—actually in facsimile reproduction—coincides so closely with the new architectural vision of warmly textured surfaces that the argument of a creative connection in the 19th century among rendering, reproductive techniques and architecture itself is strongly reinforced. Each art affects the other and partly creates it. This must be considered one of the reasons why none of the mid-century eclecticisms, however occasionally based upon archaeology, is ever wholly unoriginal. Always the factor of graphic technique intervenes and transforms the copy, and the archaeological object reaches the architect through a constantly metamorphosing chain of 19th-century techniques. With the perfection of methods for reproducing photographs and the beginnings of a heavy use of photographic material in the architectural magazines in the middle 80's, a new factor comes on the scene, for now the object to be copied appears before the architect untouched, as it were, by 19th-century hands—recorded but only meagerly re-evaluated by 19th-century vision. In this process the Beaux-Arts water color wash

Leyes Wood must have been an aesthetic revelation to all who saw them, and while Leyes Wood is by no means the first of Shaw's houses, whether done alone or in collaboration with Nesfield, it is the first with which we need concern ourselves here, since only this house and those published after it can be considered especially influential upon the domestic development in America.[36]

In general Leyes Wood explicitly revives late medieval domestic forms with an added plaster decoration of semiclassical Renaissance motifs. Its gables and its window bays with small, leaded panes recall Tudor domestic practice, as does its great two-storied hall.[37] Leyes Wood, therefore—domestic in scale, freely planned, richly surfaced, and coherent in design—was nevertheless an eclectic house, unashamedly derivative.

A comparison with Philip Webb's Red House for William Morris, 1858–60, is instructive in this respect. The Red House is a kind of simple farmhouse, built of brick, without any extraneous tiles, straightforward in its adjustment to function, integral and expressive in construction.[38] There is a simple state-

---

of the 90's and after—less specifically architectural than the earlier techniques and, partly through the concomitant use of photographic material, accepted largely as a picture relating only to itself—must probably be considered of comparable importance.

36. For a fuller but by no means satisfactory account of Shaw's work see Sir Reginald Blomfield, *Richard Norman Shaw, R. A.*, London, 1940. Blomfield's academic prejudices cause him to be little interested in Shaw's early work. Although he does include some plans and sections of Shaw's earlier and more medieval houses, his main intention is to show how Shaw later fortunately turned away from such nonsense in favor of classicistic design. Similarly, the only book on Philip Webb—William Richard Lethaby, *Philip Webb and His Work*, London, 1935—is also unsatisfactory. Though Lethaby is probably a more sensitive critic and creative thinker than Blomfield, he includes no plans and is discursive and unmethodical in his presentation. Henry-Russell Hitchcock's *Early Victorian Architecture in Britain* (New Haven, 1954) deals only with the pre-Webb and Shaw period.

The plan of Leyes Wood has been published, to my knowledge, only twice, first in Herman Muthesius, *Das Englische Haus*, Berlin, 1908; and second in P. Morton Shand, "Looping the Loop," *Architectural Review*, 77 (March, 1935), 99–104.

37. As a matter of fact *Building News* (March 31, 1871; p. 244) says of Leyes Wood, "in arrangement it is like any other modern house." This shows that the hall itself was not considered unusual, but that the house as a whole was felt to be archaizing enough so that the fact of its modern planning had to be stated explicitly. The *Builder* earlier had said, without reproducing a view: "admirable specimen of the peculiar style at which he is proficient, embodying so much of old English sentiment, a revival of the past which it is more lawful to indulge in a private house for the gratifying of a man's own taste, than in more public places." *Builder* (1870), p. 359.

38. Lethaby, pl. 1.

ment of essentials in the Red House. It faces up to the nature of vernacular construction in brick. It was thus comparable in intent and "reality" to the American stick style and grew from similar romantic-rationalist principles.[39] At the same time it used a small living hall.[40]

But Leyes Wood is different. Although it developed the living hall, the domestic scale, and the adjustment to domestic function characteristic of the Red House, the style had now become overtly traditional, openly Old English. With their tile hangings or half timber over perfectly sound brick walls, Shaw's houses were no longer true in the sense in which the midcentury had used the word, nor were they "real" according to that usage. In the intrinsic meaning of the English Gothic revival and American stick style they were antiquarian and decoratively conceived houses: architectural pastiches, though wholly charming. This dual nature of Shaw's early Queen Anne houses needs to be kept in mind. If they inspired later original work in America and England, they also gave rise to thousands of Tudor cottages both here and in England. Also, with their classical details and their break with Gothic revival "truth," they set the stage for the eclectic manifestations of the late 19th century, into which Shaw himself eventually moved.

Their charm, aided by the marvelous technique of Shaw's sketches, was immediately potent, and from 1871 on, *Building News* published them regularly. In August of 1871 appeared Preen Manor, built in 1870–71. Though no plan was included, it was stated that Preen had a "hall and staircase about 35 ft. by 18 ft. from which enter [*sic*] the drawing-room and library." [41] At this time sketchy views of old half-timbered streets began to appear in *Building News,* as evidence of the antiquarianism which formed part of Shaw's appeal.[42] *Building News,* to be sure, did not surrender to this trend without some struggle. In May, 1872, it published a review of the Royal Academy Exhibition of Architecture of that year, mentioning "Grim's Dyke," Harrow Weald, for T. Goodall, R. A., as well as "Cragside," Lothbury, Northumberland, both of which Shaw had exhibited. It accompanied the text with a perspective view of Cragside, again with no plan. *Building*

39. Scully, "Romantic Rationalism," pp. 135–8.

40. This can hardly have had an effect in America, since it was not published.

41. *Building News,* Aug. 11, 1871. A large two-page view. The *Builder* (1871), p. 340, said of Preen, "one of Mr. Shaw's admirable etchings in the picturesque style he has made his own." It admired "the domestic quiet and homeliness, though belonging more to the past than to the present."

42. *Building News* Aug. 18, 1871; Nov. 10, 1871. Mention should be made here of Richard Norman Shaw's picturesque book *Architectural Sketches from the Continent,* first published in London in 1858 and as a second ed., because of Shaw's growing popularity, in 1872.

News extolled these houses, but added, "The design of the two works criti-cized above is, however, quite open to the observation that it is hardly at all modern. It is a reproduction of past times; but it *is* a reproduction, pure and simple. This, we think, can hardly be said of Mr. Street's work." [43] That *Building News* was alluding to Street's Law Courts may confuse modern readers, but it shows how critics in 1872 felt that Victorian Gothic was pre-sumably produced from a set of principles, while Shaw's work was held to be eclectic and unprincipled.

The semi-Tudor, tiled, and half-timbered designs that now began to flood the pages of *Building News* point up the current popularity of the Queen Anne style.[44] Yet none of those published offered anything really new that could have exerted positive influence upon American architects beyond Shaw's own example. Plans especially, some of which were published, were unexceptional and cannot be considered significant. But by the end of 1873 and early 1874 not only Godwin but also Street, fresh from the accolade bestowed upon him by *Building News* for his freedom from Queen Anne antiquarianism, had succumbed to the Queen Anne, and he published de-signs that revealed the direct influence of Shaw's work.[45] Consequently, wherever Americans might have looked in the pages of *Building News* dur-ing 1873 and 1874, they would have been faced by the brick, the half timber, and above all the tile hangings and leaded casements in generous banks, of the Queen Anne. And though in 1873 they might have seen the magnificent full-page lithograph of Shaw's New Zealand Chambers (Fig. 7)—a monu-

43. *Building News* (May 10, 1872), p. 381. Harrow Weald was illustrated by a lithographic view in *Building News*, September 6, 1872. Again no plan. Of this the *Builder* (1872), p. 358, said, "the architect's usual manner in plain and unpretentious mansions; usual simple picturesque treatment of windows, usual cutting up of roof and walls in a somewhat exaggerated effort at piquant and picturesque expression."

44. Another indication of the full arrival of the Queen Anne was its acceptance at this time by that belated champion of the Gothic revival, Charles Locke Eastlake. In his book, *The Gothic Revival* (London, 1871), Eastlake reproduced views of Cloverley Hall and Leyes Wood and stated that Shaw had broken through many prejudices concerning the expression of construction, often concealing his ceiling construction beneath molded plaster ornament.

45. George Edmund Street's design was the New Rectory House, Wigan. *Building News,* Oct. 3, 1873. Edward W. Godwin built a wild one, somewhat similar in feeling to a later house in America by Bruce Price ("The Craigs," Mt. Desert, 1879) but characteristically with not so open a plan. *Building News,* July 3, 1874. Godwin's importance in the development of the English Queen Anne was certainly considerable, especially in its later phases. Dudley Hebron's recent book establishes Godwin's importance but suffers from a lack of pertinent illustrations. Dudley Hebron, *The Conscious Stone,* London, 1949.

ment of the urban Queen Anne in red brick, gables, white trim, and bayed casements that was to provoke a flood of imitation in American urban architecture—for our purposes it is more significant that in May, 1874, *Building News* published a perspective and plan of "Hopedene," Surrey (Fig. 8), just completed by Shaw.[46] The horizontal divisions of the mass of the house into brick below, tiles above; the banked, leaded casements; and the plaster ornament were undoubtedly familiar to many people in America by this time, but the plan was probably the first of Shaw's domestic plans to be seen by most American architects. As in Richardson's Codman House, but much more simply arranged, the specialized spaces of library, drawing room, and dining room open off the hall, whence a corridor leads to the service area. This kind of planning may be called peripherally additive, controlled by the center. That is to say, the individual spaces develop as needed, without regard to rule, around a more or less central hall, a freely placed volume of space containing entrance, fireplace, and stairs.

Contemporaneously with the publication of Hopedene Richardson built his one and only overtly Shavian house. This was the Watts Sherman House at Newport, 1874, in which he brought Queen Anne on American soil forcibly to the attention of American architects. Richardson's earlier planning innovations had apparently affected nobody, while the use of shingled surfaces, as in the Andrews House, seems to have influenced only those architects in close association with him, such as Gambrill, his partner, and Charles Follen McKim, the young draughtsman who was with Richardson from 1870 to 1872.[47] Upon houses built by these men in 1874, such as McKim's Blake House in Newton Lower Falls, Massachusetts, or Gambrill's Tinkham House in Oswego, New York, shingles appeared as the surfacing material of the upper floors, but no hint of the new space opened up the interiors. Shaw's English tiles were difficult to manufacture in America.[48] Shingles, a native

46. *Building News,* May 8, 1874.

47. Charles Gambrill was Richardson's partner from 1867. His was a "dim" artistic personality, according to Hitchcock, and the partnership seems to have been purely for business and office-space purposes, a not uncommon practice among architects. Cf. Hitchcock, *Richardson.* Charles Follen McKim, 1847–1909, spent one year at Harvard (1866–67), where he distinguished himself at right field for the baseball team, attended the Beaux-Arts in Paris from 1867 to 1870, entered Richardson's office in 1870, and left it in 1872. For further information see Charles Moore, *The Life and Times of Charles Follen McKim,* Boston, 1929.

48. The attempts to introduce the manufacture of tiles in America in the early 70's were never very successful, and though some houses were tiled during the 70's the use of the foreign material was much overshadowed by the use of shingles.

but generally neglected material, offered a practical substitute. On McKim's and Gambrill's houses, as on Richardson's, shingles were without doubt an Americanization of Shaw's tiles. At any rate, William R. Mead, shortly after entering into partnership with McKim in 1872, took up the fashion in a small house at Peekskill, New York, and in a summer hotel on Cayuga Lake. Again the shingling was confined to the upper zones, and no new sense of space was apparent in the plan.[49]

With the Watts Sherman House (Figs. 9, 10, 11, 12) Richardson went beyond what he or anyone else had done and produced a design that adopted all aspects of Shavian domestic architecture. Of all Richardson's or his associates' houses up to this point the Watts Sherman House is undoubtedly the most mature in design, and also the most immediately derivative. But the planning itself was by this time as much Richardson's as Shaw's, and it is more open. The living-hall arrangement of monumental fireplace and monumental stair has scale, unity, amplitude, and calm. The beamed ceiling is rather lower than those of the vertical midcentury houses. This space creates a sense of horizontal extension and relaxation that is Richardsonian, since he could not have known any such device in Shaw's work. In the midcentury houses the very verticality of the rooms is usually enhanced by a plain plaster ceiling, but in the Watts Sherman House the beams stress the ceiling plane, bring it down, reduce verticality, and accent the horizontal. The mass of the house, seen as Richardson designed it and before the later additions (Fig 9), was much more vertical and thereby less Queen Anne than the horizontal spreads of Shaw's English houses.[50] Yet all the elements of the exterior are of direct Queen Anne derivation—the entrance porch, the high brick chimney, and

49. *New York Sketch Book of Architecture,* 1874. William Rutherford Mead graduated from Amherst in 1867, spent a year in an engineer's office, and from 1868 to 1871 was in the office of Russell Sturgis (who built Farnam, Lawrence, and Durfee Halls on the Old Campus at Yale), under the direct supervision of George Fletcher Babb (whose firm—Babb, Cook, and Willard—built the Atwater-Ciampolini House on Whitney Avenue, New Haven, in 1890). Mead then spent part of 1871 and 1872 in Florence, studying at the Accademia delle Belle Arte. In 1872 he returned and entered into a kind of loose partnership with McKim and William B. Bigelow, to whose sister McKim was briefly married. Moore, pp. 40–1.

50. No Shaw interior views had been published, nor can I find anywhere any statement which Richardson might have seen concerning the height of Shaw's ceilings. He could have deduced it from published views already discussed, as he might have deduced exposed beams as a medievalizing adjunct. The low ceiling thereby becomes at least partly an original creative process on Richardson's part. The greater verticality of the exterior can be seen in the *New York Sketch Book of Architecture* for 1874, which published Richardson's perspective almost as originally built.

the horizontal window bands in the gable above the entrance, filled in with stucco and half-timbered panels to keep the horizontal continuity of surface in that area.

The Watts Sherman House has qualities of its own. The texture of the shingled surface is warmer, rougher, and more painterly than the smoother English tiles of Shaw's work. The stucco in the half-timbered panels is rose-red, rich and deep in tone, and the mortar joints of the random ashlar masonry of the ground floor are slim, sinuous veins of red. The gable stucco is warm beige, to which, perhaps fortunately, the plaster ornament of the main gable was never added. The porte-cochère is low enough for one to sense the light pressure of its presence overhead and yet high enough so that the scale is not unduly forced. Entering under this into the main hall, one must turn to the right a little awkwardly to avoid the stairs and thus faces, across the hall, the high fireplace with its projecting hood. This noble monument appears to be free standing because of the wide openings on either side through which space flows into library and drawing room (Figs. 10, 11). In these relationships of simple and monumental elements, of ample stairs turning as they rise, of high fireplace, the space takes on palpable order and quiet. Light comes into the hall through the great window wall on the entrance side, filled with richly handled stained glass by LaFarge. Though a sense of Richardsonian unity pervades the whole, certain elements in the house reveal the painterly hand of Richardson's young assistant, Stanford White.

Desiring as a youth to be a painter, and with considerable gifts in that line, White had been advised by John LaFarge to give up the idea as unremunerative. As a result he had entered Richardson's office as a draughtsman in 1872, the year in which the building of Trinity Church in Boston began.[51] White had no architectural training when he came to Richardson, but he rapidly made himself useful as a draughtsman and design assistant. The drawing of the living hall of the Watts Sherman House (Fig. 12) which appeared in the *New York Sketch Book of Architecture* of 1875 is probably his.[52] White's

51. For further information on Stanford White see Baldwin's biography, appropriately less pompous than Moore's biography of McKim. Charles Baldwin, *Stanford White,* New York, 1931.

52. *New York Sketch Book of Architecture,* 1875. Reprinted in *Examples of Architecture,* 1880. The drawing is unsigned but looks like White's work, and it has always been assumed that it is his. The sense of light and space that White captured in this drawing is only a little marred by the fact that no such view of the living hall is actually possible from any point in the house. It is instructive to compare this atmospheric and brilliant creation of White's with two drawings of this period by men who were later to become his partners. Mead's interior perspective of the hall of his small house at Peekskill (in *Sketch Book,* above; also reproduced in *Examples of Archi-*

decorative skill and sense of delicate scale at this time, disciplined by Richardson's sense of the architectonic relationships of simple elements, can be seen nowhere more convincingly than in the Watts Sherman House. The library, redecorated by him before 1880 (Fig. 13), is paneled in green, picked out by linear designs in gold. Though the paneling itself is probably colonial in inspiration, it seems also to owe something to Hispano-Moresque prototypes. Some of the designs, especially those over the doorways, can be considered proto-Art Nouveau and even to some extent proto-Sullivanian. Thin, sinuous plant stems of gold whip in curving lines across other curves, in a way similar to the Art Nouveau decoration of the Victor Horta House of 1893 in Brussels, or even to Sullivan's ironwork ornament on the lower floors of the Carson Pirie Scott Store of 1899–1904.[53] The light blue and white Dutch tiles of the hall fireplace may also be a White touch, and to him may be due, on the exterior, the enlivening red tint of the stucco and the mortar.[54]

The Watts Sherman House must have said two things to architects in 1875: first, that it was a work of art of a quality few had attained; second, that it was an English manor house. It would be easy to take the next step and assert that it was the work of art *because* it was an English manor house. For this duality in the Watts Sherman House the talented Stanford White may probably be held responsible. It would appear that Richardson—who was experimenting, as has been shown, with a style parallel to Shaw's Queen Anne and who by the time of the Andrews House of 1872 was certainly influenced by Shaw—turned to a close adaptation of Shaw's Queen Anne only under what may loosely be called he influence of Stanford White. Indeed, it may be

---

tecture) is hard, linear, awkward, honest. Without atmospheric effects or any sense of space and light it is accurate but unimaginative and unattractive—an engineer's drawing without sensitivity. On the other hand, the McKim interior perspective of the hall in his Livermore House, Montclair, N. J. (also reproduced in *Examples of Architecture*), while it laboriously attempts to reproduce those varieties of light so effortlessly created by White, is nevertheless awkward, confused, and basically as hard and unimaginative as the Mead drawing, although it attempts an atmospheric effect. Yet McKim brings one directly into the architectural space and makes him feel the actual volume. Like Mead's drawing, but unlike White's, McKim's is architecturally honest in a professional sense. The three men somehow emerge as personalities from this comparison: White extraordinarily talented but tending toward architectural irresponsibility; Mead solid and direct but without any particular gift for design; McKim attempting not very successfully to be what he is not, but with a real feeling for space and control.

53. Giedion, *Space, Time and Architecture* (pl. 127), reproduces the Horta interior, 12 Rue de Turin, Brussels. For the Sullivan ornament on the lower zones of the Carson Pirie Scott store see Hugh Morrison, *Louis Sullivan* (New York, 1935), pl. 61.

54. Hitchcock believes White responsible for all the decorative detail. *Richardson*, pp. 156–61.

recalled that an analogous situation arose with respect to the tower of Trinity Church. Richardson, involved with structural difficulties as the building began in 1872 and needing a new tower to cap the design, finally accepted an adaptation by White of the Spanish Romanesque towers of Salamanca Cathedral, based on a photograph originally sent to Richardson by the painter LaFarge.[55] In 1877, when a correspondent wrote to the *American Architect and Building News* that the tower of Trinity was successful precisely because it was borrowed from that of Salamanca, the *Architect* agreed.[56] This attitude toward the virtues of archaeological borrowing, so foreign to midcentury ideals of assimilation and experiment, was therefore a new phenomenon in the middle 70's. It was probably unfortunate that two of the early monuments by which Richardson began to exert a wide influence were thus categorized.

Certainly a quality of decorative superficiality characterizes the few Queen Anne designs that appeared in America between 1874 and early 1876. Apart from two emanating from Richardson's office (but probably the work of White) [57] the most interesting project was by Oakey and Jones of New York. This project, dated 1874 and therefore an exact contemporary of the Watts Sherman House, is really a high, wild, stick-style mansion covered with shingles on its second story and sporting Queen Anne bays and gables with diamond-paned windows.[58] Although a large hall runs through the house and contains a fireplace, the plan as a whole is undistinguished and boxy. The cohesion of design which gave the Watts Sherman House such power is not present here. The Queen Anne elements are blatantly eclectic, pasted on a shell of vernacular forms.

55. *Ibid.*, pp. 139–40. One notes at this moment a painter, or rather two painters (White and LaFarge), endowed with a flair for the attractive pastiche, exerting a negative effect upon the originality of American architecture. Later academic painters and sculptors, all entangled as they were in their late 19th-century dichotomy between the real and the ideal and partly divorced by Beaux-Arts practice from the creative possibilities of materials and techniques, were to overwhelm American architecture by the early 90's with projects, monuments, and memorials—where architecture as such seems smothered by academic painting and sculpture. The distrust of Wright for other artists, unless strictly under the architect's supervision, though certainly regrettable, thus becomes historically understandable and important for his own development.

56. *Am. Arch. and Building News*, 2, March, 1877.

57. The Blake and Cheney projects of 1875 and 1876. Hitchcock, *Richardson*, pls. 49, 50.

58. Published in the *Architectural Sketch Book* (May, 1874), pl. 41.

2· Queen Anne and Colonial Revival, 1869–76

The Centennial Exposition at Philadelphia from May to November, 1876, next brought the Queen Anne fashion clearly into the limelight. Here was an event where evocations of the past, supposedly more virtuous and desirable than the present, suddenly became dominant themes. It is not my intention to consider the Centennial as a whole, since its general aspects have already been examined in considerable detail.[1] Only a few facts concerning the Centennial are of importance here. The first is that the two British Government buildings at the Centennial, one serving as the Commissioner and Delegates' Residence and Staff Office and the other as Staff Quarters, were built in a half-timbered, Old English cottage style which was at least called "Queen Anne." These were the work of Thomas Harris, High Holborn, one of the many architects who were working in the Shaw manner. They appeared in *Building News* in November, 1875 (Fig. 14) and were republished in the *American Builder,* with enthusiastic comment, in April, 1876.[2] The *American Builder* burbled:

> The most interesting and by far the most conspicuous and costly buildings erected by any foreign Government on the Centennial grounds are those belonging to Great Britain. Ample space was awarded to them for the purpose in the northwestern part of the inclosure, and the structures

1. Christine Hunter Donaldson, *The Centennial of 1876,* unpublished Ph.D. dissertation, Yale University, 1948.

2. *Building News,* November 12, 1875; *American Builder, 12* (1876), pls. 18, 19. That Thomas Harris was doing Old English work at this time is an indication of the power of the movement in England, since Harris had always been very Gothic and "original" in the typical midcentury way—to such an extent that his best known nickname has always been "Victorian" Harris.

which they have reared will commend themselves to thoughtful persons, and to professional builders, by the quiet lesson they preach of the thorough adaptability of Gothic [*sic*] to modern residences. The houses, therefore, within the British part of the grounds, may be considered rather as an exemplification of the manner in which houses essentially Elizabethan in character may be built at the least possible expense, and with the cheapest materials.

. . . The body of the building (the larger) seems to be entirely window, for the casements of the rooms and of the corridors in the two stories of the building are connected and form an uninterrupted line of windows. . . . The casements in the wings are bay windows, and one of them has a queer pent top, but the great beauty of these is that no two are alike in construction. For this, which is the national architecture of England, positively revels in fullness of invention; and, indeed, in fertility and wide scope to the fancy, it is as far superior to the cold, pale, barren Ionic, as the heavens are above the earth.

. . . Inside the grand hall the eye is first arrested by the dado, which is everywhere paneled in painted pine wood of chocolate color. The great fireplace is to the left, and the staircase to the right. . . . The fireplace is handsome, but in the modern development of the old style. The mantelpiece is of dark walnut, seven feet high, with finely carved cornice of the old egg and tongue and dentil patterns. In the frieze are panels of painted tiling very beautiful to see. . . .

. . . the large reception room . . . will be famously lighted, for the casement window extends the whole width of the room. . . .

It will be observed that the decorations of this building are strictly constructional, and this is the second important feature of English Gothic. Nothing is hidden, but everything is made available for purposes of ornamentation. . . . The fireplace does not dwindle into a chaufferette and get huddled under my lady's skirts as in the Renaissance, but stands out as the chief ornament of the room. And, instead of being dark and gloomy, as some believe, positively there is such a flood of light as may be embarrassing when the hot sun dominates the summer months. But the chief thing that will strike the observant eye in this style is its wonderful adaptability to this country, not to the towns, indeed, but to the land at large. Its one fault . . . is in the enormous amount of timbering and plastering required, from the space covered. . . . It is to be hoped that the next millionaire who puts up a cottage at Long Branch will adopt this style, and he will have a house ample enough to entertain a Prince, yet exceedingly cozy, cool in summer, and yet abundantly warm in winter, plain enough, and yet capable of the highest ornamental development.[3]

Thus the rough and ready *American Builder,* champion of practicality and hardheadedness—and in the early 70's of a rigidly utilitarian positivism—fell head over heels in love with the Queen Anne in its most antiquarian aspect, the half-timbered. Although the *American Builder* invoked the rationalism of the old Gothic revival in explaining these buildings, it was nevertheless not only formal elegance but also quaintness and values of association which had effect here, as in the expression, "the national architecture of England." It should also be noticed that the *American Builder* heartily recommended this sort of thing for American use, saving only the difficulty a builder might have with authentic half-timbering and plastering—a problem that could easily be solved by covering the surface with shingles.

Queen Anne shingles, panel work, and open interior space were reinforced by the architectural influence of another country represented by wooden buildings at the Centennial; that is, Japan. The Japanese buildings, a "Bazaar" and a "Dwelling," were of frame construction with overhanging eaves, and their structural articulation in some ways recalled the American stick style. The *American Architect* wrote of the "Dwelling," "A bird is handsomely carved in bas-relief on the wooden panel between the top of the front door and the overhanging porch." [4] This feature relates to Queen Anne decorative motifs, as, for example, to its carved barge boards and plaster panels. In another article, apparently instigated by the interest in Japanese architecture that had been aroused by the Centennial, the *Architect* described types of Japanese shingle work as "very small shingles, hardly more than two inches wide, and showing three or four inches to the weather." More importantly, of Japanese interior spatial organization, the *Architect* stated: "Thus at any moment any partition can be taken down, and two or more rooms, or the whole house, be thrown into one large apartment, broken only by the posts which marked the corners of the rooms. Doors and windows,

3. *Ibid.,* pp. 81–2. A drawing of the hall described in this article was published in a popular book on the Centennial Exhibition. P. J. Sandhurst, *The Great Centennial Exhibition Illustrated* (Philadelphia, 1876), p. 541.

4. "Japanese Building at the Centennial," *Am. Arch., 1* (1876), 136. Morse stated in 1885: "The Japanese exhibit at the Centennial Exhibition in Philadelphia came to us as a new revelation. It was then that the Japanese craze took hold of us." Morse, *Japanese Homes,* p. xxvii. The Japanese buildings have recently been published in Clay Lancaster, "Japanese Buildings in the United States before 1900: Their Influence upon American Domestic Architecture," *Art Bulletin, 35* (1953), 217–24, pls. 1–3.

as we use them, there are none." [5] Consequently, Queen Anne materials and general spatial direction received, by 1876, the support of influences from similar aspects of Japanese domestic architecture. These had already been allied, through comparable—though in Japanese hands more sensitive and integral—handling of the wooden frame, to the American stick style itself.

Acceptance of Queen Anne depended in 1876 upon still another factor, which seems at first glance entirely unrelated, yet which became inseparably connected. As the Queen Anne purportedly revived vernacular English domestic architecture of several centuries past, it began to be related in the minds of Americans to their own colonial building of one hundred to two hundred years before. Interestingly enough, both interests illustrate a preoccupation with the same moment in architecture, the period of transition from the medieval to the Renaissance, from a freer to a more ordered way of building, from a more "organic" to a more abstract. The first indication of this relation of English Queen Anne to American colonial occurred in an editorial in the second issue of the new *American Architect and Building News,* January, 1876. Speaking of the Centennial, the article stated that New York had considered putting up "a model of an old Dutch Colonial house, and Massachusetts had it in mind to build an old-fashioned New England country house," but

> It might perhaps be feasible, and it would certainly be more interesting, to buy such a house (of which there are many at this day perishing of neglect), and transport it to Philadelphia. The New England farmhouse is something *sui generis;* it would be interesting to have one with a history. The English commissioners have built, for their own occupation, two half-timbered houses in the style of two centuries ago. Illustrations of these have already appeared in the *Building News.*[6]

In the same breath with the discussion of New England farmhouses with a "history" the *American Architect* mentions the English Queen Anne houses. The Queen Anne thus rode into America on a wave of nostalgia, and that nostalgia was a new and suddenly poignant American longing to recall its 17th- and 18th-century past. The longing became a powerful force in the early 1870's and culminated in the colonial enthusiasm aroused by the Centennial of 1876. Yet certain indications of an awakening interest in the colonial past and its architecture had existed earlier.

Arthur Gilman of Boston had expressed his admiration for colonial churches in an article appearing in 1844, but his interest in these was only

5. *Am. Arch., 1* (1876), 26–7.
6. *Am. Arch., 1* (January 8, 1876), 9.

a parenthetical inclusion in the general rationalist attack upon the Greek revival and did not indicate colonial revivalist enthusiasm.[7] In 1852 Lewis Falley
Allen in his book *Rural Architecture* expressed a preference for the farmhouses of the past century with their capacious fireplaces, low ceilings, and
sense of shelter.[8] In 1858 Nathan Henry Chamberlain, in what is probably
the first separate publication devoted to colonial architecture, published
A Paper on New England Architecture, originally read before the New England Historical and Genealogical Society on September 4 of that year.[9]
Chamberlain's pamphlet and its original audience illustrate two different
sides to the interest in colonial architecture that continued to be of importance. On the one hand was Chamberlain himself, who saw this architecture creatively through the eyes of his own time. He called it "organic." To
him it was full of dark nooks and sheltered spaces. In it he found the perfect
expression of his longing for the picturesque. On the other hand there was
his audience, not primarily interested in architecture, neither creative nor
really historically minded, but rather a group of Americans yearning for
roots. To them colonial architecture was soon to take on tremendous value
as symbol. Its meaning was to become that of security and of memory, a
common fund of approved and communicable experience.

In 1869 Richard M. Upjohn, first president of the American Institute of
Architects, gave a short talk entitled "Colonial Architecture of New York and
the New England States," at the third annual convention of that organization.[10] It is of interest that the newly founded, avowedly refined A.I.A. should
so soon have come into contact with the kind of historical study that was
eventually to provide the livelihood of so many of its members; but in reality
little discernible interest in colonial architecture had as yet merged. Gilman,

7. Review of *Shaw's Rural Architecture* by Arthur Gilman, *North American Review,*
April, 1844. It should be added that the rear of Gilman's Boston State House and his
Arlington Street Church, both built in the 50's, show certain influences from Gibbs.

8. Lewis Falley Allen, *Rural Architecture* (New York, 1852), p. 20. Much more typical of
the attitude toward colonial architecture of the 40's, 50's, and much of the 60's as well
was Louisa Tuthill's comment concerning colonial farmhouses: "Happily, they were all of
such perishable materials that they will not much longer remain to annoy travelers, in
search of the picturesque through the beautiful villages of New England." Louisa Tuthill,
History of Architecture from the Earliest Times, Philadelphia, 1848.

9. Nathan Henry Chamberlain, *A Paper on New England Architecture,* Boston, 1858.
For a bibliography of later publications see Frank J. Roos, *Writings on Early American
Architecture* (Columbus, 1943), *passim.*

10. Richard M. Upjohn, "Colonial Architecture of New York and the New England
States," *Proceedings of the Third Annual Convention of the American Institute of Archi-
tects* (Nov. 17, 1869), pp. 47–51. For a discussion of Upjohn's part in the founding of the
A.I.A. see Everard Upjohn, *Richard Upjohn, Architect and Churchman.*

Allen, Chamberlain, and Upjohn, widely scattered in time, do not constitute a revival, and their passing interest in the colonial during the midcentury is noteworthy only because of its rarity at the time.[11] Only in the early 1870's did interest in colonial life and architecture begin to assume some of the proportions of a genuine revival. This interest at first was predominantly popular and would seem to have been inspired by two factors: the rise of the summer resort and the approach of the Centennial year.

The growing popularity of seaside vacations, noticeably increasing after the Civil War, began by the early 1870's to focus attention upon the resort towns, many of which had changed very little since colonial days.[12] In such surroundings the call of the picturesque and the romantic could easily be strengthened by a growing appreciation of the ancient architecture to be found there. One of the earliest indications of this new orientation was H. T. Tuckerman's article published in *Harper's New Monthly* in 1869 and entitled, appropriately enough, "The Graves at Newport." [13] Tuckerman recalled the spirit of Newport's past in architectural terms:

> The low ceilings, wainscot panels, the French plate mirrors with heavy frames . . . the straight-backed mahogany chairs, old English prints on the walls, the small window-panes often set in cedarwood, the green painted floors, the snug and sunny window-seats, and broad hall and easy staircase, the high mantels and vast chimney, quaint sideboard, portraits by Stuart or miniatures by Malbone, fresh geraniums, ancient sampler— a mourning piece "in memory of Hamilton"—cut glass decanters, and old silver, are insignia of the old households which vividly contrast with the

11. One should recall the remodelings of George Evertson Woodward, *Woodward's Country Homes* (New York, 1865), e.g. figs. 63, 64, 123–5. See also n. 8 above.

12. Newport, Marblehead, Portsmouth, and many others come into this category. Others, like Mount Desert, where in the 60's a thriving summer colony began to grow up, had less colonial architecture but many of those qualities which shortly came to be associated with colonial style, namely picturesqueness, unspoiled simplicity, the sense of an older way of life brought to mind by its solitudes. Its rise as a summer resort is typical of the whole development, with the exception of Newport, which had been a summer resort as far back as colonial times. (George C. Mason, *Newport Illustrated*, Boston, 1854.) In 1850 the painter Frederick Church, while on a summer cruise, landed on Mount Desert, found the place unspoiled, and painted there. His picturesque vision, like that of the rest of the Hudson River School, opened the eyes of Americans to the beauty of their landscape as a place of refuge. Consequently, to some extent in the 1850's but more and more after the Civil War, summer visitors began to flock to Mount Desert and elsewhere. By 1870 Bar Harbor on Mount Desert was a thriving resort. George E. Street, *Mount Desert, A History*, Boston, 1905.

13. *Harper's, 39* (1869), 372–88.

verandas, lawns, croquet grounds, French chairs, marble centre-tables, ottomans, photograph albums, and conservatory flowers of the modern villas.[14]

This account of the old houses reads much like descriptions of some of the houses of the 8o's. Notice should be taken of the "broad hall and easy stair-case," "the vast chimney," "the snug and sunny window-seats." Tuckerman patently felt the old houses to be simpler, more homelike, and richer in warm associations than the modern buildings. All these details were to be-come architectural elements in the architecture of the 8o's.

In 1871 *Harper's* published a romantic account of Montauk Point on Long Island, which told sentimental tales of the early inhabitants and reproduced a drawing of a picturesque kitchen fireplace from an old house as well as the "old church" at East Hampton, built in 1717.[15] In 1872 there appeared an article on Mount Desert, Maine, but here the author confined himself to scenery and ignored the local architectural color.[16]

In 1872 this growing colonial revival, centering in the watering places, first took architectural form. In that year Charles Follen McKim, living at New-port, restored and rebuilt rooms in an 18th-century house on Washington Street, just north of the old town at the shores of the bay. His *chef d'oeuvre* in this project was a spacious and eminently colonial fireplace, surrounded by appropriate paneling.[17] At this time also he used, in several houses he built in New Jersey, a system of interior decoration that can only be called imitation colonial. Photographs—not drawings—of the interiors were published in the *New York Sketch Book* of 1874.[18] These rooms by McKim must be considered the first actual example of the use of 18th-century forms in the 70's, either in restoration or in new work. The early date of these rooms makes their com-parative "correctness" all the more striking. They are an excellent indication of those predilections of McKim which were to reveal themselves so fully by the end of the 8o's. His personality seemed to require clear prototypes for ac-tion, and in the early 1870's he was already turning to the 18th century for precedent and example. In the linear exactitudes of 18th-century work he found also that rather dry and academic classicism which seems to have been

14. *Ibid.,* p. 382.

15. Charles Parsons, "Montauk Point, Long Island," *Harper's, 43* (1871), 481–93.

16. George Ward Nichols, "Mount Desert," *Harper's, 45* (1872), 321–41.

17. This was the Robinson House. A photograph of the fireplace was published in the *New York Sketch Book of Architecture* and republished in *Examples of Architecture,* 1880. Downing and Scully, fig. 192.

18. *New York Sketch Book.* Page House, Montrose, New Jersey. Reprinted in *Examples of Architecture,* 1880.

his real aesthetic preference. At the same time he was developing a sensitivity for order, space, and scale which had a potentiality for wider results than mere antiquarianism.

From 1873 to 1876, the year of the Centennial, the pattern of revival continued to expand and grow. In 1873 Thomas Wentworth Higginson published a book called *Oldport Days,* an antiquarian compilation of Newport colonial stories, redolent with nostalgia for the good old times.[19] Newport in consequence continued to be the hub of revivalist energy—a phenomenon not surprising, since it was at once the most celebrated summer resort in America and one of the richest towns in the country in respect to colonial buildings. Moreover, it was for Newport that Richardson had designed his F. W. Andrews House of 1872 and his Watts Sherman House of 1874. Colonial and Queen Anne thus seem to have risen together in Newport in the early 70's, affirming their affinity to each other and suggesting the creative amalgamation of the two that was eventually to occur. In 1874 Newport continued as the center of colonial revivalism. In that year the *New York Sketch Book* published a photographic reproduction—again not a drawing—of Bishop Berkeley's House in Newport, built in 1728.[20] The photographer ignored the symmetrical façade and concentrated upon the long, shingled slope of roof in the rear (Fig. 15). The *Sketch Book* stated that this house was typical of most old houses then lamentably falling into ruin. These should be preserved or at least recorded, the *Sketch Book* advised, and the responsibility belonged to architects, since the houses were not only quaint and picturesque but possessed "merit as architecture, and the architects are their true historians."

Such specifically architectural interest in colonial buildings as set forth in the most influential and advanced architectural publication, along with McKim's overtly colonial interiors published in the same periodical, served to excite further popular interest in things colonial. This interest became noticeably stronger between 1874 and 1876. In 1874 *Harper's* published long articles with copious illustrations on Newport, "The Queen of Aquidneck," on Marblehead, and on Portsmouth, New Hampshire. The Newport article stresses both that town's excellence as a summer resort and its distinguished historical and architectural past.[21] Picturesque sketches are reproduced of the Governor Coddington House of 1641 and of other nondescript picturesque piles, as well as of Peter Harrison's 18th-century masterpieces, the Redwood Library and the Jewish Synagogue.[22] The Marblehead article,

19. Thomas Wentworth Higginson, *Oldport Days,* Boston, 1873.
20. *New York Sketch Book, 12* (1874), pl. 45.
21. Junius Henri Browne, "The Queen of Aquidneck," *Harper's, 49* (1874), 305-20.
22. See Henry-Russell Hitchcock, *Rhode Island Architecture* (Providence, 1939), pls. 9,

though less rich in illustrations than that on Newport, deals appreciatively
with the atmosphere created by the old houses of the town and makes it clear
that historical values and old associations had much to do with their appeal.[23]
The writer approves of "the snug sitting-rooms and the polished kitchens"
of the old houses and decides that though some of the new houses "are certainly handsomer than the old ones . . . they are very uninteresting in
comparison with the houses that have tasted the salt air of the old town for two
and three half centuries . . . [and] have a history . . . [and] associations."[24]
The Portsmouth article is the richest of all in drawings, atmosphere, and
comments. Its title, "An Old Town by the Sea," perfectly expresses the dual
intent that can be noted behind all these articles: the glorification of the
summer resort and the yearning for the old.[25] Drawings of old graves, old
gambrel-roofed houses shaded by trees, big chimneys of weathered masonry
covered by vines, landscapes with ancient houses stretched out as if rooted
there, and even of fireplaces covered with 18th-century detail—all these drive
home in this article the reality of the nostalgia they aroused. This nostalgia
was not only sentimental or antiquarian—and the point needs emphasis—
but also the product of an intense vision of the architecture itself. It fastened
upon those elements which have already been noted and which were to become of importance in later original developments—the wide halls, the easy
stairs, the fireplaces. An excellent drawing of the hall of the Warner House is
included, and of that house the article has this to say:

> The interior is rich in paneling and wood carvings about the mantel
> shelves, the deep-set windows, and along the cornices. The halls are
> wide and deep, after a gone-by fashion, with handsome staircases, set at
> an easy angle, and not standing nearly upright, like those ladders by
> which one reaches the upper chambers of a modern house. The principal
> rooms are paneled to the ceiling, and have large open fireplaces adorned
> with the quaintest of Dutch tiles.[26]

In such nostalgia was something of a real desire for a new simplicity, associated with an old simplicity, as well as a seeking for amplitude and ease.

10; Carl Bridenbaugh, *Peter Harrison, First American Architect* (Chapel Hill, 1949), *passim;* and Downing and Scully, pp. 25, 72–85.

23. John W. Chadwick, "Marblehead," *Harper's, 49* (1874), 181–202.

24. *Ibid.,* p. 187.

25. T. B. Aldrich, "An Old Town by the Sea," *Harper's, 49* (1874), 632–50.

26. *Ibid.,* p. 644. It will be recalled that Stanford White used 18th-century white and
blue Dutch tiles on the sides of the hall fireplace in the Watts Sherman House at just
about this time.

The longing for the sea in the early 1870's, perhaps a longing for escape from an industrial civilization grown complex and brutal, from cities grown too dense and hard, was a genuine emotion. The new yearning for colonial architecture was also not only fashion or antiquarianism but something deeper as well. In an article in *Harper's,* also in 1874, John Chadwick, who had written the article on Marblehead, ably summed up the desire for smaller, simpler, and more "natural" things, which lay behind the whole revival: [27] "After having staid [sic] here for a few days the towns and cities of the continent become a dream, a myth, to you. Going back to Boston you are surprised to find the State Houses still standing. One's experience here begets a feeling that our ordinary world is too large." [28] For the America of Boss Tweed, the Grant Administration, and the financial adventurers who had lately dragged the country into a disastrous depression, the sea apparently meant something clean and simple, with good memories.[29] It evoked ancient, archetypal patterns of life. And to the sea, the summer resort in general, and the country suburb, as will be shown later, the best of what was the true colonial revival remained more or less tied. Here again a longing for Jeffersonian agrarianism—or for the frontier or its available substitutes—arose during difficult times as a reinvocation of outgrown but remembered cultural objectives.

To the rising fire of colonial enthusiasm the approach of the Centennial of 1876 now added fuel. *Harper's* published an article in 1874 entitled "A Glimpse of '76"; it gave a romantic account of the trials and tribulations of the Revolutionary fathers and reproduced as well many illustrations of colonial furniture and firesides, spinning wheels and silver.[30] Across the page from a drawing of the low-ceilinged, puncheon-floored room which was Washington's headquarters at Newburgh the writer stated:

> As the one hundredth anniversary of our national independence draws
> near, the thoughts of our people are eagerly turned . . . to a more
> familiar observation of the men and women who were actors in that

27. John W. Chadwick, "The Isles of Shoals," *Harper's, 49* (1874), 663–76.

28. *Ibid.,* p. 676.

29. The corruption of government and business in the early 70's is too well known to need discussion here. A desire to escape spiritually from the morass, and an obscure sense of guilt at being associated with it, would seem to have played dominant parts in the whole drive toward both summer resorts and colonial architecture—the resort as a place close to that pure and romantic nature which the Hudson River School painters had made known, and colonial architecture as the concrete embodiment of a supposedly purer, certainly simpler, age.

30. Charles A. Deshler, "A Glimpse of '76," *Harper's, 49* (1874), 230–45.

great event . . . to take note of their appearance, manners and customs; to cross their thresholds and see . . . what entered into their domestic appointments and belongings.[31]

Centennial enthusiasm thus reinforced the interest in colonial architecture and artifacts, and emphasized that craze for colonial furniture which by the 80's would supplant to a large degree the more or less Eastlakian interior appointments of the early 70's.[32] In 1874 *Harper's* began a series of articles called "The First Century of the Republic." The lead article was entitled "Our Colonial Progress."[33] The series extended into 1875 and was supplemented by other articles extolling the virtues of colonial heroism. Here colonial architecture was discussed, or at least formed a conspicuous feature of the *mise en scène,* as in "The Concord Fight" or "Echoes of Bunker Hill."[34] These new reasons for interest in things colonial did not prevent the continuing growth of the resort town, with colonial architecture as a factor in the revival. In 1875 Cape Cod, Nantucket and the Vineyard, Gloucester, Cape Anne, and Newburyport were subjects of enthusiastic articles with copious illustrations.[35] These places were presented richly and with a typically picturesque vision. Everything is shadow and texture, bowered in trees. The appearance of the article on Newburyport is especially interesting because here McKim, Mead, White, and Bigelow were to spend most of their time on their "celebrated" trip in discovery of the colonial

31. *Ibid.,* p. 230.

32. Charles Locke Eastlake was less important in American architecture in the 70's than has occasionally been supposed. Although his *Hints on Household Taste* (London, 1868) had seven American editions from 1872 to 1883, its influence was primarily toward a kind of heavy, notched, and incised wooden furniture and hardly affected the architectural shell itself. His furniture, not so widespread as would appear from the number of American editions of his book, was soon supplanted by colonially inspired pieces. Probably the main importance of his book arose from its popularization of the ethical-aesthetic principles of Ruskin and Morris.

33. *Harper's, 49* (1874), 861–78.

34. Frederick Hudson, "The Concord Fight," *Harper's, 50* (1874–75), 777–804; Samuel Osgood, "Echoes of Bunker Hill," *Harper's, 51* (1875), 230–8.

35. Charles Nordhoff, "Cape Cod, Nantucket, and the Vineyard," *Harper's, 51* (1875), 52–66; Harriet Prescott Spofford, "Newburyport and Its Neighborhood," *Harper's, 51* (1875), 161–80; S. G. W. Benjamin, "Gloucester and Cape Ann," *Harper's, 51* (1875), 465–74. The article on Moosehead Lake which appeared that year, although it contains no colonial architecture, should nevertheless be considered of importance, since it stresses that sense of the cleanness and fineness of outdoor, simple life which played so large a part in this whole development. Julius H. Ward, "Moosehead Lake," *Harper's, 51* (1875), 350–65.

in 1877.[36] Other articles, such as "Concord Books," "Cambridge on the Charles," "The Romance of the Hudson," and "Old Philadelphia" played their part in adding to the intellectual and emotional attitudes of the revival. All amply illustrated 17th- and/or 18th-century architecture.[37]

Such channeling of colonial enthusiasm into colonial architecture received added impetus at the Centennial itself. At the great exhibition in Philadelphia, which was attended by unprecedented crowds,[38] could be seen not only the English Queen Anne buildings with their open halls, great fireplaces, and continuous banks of windows but also a complete "New England Kitchen of 1776." Intended as a foil to the "Kitchen of 1876," its effect was to bring sharply to public attention, in three dimensions, the beamed ceilings, leaded casements, and masonry hearths of colonial farmhouses. It was stocked with colonial furniture and colonial housewives in full regalia, and was extremely popular.[39]

Our conclusion, then, must be inescapable. First, beginning roughly in 1869 but gathering real force only in the early 70's and especially from 1874 on, a combination of enthusiasm for summer resorts and for the Centennial had created, at least by 1876, the popular basis for the colonial revival. Second, that revival seems to have had a dual nature: it was nostalgic and antiquarian, but it was also sincerely re-creative, born of a profound need and fed by new broadenings of picturesque vision. In the wide halls and capacious fireplaces of colonial houses, in their low ceilings and rough materials, popular observers had somehow vaguely felt the answer to a need for space, shelter, and simple life. It remains for us to trace the progress of this burgeoning revival and to examine how—in one of those curious alchemies

36. William Rutherford Mead later said of this trip: "In our early days all of us had a great interest in Colonial architecture, and in 1877 we made what we afterwards called our 'celebrated' trip to New England, for the purpose of visiting Marblehead, Salem, Newburyport and Portsmouth. . . . We made sketches and measured drawings of many of the important colonial houses, which still remain in our scrap-book." Moore, *McKim*, p. 41. It will be observed that the great men went exactly where *Harper's*, several years before, had directed them.

37. H. R. Hudson, "Concord Books," *Harper's, 51* (1875), 18–32; Charles F. Richardson, "Cambridge on the Charles," *Harper's, 52* (1875–76), 191–208; Benson J. Lossing, "The Romance of the Hudson," *Harper's, 52* (1875–76), 633–50, 822–37; Rebecca Harding Davis, "Old Philadelphia," *Harper's, 52* (1875–76), 705–21, 868–82.

38. For an exhaustive account of the Centennial's phenomenal attendance see Christine Donaldson's dissertation, *passim.*

39. Its popularity can be attested by the fact that it was illustrated in Sandhurst's book on the Centennial exhibitions, as was the hall of the English building already noted, whereas the "Kitchen of 1876" was not. Sandhurst, *The Great Centennial Exhibition Illustrated*, p. 542.

which are so common in the history of art—it merged with the so-called Queen Anne to produce a new and original domestic architecture.

Thus, while the colonial revival appeared in 1876 as the chief characteristic of popular feeling about the Centennial, the Queen Anne itself was also brought into sharper public focus at the same moment. In May of 1876 *Harper's* began a series of articles by Henry Hudson Holly, entitled "Modern Dwellings: Their Construction, Decoration, and Furniture." [40] Holly's first article begins with a plea for the use of Queen Anne as the natural building style for America. Advancing the usual arguments about the necessity to meet specifically American requirements of climate, landscape, function, and so forth, Holly declared that the Gothic, the last of the styles adapted for that purpose, was now dead so far as domestic architecture was concerned and that the Queen Anne answered all requirements nicely.

> . . . within the last three years . . . it has been discovered that the Gothic, however well adapted to ecclesiastical purposes, is lacking in essential points for domestic uses; and Norman Shaw, J. J. Stevenson [41] and others have openly advocated the heresy. . . . These writers, then, exempt themselves from a slavish conformity to the Gothic. . . . One of the principles upon which the promoters of the Gothic revival insisted with energy and eloquence was *"truth* in architecture." . . . But these new reformers say that truth is not the peculiar possession of Gothic architecture. . . . They claim that in what is loosely called the "Queen Anne" style we find the most simple mode of honest English building, worked out in an artistic and natural form, fitted with the sash windows and ordinary doorways, which express real domestic needs (of which it is the outcome), and so in our house building conserving truth far more effectively than can be done with the Gothic. One great practical advantage in adopting this and other styles of the "free-classic" school is that they are in their construction and in the forms of the mouldings employed the same as the common vernacular styles with which our workmen are familiar. They are described by Mr. Ridge

---

40. *Harper's, 52* (1875–76), 855–67. This was the first article of a series which ran in *Harper's* through the rest of 1876 and was published as a book, somewhat expanded and significantly altered, in 1878: Henry Hudson Holly, *Modern Dwellings in Town and Country Adapted to American Wants and Climate. With a treatise on furniture and decoration,* New York, 1878.

"Jock" Stevenson was instrumental in the building of the board schools in the Queen Anne manner in the early 70's. Stevenson's best known design, done with his partner Robeson, was the Red House, Bayswater. Stevenson's and Ridge's point of view in the Queen Anne controversy can be found in *Building News* (March 13, 1875), p. 285.

somewhat as follows: "The Queen Anne revival shows the influence of the group of styles known as the Elizabethan, Jacobite, and the style of Francis I, which are now, indeed, to be arranged under the general head of 'free classic', but the Queen Anne movement has also been influenced by what is known as the 'cottage architecture' of that period." These cottages are partly timbered, partly covered with tile hangings, and have tall and spacious chimneys of considerable merit. They have really nothing by which to fix their date. Their details partook strongly of the classic character, while the boldness of their outline bore striking resemblance to the picturesque and ever-varying Gothic. Nevertheless they were very genuine and striking buildings, and have been taken freely as suggestions upon which to work by Mr. Norman Shaw at Leyeswood, Cragside, and a house at Harrow Weald, which are certainly some of the most beautiful and suitable specimens of modern cottage architecture in England; and the cottages erected by the British government on the Centennial grounds at Philadelphia are adequate illustrations of this style.[42]

Holly's long and confused statement is worth quoting because it shows the nature of the argument whereby the case for Queen Anne was presented.

The rationalism which had been at the root of Gothic revival theory was still held to be the arbiter of excellence. The Queen Anne was better for domestic purposes because supposedly more rational. Yet the insistence upon the link with classicism in the "classic detail" of Queen Anne building was a break with the Gothic revival principles of "originality" and "reality." Here Holly actually rejected the whole ethical basis for Gothic revival theory. Most significant perhaps was the appeal for the return to Queen Anne as a national vernacular of a century or two earlier. This certainly made it possible to associate the whole movement with colonial architecture itself, and especially the "classic detail" with 18th-century American wooden adaptations of Palladian-English originals. Holly's entire argument, possibly the first introduction to Queen Anne for most educated Americans, must be regarded as an attack upon the general architecture of the time. That architecture, as I have tried to show elsewhere, could scarcely be characterized as purely "Gothic"; it was instead based upon Gothic revival ideas of originality, expression of site, construction, and so on.[43] Holly's argument was thus an

42. "Modern Dwellings," p. 856.
43. See my "Romantic Rationalism," pp. 121–42, *passim*. Note pp. 127, 140–2.

attack upon the whole intellectual basis of this architecture and a call to antiquarian revival.[44]

Holly's designs in the *Harper's* articles are undistinguished if typical stick style structures, with a few added Queen Anne details such as window bays, shingles, tiles, and sunflower designs in *sgraffito*. The plans reveal little of the new sense of space. There are no living halls, no fireplace and stair combinations.[45] For the general public at this time, therefore, the Queen Anne must have emerged only as a kind of pictorial composition that used shingles and designs in plaster. By a process not entirely clear, it seemed vaguely allied to the colonial.

What that alliance really might be was demonstrated by Charles Follen McKim in 1876. In that year he remodeled the 18th-century Dennis House on Washington Street in Newport.[46] He removed the stairs from their original position by the front door and placed them in the former kitchen at the rear, which he enlarged and to which he added a capacious bay window. This large room, now with fireplace, stairs, and window wall, became in consequence a Queen Anne living hall (Fig. 16). McKim's colonial enthusiasms, as already displayed in the Robinson House at Newport, here merged with Queen Anne influences to produce a distinguished example of the new space.

In consequence, by 1876 Queen Anne and colonial influences both worked to promote revivalism. I shall seek in the next chapters to show how these influences were temporarily united into the intellectual and aesthetic basis for a new domestic architecture. In that process certain types of academic thinking also began to take shape, and would become significant in the later academic reaction against the new architecture itself.

44. Holly's argument concerning Gothic was of course absurd so far as America was concerned and is really an argument that made sense only in the English controversy of the early 70's. Yet it is typical of the kind of confused thinking which began to take place and is therefore significant.

45. When Holly's book appeared in 1878, ten new designs with large living halls and fire and stair combinations had been added, as will be mentioned later. *Modern Dwellings,* designs 2, 3, 8, 9, 11, 15, 18, 20, 21, 22.

46. Now St. John's Rectory. Never published or discussed in its time.

3. Romantic Rationalism and the Assimilation of Queen Anne and Colonial Influences, 1876–77

In an atmosphere of hazy enthusiasm for Queen Anne and colonial the *American Architect and Building News* began publication in January, 1876. Designed as a vehicle of expression for the architectural profession, it professed a lofty idealism, concerning both architecture as an art and the dignity of the architect as an artist.[1] Unlike the *American Builder,* its older rival, it regarded itself from the beginning as a molder of taste, a clearinghouse of aesthetic speculation, and the catalytic agent in a renaissance of American architecture. It was consciously concerned from the first with questions of style and so marked a shift from that antistylistic, utilitarian pattern of thought which had been a product of midcentury romantic rationalism and which reached its middle 70's peak in E. C. Gardner. Thus the *American Architect* forms an excellent base for an investigation of the intellectual and formal developments through which the new domestic architecture came into existence between the years 1876 and 1882. This journal not only reproduced elaborate plates illustrating the work of the rising young architects

1. William Rotch Ware, its first editor, was a graduate of the Beaux-Arts. He guided the magazine and shaped its policy until 1880. These were not only its critical years but, as a study of the magazine tends to show, possibly its most productive years. During this time the *American Architect* was, according to its lights, a crusading and courageous publication. One might point out that its quality showed a slow but steady deterioration after it began to accept quantities of advertising in the early 90's. Originally, to preserve the architect's impartiality and freedom, it had accepted none.

but also published articles, letters, and editorials yielding a further insight into the intellectual atmosphere which fostered the designs. As it is now useful to the scholar because it brings so many elements together, so it must also have been of considerable importance as a positive factor in the development of its own time. It will be worth while, therefore, to discuss at some length the intellectual and design processes of the years 1876–83, through which the assimilation of Queen Anne and colonial influences took place, as they are revealed primarily in the *American Architect*.

In the process of assimilation two divergent general approaches to architecture began to make themselves felt. On the one hand, there were antiquarian and academic tendencies, and on the other, free and creative ones. The two streams mingled, complemented each other, developed further, and again diverged. By 1883 the creative side seems to have carried the day, and indeed to have led directly into an original architecture. But the academic approach, bred in those years, while it seemed for a time to have gone underground for most architects, emerged very shortly to usurp the whole.

The entire development must be seen as beginning from the solid base of midcentury romantic-rationalist criticism. This was the point of departure. In its second month the *American Architect* began the publication, as a serial, of Viollet-le-Duc's *The Habitations of Man in All Ages*. Straightforward, rational, based upon a clear-cut theory of functionalism and structural expression, the great Frenchman's architectural philosophy was part of the same stream of realistic thought that had been important in the free American development of the midcentury. At the same time Viollet-le-Duc's preoccupation with many kinds of building techniques constantly opened up avenues of plastic experience, as in his "Fat Fau's House," reproduced in the *American Architect* (Fig. 17) to illustrate the framing techniques used in the Orient. A sense of these had already been present in the Sturtevant House of 1872, and their interwoven quality was to continue to have an important effect upon the American development.[2] Tied to the Gothic revival as the main core of its theory, although not always answerable to it for its forms, Viollet-le-Duc's philosophy created a solid foundation for experimental thinking of the most decisive kind. Rooted in a sense of materials and their

2. *Am. Arch. and Building News, 1* (Feb. 26, 1876), 68–70. One interesting point should be noted here: the bamboo posts, illustrated by Viollet-le-Duc in Fat Fau's House and discussed in this portion of the *Habitations* may very well have served Stanford White as models for his later use of posts which imitate bamboo, as on the porch of the Bell House, Newport, 1882–83. The long range effects, however, were more important, involving the whole sense of interpenetrating and interwoven spaces, as in White's designs of the 80's, and later in those of Frank Lloyd Wright. For a discussion of the articles in the *American Architect* in 1876 concerning Japanese architecture see above, Ch. 2, pp. 21–2.

properties, it regarded architecture as a rational creation. Such intense materialism was at once its greatest strength and its severest limitation. The nature of this philosophy is indicated by an attack which was made upon Ware and Van Brunt's use of wooden vaulting in the ceiling of the Harvard Memorial Hall of 1875–77.[3] The polemic, after a short exchange of articles on both sides, concludes as follows:

> An arch is not merely a form; it is a form expressive of a certain mode of construction, which mode of construction is the most direct and economical way of getting over an opening in stone or brick, but is wasteful and ridiculous excess when it is imitated in wood. The form becomes then an empty form, expressive of nothing save by traditional association, or something of that sort. Imitation does not consist in falsely representing the surface of a material only: it consists as here, in denying *the nature of a material*. . . . If there is a necessary alliance between stone and this form, as there is, there cannot be a necessary alliance between wood and the same form. It is simply out of the question that a design for a ceiling can be equally right and expressive whether it is executed in wood, or stone, unless it is utterly wrong and inexpressive in either. . . . It follows either that the thing is nonsensical, as I said it was, or else that bad engineering may be good architecture,—a proposition which I trust Mr. Van Brunt will not distress me afresh by maintaining.[4]

This is an extremely lucid statement of romantic logic, popularized by Pugin and developed throughout the Gothic revival. Viollet-le-Duc and Ruskin, in their respective ways the two best known protagonists of that point of view, remained the basic reading of all architects in America during the 70's, and during this period they were rarely mentioned with less than profound respect.[5] Romantic rationalism (or can one call it moral materialism?) was a basic part of the American architect's intellectual equipment in 1876. The *American Architect* itself demonstrated this in an editorial comment

3. The Ware of Ware and Van Brunt was a relative of William Rotch Ware and head of the architectural school at the Massachusetts Institute of Technology. This school generally turned out Beaux-Arts academic projects at this period and was also responsible for the measuring and drawing of colonial church steeples in Boston. Hitchcock, *Richardson*, pp. 150–1. However, its influence can hardly have been completely antiquarian, since Wilson Eyre, later one of the best of the shingle architects (discussed in Ch. 7), attended M.I.T. in the late 70's.

4. "The Critic of Memorial Hall," *Am. Arch., 1* (1876), 71. The italics are mine.

5. Even McKim once had a desire to translate Viollet-le-Duc's *Dictionnaire raisonné* into English. Cf. Baldwin, *Stanford White*, p. 354.

which stated that American architects were "in general more successful in their country houses than in their other work . . . and . . . it is likely they will succeed better still . . . [because our] domestic life is a type by itself; our way of living is not like that of any other people, and modern household conveniences essentially modify the plan and uses of a house." [6]

Yet into the field held by this utilitarian rationalism other forces were moving: the nostalgic entities "colonial" and "Queen Anne." A touch of cold antiquarian academicism sits icily on the *American Architect*'s first mention of colonial architecture. In March of 1876 it suggested that architects should spend their holidays making notes on colonial buildings, now all too rapidly passing away, because these represented an architecture "which, with all its faults of formality and meagreness, was, on the whole, decidedly superior in style and good breeding, if we may say so, to most that has followed it." [7] The association of colonial architecture with "good breeding" is typical of both an antiquarian and academic point of view, since the phrase, with all its connotations, expresses the psychological drives leading toward both positions. [8] At any rate, the *American Architect* in July made clearer exactly what it meant by the phrase and what its real feelings about colonial architecture were. In an article "American Architecture—Past" (which I have discussed elsewhere in connection with Andrew Jackson Downing), [9] the *American Architect* states:

> The architecture of the Colonies was, of course, derived from England; and it was drawn off at a pretty low ebb, just when the vagaries of the Queen Anne style, the last trace of the sturdy independence which had for a hundred and fifty years resisted the growing rigors of the Renaissance, had given way to the narrow formalities of the Georgian period. The style inherited here, therefore, was pretty narrow, formal, and lifeless. Nevertheless, it had been formalized by the great artists of the Renaissance from whom it had been handed down, and who had given great study to the most careful and elegant adjustment of its details and

6. "Some of the Practical Conditions of American Architecture," *Am. Arch., 1* (1876), 266–7.

7. *Am. Arch., 1* (1876), 90.

8. This proposition, I believe, does not need to be defended extensively. Much of the impetus leading toward the establishment of academies in the 16th century was apparently a desire for security, and the *American Architect*'s statement in 1876 reveals a distrust of the ever-changing present which feeds at similar sources. Pevsner relates this attitude to what he calls the "totalitarian" side of Mannerism. Nikolaus Pevsner, *Academies of Art* (Cambridge, 1940), p. 66.

9. See my "Romantic Rationalism," pp. 121–2 ff.

its rules. It was a style whose ancestry was good, and whose breeding had always been careful. . . . Work done in this way always retained the mark of its good descent. It might be monotonous and uninteresting, but never lost the character of good breeding and refinement which its progenitors impressed upon it.[10]

Thus a sharp split in feeling finds expression. On the one hand the writer, bred in the picturesque variety and "organic" freedom of the mid-19th century, feels Georgian architecture to be formal and lifeless. On the other hand, he seems hypnotized by its "good breeding," which he certainly desires. He longs for its order, but he fights shy of its formality, or, in a deeper sense, of the psychic implications of order.

An important semantic point emerges. As noted earlier, the term "colonial" or just "old" had been applied indiscriminately in the popular articles in *Harper's Monthly* to both 17th- and 18th-century architecture in America. Whether the house in question happened to be of the earlier, more medieval, or later, more Palladian type seems to have made no difference to the writers; it was all old, colonial, and picturesque. But as I have pointed out, these writers were generally preoccupied with features which, although they were shared to some extent by both types, would nevertheless be considered by modern critics as characteristic of the earlier, freer, and more medieval houses—or of the later houses which were the smallest, the simplest, the least Palladian, and closer to the earlier ones. These features are the capacious fireplaces, low ceilings, sheltered nooks, simple materials, and so on.[11] While the writers of the popular articles lumped both types together and certainly liked very much the moldings, tiles, and halls of the later houses, they reacted most strongly to those aspects of space and materials in colonial architecture which were earliest in time and most medieval.[12] The writer in the *American Architect,* however, when he says colonial, means only "Georgian," or the later, Palladian type; he seems unaware that any earlier kind had existed in America. He is also fascinated by Georgian details with their "elegant adjustment."

The question arises: what was colonial to these people? The answer seems to be that from 1876 on the word generally came to mean "Georgian," or "Palladian," and the phrase "colonial detail" meant more or less 18th-century Palladian details. These became the "classic details" of some of the American Queen Anne houses. Yet these houses were essentially freer and more me-

10. *1* (1876), 242–4.

11. See above, Ch. 2, pp. 24–25, 28.

12. See Fiske Kimball, *Domestic Architecture of the Colonies and of the Early Republic* (New York, 1922), pp. 9–52.

dieval, like the earlier colonial houses, of which some, as I shall show, were actually published. Therefore one can only assume that although at first the important re-creative experience of colonial architecture was actually addressed to the medieval colonial, the word itself very shortly came to mean "Georgian," that is, for modern critics the Palladian and more academic period in colonial architecture. It is so used here by the *American Architect*.

The duality in the colonial revival of the late 70's must be kept in mind. It was at once a creative experience and a revival in the 19th-century sense, and it was at the same time a phrase weighted by the academic virtues of good breeding. These at first applied only to details and would take over the whole of architecture only when the climate of taste became itself academic.

The whole process, however, represented a rebuff to the nonantiquarian development which had stemmed from Gothic revival rationalism. This fact is well illustrated by a letter from England printed in the *American Architect*. A remarkably percipient work (and unfortunately unsigned), it decisively points out the academic possibilities which lurked in the dual aspect of Queen Anne growth. It claims that Gothic revival principles had been developing well, with workmen beginning to be trained according to the ideals of Morris and Webb and with industrial design progressing satisfactorily, when

> . . . suddenly a clever young practitioner [Shaw] started out with some picturesque adaptations of the work of a century and a half ago; the mobile part of the profession began to imitate him; the fashion took; and the "Queen Anne" style, as they called it, began to be the rage. . . . And now there are signs in the air of a second Greek revival. Such a revival may not come, and it would not, after the experience of this generation, be the formal thing that it was before; but that it is thought likely to recur at all, shows the more clearly the want of solidity in the movements of this whole generation.[13]

The strictures of this writer may be partially dismissed as those of a die-hard Gothicist. On the other hand, future events were to bear out his intuition that the new movement in England and America, potentially so creative (which he does not admit), held within itself at the same time certain seeds of academic classicism.[14] Certainly there was some "want of solidity

13. "In Search of a Style," *Am. Arch., 1* (1876), 259–60. This writer (p. 258) also quotes Kerr, who, in an article entitled "Renewal of the Study of Greek Architecture," had felt a new classicism on the way.

14. As early as 1876 the passion for the preservation of old structures had begun. Old South Church, Boston, threatened at this moment, was saved by a popular movement in

in the movements of this whole generation," and it was perhaps inevitable that the original creative adjustment, when it did arrive, was to be precarious and short lived, although laden with possibilities for future growth. One of those possibilities, beyond classicizing academicism, was to be the rediscovery of "classic" order itself.

Notwithstanding the critical furor, only a few of the houses published by the *American Architect* in 1876 reveal any Queen Anne influences whatever. A house near Boston by Peabody and Stearns; the Humeston House at Holyoke by Henry F. Kilburn; Westerly Prospect at Beverly Farms, Massachusetts, by W. G. Preston; and a cottage at Seabright, New Jersey, by R. H. Robertson— these are typical examples of the developed stick architecture of the early 70's. The Bennett House in Wilkes-Barre by Bruce Price is an excellent instance of a similar sensitivity transposed into brick.[15] Of interest are the remarks of the *American Architect* concerning the Lee House at Beverly Farms, Massachusetts, by Cabot and Chandler: "The frame construction of the upper stories gave so good a motive to its decoration in half-timbered work, that this means of emphasizing the construction has been carried throughout the design." [16] This is pure stick style rationalization. Thus these houses as a group may be said to constitute the background from which the new formal development was about to spring, corresponding as they do to the background of the new intellectual development, which was the romantic-rationalist architectural theory of Pugin, Ruskin, Downing, Wheeler, and Viollet-le-Duc.

Exemplifying a movement toward the surface texture that characterized the new formal development is the T. G. Appleton House at Newport, built by Richard Morris Hunt in 1875 and published by the *American Architect* as the

---

which architects heartily joined. *Am. Arch., 1* (1876), 273. On October 7 the magazine reproduced an interior view of this building and a section showing the framing of the main roof trusses. It is not argued that the desire to preserve old buildings necessarily indicates an academic or antiquarian moment in architectural creation. Indeed such a desire probably marked a necessary phase of self-awareness in the United States of the 70's. But the attitude had been foreign to the midcentury, which preferred to remake the old in its own image. To venerate the old was a new phenomenon in 1876, and as previously noted was already linked with academic design in Ware's classes at M.I.T. See n. 3 above.

   15. 1. House near Boston, Peabody and Stearns, *Am. Arch., 1,* Jan. 15, 1876.
       2. Humeston House, Holyoke, Mass., Henry Kilburn, architect, *op. cit.,* April 22.
       3. Westerly Prospect, Beverly Farms, Mass., by W. G. Preston, *op. cit.,* June 17.
       4. Cottage at Seabright, New Jersey, R. H. Robertson, *op. cit.,* July 22.
       5. Bennett House, Wilkes-Barre, Pa., Bruce Price, architect, *op. cit.,* May 6 (the first published work by this extremely important architect, who was also the father of Mrs. Emily Post).
   16. *Am. Arch., 1* (1876), 109.

first design reproduced in its first issue (Fig. 18). It is one of Hunt's best houses, awkward but expressively rugged and without Hunt's usual eclecticisms.[17] While basically in the midcentury stick style, it was described as having a "rubble-stone" lower floor, and an

> upper, of wood covered with slates laid in colored patterns, a mode of construction which is becoming not uncommon at Newport of late. It is a common habit there, to use slate only for the wooden walls of houses, using shingles for the roof, which make a tighter and securer covering; an important point in a climate so wet as that of Newport, and where many of the houses are left unoccupied for a great part of the year.[18]

Although Hunt here, perhaps characteristically, used the heavier slates rather than the native shingles as wall covering, the *American Architect*'s comment concerning the use of shingles in summer houses was to the point. The simple fact of necessary protection against weather, especially over a light frame skeleton with thin sheathing, was undoubtedly of importance in the whole rise of shingles, which indeed had been used in Rhode Island since colonial times.[19]

More significant than the Hunt House, however, is one by A. F. Oakey at Lenox, Massachusetts (Fig. 19). While rather frenzied, it expresses a much more advanced development of Queen Anne inspirations than does Hunt's Appleton House. It has also the distinction of being the only house published in the *American Architect* in 1876 of which the plan is in any way advanced. Open in space and with a large living hall and fireplace, this house also used "pine shingles soaked in linseed oil" on its second story.[20] It represents one of the first of Oakey's ebullient productions, of which further examples were soon to appear.[21]

17. Hunt never advanced much further in the free design, and his best work probably remains the few stick style houses he built in his younger days, the J. N. A. Griswold House at Newport, of 1862, being an early example, and the Appleton House, discussed above, a later one. See my "Romantic Rationalism," pp. 138–9.

18. *Am. Arch., 1* (1876), 5.

19. Were it not for the fact that Richardson's Andrews House, with its shingled upper story over clapboarded lower story, appeared only shortly after the first publication of Leyes Wood with its tiled upper and brick lower stories—as discussed earlier—one might be tempted to believe that Richardson, in first using shingles, had acted upon the inspiration of a long-standing Rhode Island tradition. Whatever his inspiration, he initiated anew a type of wall covering entirely in keeping with damp seaside conditions in general, and old Rhode Island practice in particular.

20. *Am. Arch., 1* (1876), 99.

21. In 1876 William Ralph Emerson of Boston also published a project showing Queen Anne influence. A simple, thin-sided wooden house, it timidly used a shingle covering, carefully retained within panel stripping, on portions of its upper story. *Architectural Sketch Book* (Boston), *4,* November, 1876.

In 1876, therefore, while the theoretical basis of a new architecture was beginning to take form, the new architecture itself had not advanced very far. The year 1877, after the influence of the Centennial had had time to spread, saw very broad advance on all levels. In that year the relation of Queen Anne to colonial was defined more exhaustively, and the whole nature of the architectural revival began to take definite shape. At the April meeting of the Boston Society of Architects R. S. Peabody, of the Boston firm of Peabody and Stearns, read a revealing paper entitled "A Talk about 'Queen Anne.' " This was reprinted in the *American Architect* in the same month. Peabody regarded the Queen Anne as a definite break with the Gothic revival, eclectic in inspiration but tending toward the classic, a gay and affected style influenced by "odd bits" of handicrafts, Morris wallpapers, and artistic bric-a-brac. He ends with this significant paragraph, which links English Queen Anne to American colonial:

> Thus I have meant to show that this movement is very strong and well established in England, and consequently of importance to our designers; that bric-a-brac, and Japan, and India, and classic mythology, and odds and ends, inspire it quite as much as Queen Anne; and that after all it is a curious support to our American eclectic notions. But lastly to those who do believe in revivals, "Queen Anne" is a very fit importation into our offices. There is no revival so little of an affectation on our soil, as that of the beautiful work of the Colonial days. Its quiet dignity and quaintness, its cosiness and elegance, always attract us. It is our legitimate field for imitation, and we have much of it to study right in our own neighborhood. In fact, anyone who in summer drives over the ancient turnpike from Hingham to Plymouth will not only pass through a beautiful country full of old homesteads, but will find the sun-flowers still nodding behind the gambrel-roofed houses that line the road through Queen Anne's Corner.[22]

This article of Peabody's was soon answered by an Englishman signing himself "J. M. B.," in "A Few More Words about 'Queen Anne,' " published in October. His article is fairly confused, but the point emerges that the Queen Anne in England had developed into a complete rejection of the

22. *Am. Arch.*, 2 (1877), 133–4. The "Japanese" reference is also important, as indicated earlier. Notice the immediate and effortless association of colonial with Queen Anne, simply the same thing to Peabody. Robert Swain Peabody was born in New Bedford, Mass., in 1845; he took his A.B. at Harvard in 1866, and his A.M. there in 1870. He studied at the École des Beaux-Arts in 1868 and began practicing architecture in Boston in 1870. He was president of the A.I.A. in 1900–01, and of the Boston Society of Architects in 1902–05 and again in 1907. He died in 1917.

Gothic revival and was now regarded as the continuation of 18th-century building, before any of the revivals began.

> The study of the subject proved the fallacy of the so-called revivals, and showed the gradual development of the old work to be so complete, that instead of stopping the sequence as was done when we tried to put a Greek temple in a London park, it would have been more to the purpose to take up the story and carry it on from the point it had reached, and with the material lying ready to our hands. That is what the so-called revival of Queen Anne really is; an attempt to continue the work of English domestic architecture in the true spirit of English work. . . . Some classicists say it will end in all becoming classic.

The "true spirit," for this correspondent, had now become 18th-century and classical. He claimed the New Zealand Chambers (Fig. 7) for the Queen Anne but rejected Leyes Wood and Cragside. Quoting Peabody, he urged Americans to do as the English had done.

> You, like us, have a heritage of the key-work on which it is all founded; and if ever America is to become possessed of an historical style, it must spring from the work of the old colonists. . . . Preserve then your old colonial architecture, and it may yet bring fruit of which all the world of art may be proud.[23]

This is an important article. It indicates the classicistic point which some English Queen Anne thought had already reached, and it points out the way, along similar lines of antiquarian research, that America might be expected to follow. However, that America was still in an earlier stage of revival and might follow a different path toward classicism was indicated by a letter signed "S. S.," who snapped back at J. M. B.: "is it not fair to say that if Cragside and the Wispers are not Queen Anne, and Lowther Lodge [Fig. 20] is, so much the worse for Queen Anne?" [24]

23. *Am. Arch.*, 2 (1877), 320–2. J. M. B. was the English architect J. M. Briden, who later, quite naturally, became a mainstay in England of the monumental Queen Anne, the Georgian revival, and the classicistic in general.

24. *Ibid.*, p. 339. Cragside and Wispers were two of Shaw's earlier, more medieval country houses. Lowther Lodge, 1873 (publ. *Building News*, 1875, republ. *Am. Arch.*, Mar. 11, 1882), is later and more classical, rather Thorpian with Renaissance pilasters, and so forth. Only a step from the Renaissance manner which Shaw was shortly to enter, Lowther Lodge stands at the turning point into the classicistic in that significant, step-by-step re-creation of the progress of the English Renaissance which Shaw carried out as his work developed. See Blomfield (who was delighted by this progress), *Richard Norman Shaw*, *passim*.

Peabody, however, had only begun his campaign, and in the same issue of the *American Architect* which contained S. S.'s small voice he published a critically important article. Signing himself, winsomely, "Georgian," he took up the cudgels for colonial revival where he had left off. His article was entitled "Georgian Homes of New England." [25] In this he developed the argument he had already presented: that the English Queen Anne architects claimed to be revising old work of a time when men never thought of styles, and that there was no reason why Americans should not do the same.

> We too have had our revivals; and if we go behind them we find in the Georgian days men working without thought of style, simply, delicately, beautifully. Many a choice wooden cornice, many a stiff mantel in our farm houses, attest this: Plancia, fascia, and soffit are still Yankee words in spite of our medieval period. With our Centennial year have we not discovered that we too have a past worthy of study?—a study, too, which we can subsequently explain and defend by all the ingenious Queen Anne arguments, strengthened by the fact that our Colonial work is our only native source of antiquarian study and inspiration.

The unabashed antiquarianism of Peabody's attitude is rather new and even refreshing, but his actual preferences in colonial architecture are also interesting; they modify somewhat the Palladian sound of his first paragraphs. He states that although there are some 17th-century houses in existence, he generally prefers those between 1727 and 1760, and yet does not admire the later, richer mansions which "seem unpleasantly angular and box-like." He likes better

> The old Fairbanks House at Dedham [Fig. 30], partly early with high-pitched roof and partly later with gambrel roof [which] forms a most picturesque pile; and so does the scattered house at Little Harbor, with gables at different heights, and floors at different levels; while the council-chamber wing runs off at an uncalled-for angle with the main building, that would delight Mr. Norman Shaw. Again, among the gambrel roofs, the great lumbering Sudbury Inn forms a most hospitable group, with its widespread barns and outhouses; while the Goodman cottage at Lenox smiles through its shrubbery, and winks its many-eyed sashes at the wayfarer. This picturesqueness I have endeavored to illustrate in the sketches with this paper, and we see that a picturesque group of

25. *Am. Arch.*, 2 (1877), 338–9. Roos claims this as the first use of the term "Georgian" (*Writings on Early American Architecture,* p. 6). But the *American Architect* had already used that term to describe colonial architecture in its 1876 article, "American Architecture—Past"; see n. 10 above.

any sort is thus not incongruous with our purpose; while of the interiors there is no need for words. We all know and like them; and it is because we too want to live amid wainscoting, nestle in elliptical arched nooks, warm ourselves beneath the high mantels at blazing wood fires, and go up to bed over boxed stairs with ramped rails and twisted balusters, and see our old chairs and pictures thus appropriately environed—it is because we like and want all this, that we seek for an excuse to do it all again. But isn't our liking reason enough?

And Peabody coos, "For once, let us reason like our clients."

One may inquire where the fierce ethical fiber of the old romanticism has gone. Peabody wallows unashamedly in sentiment, nostalgia, and antiquarianism, and in a desire for the picturesque that has now become semihysterical. He renounces principles; the old words "truth" and "reality" can recede to the ethical limbo of architectural theory whence they originally sprang. The one thing Peabody desires is emotional security, and he is prepared to achieve it as he pleases, preferably in an "elliptical arched nook." Most importantly, so far as the immediate future of the domestic development is concerned, in all Peabody's statements the need for picturesque freedom emerges as another pressing consideration. Peabody experiences the spaces, appreciates the loose and flowing masses, rolls in the textures. He has enough of midcentury originality in him to reject copying the past, even if he has renounced principles. Now finished, he says, is

> the battle of styles, and the fancies of the artist are of proportionately greater importance . . . so that we shall care for the design not for its historical accuracy, but the artist's clever art in harmonizing whatever his fancy leads him to, with itself and its surroundings. From this point of view, whatever the attractions of other sources, from no field can suggestions be drawn by an artist more charming and more fitted to our usage, than from the Georgian mansions of New England.

The architect at this moment emerges as a man who, having grown up in a demanding atmosphere of ethical principles, comes under the seductive influence of the Queen Anne and is directed from that to his own colonial. He then rejects his principles and with a kind of irresponsibility and satiric joy proceeds to imagine picturesque compositions, flowing in space and fluid in mass, which may resemble his inspirations only in details but which grow from a pictorial re-experience of their qualities. He feels himself freed, and he lays about him, sometimes daring to mock old gods, as in an article in the *American Architect,* entitled "The Doctrinaire in Art," which states:

One tires of hearing people talk masterfully about principles of art, or give the law in decoration. . . . There is no power of producing a work of art, either "high" or decorative, except in the native feeling and training of the artist, nor of judging them without a cultivated sense. Mr. Ruskin's precepts cannot answer everything . . . and Mr. Eastlake has the misfortune to have his name associated with more ugly furniture, we suppose, than the world ever saw before in equal time.[26]

Thus the architect was beginning to throw off the principles of midcentury theory, principles which had been at the root of the lively domestic development in America up to 1876. Was he, in consequence, to become purely a colonial antiquarian? Although Peabody had seemed to wish it, he had denied the necessity. But H. Hudson Holly, the very man who had begun the series of articles on the Queen Anne in *Harper's* of May, 1876, now called loudly for a specifically antiquarian and nationalistic revival. He wanted "no feeble copy of foreign styles of questionable fitness and in little sympathy with our institutions, but something distinctly American [which] might be developed." And he cries, "revive the good old types of Dutch and Puritan architecture." He continues: "In your issue of July 28, there are two designs, one intended for Albany and one for Newport (two of the oldest and perhaps most interesting cities in our country). Both are by architects of rare ability, and their efforts are praiseworthy in the extreme; but the opportunity which is here afforded to revive the good old types of Dutch and Puritan architecture has been wasted." [27] When one realizes that Holly's book on the Queen Anne had not yet been prepared for publication and that the houses he referred to were both more or less Queen Anne, the one in Albany by Potter and Robertson and the one in Newport by McKim, one wonders what measure of archaeological correctness he could possibly have had in mind.[28] As long before as 1863 Holly had called loudly for an American style, and his eagerness for tradition and regional conformity would seem to have grown over the years.[29]

In 1877 there was still an answer to Holly, and the *American Architect* made this answer in an editorial in the same issue in which his blast appeared. The journal's editorialist claimed to be as interested in colonial buildings as Holly was, and hoped that they could become better known. He refers to Holly's communication and continues:

26. Dec. 22, 1877. This is an attack upon Ruskin unusually bold for 1877.

27. *Am. Arch.*, 2 (1877), 267.

28. 1. City House in Albany, Potter and Robertson.

   2. Dunn House, Newport, 1876. Charles McKim, *Am. Arch.*, 2, July 28, 1877.

29. Cf. Holly, *Country Seats, passim.*

Certain districts we know have been carefully explored by architects whose sketch-books must be full of notes, the value of which is increasing with age. As these examples are inaccessible to most of us we trust that some of these gentlemen may be induced to give us the results of their interesting investigations, either in a separate publication or in our own pages, which of course will gladly receive any contribution of the kind. We are pleased to announce, by the way, that Mr. Charles F. McKim of New York, whose researches among the antiquities are well known, will shortly forward to us drawings of three stone colonial houses.[30] Our antiquity, although not much to boast of, and extending back to times scarcely more than a century and a half ago, should be considered a precious inheritance, and, if rightly used, can scarcely fail to be of service to architectural design, in aiding to confer upon it that sentiment of locality which, for obvious reasons, should be encouraged and cherished.[31]

All this might be as antiquarian as one could wish, but the *American Architect* goes on:

It is worthy of remark, however, that the local sentiment—the local characteristic of style—is unconsciously developed, in spite of all our attempts to masquerade in Romanesque, Gothic, or Renaissance, in Dutch or Puritan disguises. The necessities of local materials and local laws, customs, and requirements, the value of land, the degree of economy to be observed, the influence of climate—all these considerations tend legitimately to the establishment of local types. . . . [the architect] may undertake to imitate in new work one of the colonial mansions . . . but a thousand considerations conspire to interfere, consciously or unconsciously, with his loyalty to the chosen type, unless he is willing to act merely as an antiquary and not as an architect. . . . We believe that with all our intimate knowledge of works of the past, and notwithstanding all our experimental revivals of old styles, the principal element in modern work, in this country especially, is modern, born of our new materials and our new way of using old materials, of our new methods of workmanship, and of our new conditions of life, and of our restrictions to given areas in large cities. . . . To direct attention, there-

30. It was in this critical year of 1877 that McKim, Mead, White, and Bigelow took their trip along the New England coast, studying the colonial, mainly Palladian, as they went. McKim's "three stone colonial houses" never turned up in any publication.

31. 2 (1877), 261–2. Note the rise of regional sentiment, a recurrent motif in later architectural theory to the present day.

fore, to this or that range of precedent as more likely than others to lead to the development of a style distinctively American, as our correspondent [Holly] suggests, is, in our opinion, to misunderstand first, what constitutes a distinctive or representative style and how it grows; and second, what is the peculiar function of the modern architect: it certainly is not the manufacture of styles.[32]

This attitude, retaining as it does so much of that sense of building techniques and actual modern conditions that had distinguished the soundest of earlier American theory, cut through the stricter antiquarianism which was threatening the young revival and clung to the midcentury belief in architecture's necessary originality, timeliness, and modernity. Such attitudes, always present in the first years of the revival, kept the enthusiasm for colonial architecture creative and not merely antiquarian. Through this kind of vision it was possible for the men of 1877 to evaluate what they saw, to broaden but not destroy themselves in contact with the colonial. An excellent example of this was J. Cleveland Cady's reaction to the old Dutch farmhouses of New Jersey. In a talk given before the New York Chapter, A.I.A., on December 4, 1877, he stated that while attention had of late been called to the comparatively luxurious colonial work in New England, there was something also to be learned from the Dutch farmhouses of New Jersey, built very simply by common people. There is much that is prophetic of later attitudes and forms in his sensitivity:

> The Dutch houses are broad (seldom lofty); horizontal lines predominate; their roof masses are simple, expressive; and often graceful. The houses never seem ambitious or pretentious; the big chimneys, broad, well-lighted doorways, and spreading roofs suggest hospitality and good cheer. Moreover, the buildings are often singularly well adapted to their sites. . . . The color of these houses was usually quiet; the first story being of brownstone, the gable-ends and carpentry painted an olive or

32. Mention should also be made of the continual discussions in these years, too numerous to be noted here, of new mechanical contrivances, heating arrangements, ventilation, lighting, and so on. This concern with the technological facts of building, so predominant in the midcentury, continued in this period with unabated vitality. It must be regarded as another of the links with reality which characterized the American development. The rise of the open plan which Richardson had initiated in the Codman House and which formed the basis of the new sense of space could have been generally possible only with constantly improving central heating facilities. A lack of concern with these was probably one of the several reasons why English plans never developed comparable openness.

drab. Very often, however, this woodwork was in white, but there was so little of it that it was not glaring.[33]

Of one house he says:

> . . . the whole seeming to have grown out of the hillside, and to be a part of it. . . . We enter a good-sized hall . . . connecting with the drawing room by a large opening. . . . We realize that [these rooms] are not large, yet they seem extremely spacious. . . . The first assignable cause seems to be the low ceilings (about eight feet) which not only give an air of cosiness, but increase the breadth of the rooms; next we cannot but conclude that the very small trim architraves, etc., must greatly increase this effect . . . the mouldings finish is small, and the mouldings everywhere simple and delicate. . . . As we take a final survey of this homelike cosy interior, we see that the timbered and ceiled ceiling is far prettier in color and light and shade than any expanse of plaster could be; that the large fireplace suggests an ample allowance of the greatest of all creature comforts; that the low ceilings give a feeling of cosiness . . . and that the simplicity and smallness of such details as mouldings, etc., have increased the apparent size of the place very greatly.

Cady's observations are thus mainly concerned with the new sense of horizontally extended space. He looks for the reason behind each feature, not only as it reflects a specific functional requirement but also as it affects the over-all experience of space. He feels, moreover, that the construction of his Dutch houses is solid and expressive precisely because the resources of the builders are limited. Therefore each element, the solid wall and the roof to overhang and protect it, grew from an actual need accomplished as expressively as possible. His rationalism, like that of the midcentury development, enabled him to sense the architectural realities involved. This attachment to the necessary techniques of actual building and to the expressive power of functional thinking is, as in the *American Architect*'s editorial just quoted, one of the factors which enabled the late 70's to assimilate the Queen Anne and colonial creatively. Cady searches for the basic or archetypal form.

Factors which were eventually to undermine that grip on reality were already present in 1877 and were, curiously enough, not unconnected with a similar search for archetypes. As noted earlier, William Rotch Ware, the first editor of the *American Architect,* had attended the École des Beaux-Arts in

33. J. Cleveland Cady, "Some Features of the Dutch Farmhouses of New Jersey," *Am. Arch., 2* (1877), 401–2.

Paris. While there he had acquired a deep, understandable respect for European culture and for the discipline of the schools.[34] His stamp was on the *American Architect* from the very beginning. Consequently, when in March of 1877 a correspondent signed "C" claimed that Richardson's tower on Trinity Church in Boston was successful for the simple reason that it was borrowed from Salamanca Cathedral, the *American Architect,* as a periodical with pretensions to more than slight familiarity with European monuments, was inclined to agree.[35] It called attention to Richardson's own genius but said of the people of past ages:

> as first comers, they had the opportunity of appropriating the simple and natural forms that first suggest themselves for the purposes at which they aimed. They left to us who follow them the choice of using the same forms for the same uses, or taking refuge in others less natural and therefore less suitable and expressive, with the risk of being, as our correspondent says, original at the risk of being vulgar.[36]

This is the first time, to my knowledge, that any responsible architectural publication uttered a syllable against originality since Downing and Davis had overwhelmed the Greek revival; even Greek revival references to the superiority of cribbing over invention had been very rare.[37] Here was a new phenomenon in America, a defense of what was the most purely academic of architectural approaches. Its sources are to be considered as threefold—an uneasy though comprehensible cultural snobbism which must admit to pride at knowing what Salamanca Cathedral looked like, a concomitant belief that it was better to be correct if originality carried a possibility of vulgarity, and a growing desire for essential and universally applicable forms.

Thus in August of 1877 the *American Architect* editorially called for the establishment of academies of architecture in America, in order to restrain that "boldness which is impertinence." It thundered: "The obvious duty of those who would raise the standard of architecture . . . is to establish schools, in which the superabundant courage of our youth is made to understand and respect principles of art, and the true value of precedent, before it ventures upon the dangerous ground of invention and originality." The place where true principles were taught and where the value of precedent was best inculcated, it said, was of course the École des Beaux-Arts in

34. See n. 1.

35. See Ch. 1, p. 18. Here is the influence of White's pastiche having its effect.

36. *Am. Arch.,* 2 (1877), 80.

37. See Talbot Hamlin, "The Greek Revival in America and Some of Its Critics," *Art Bulletin, 24* (1942), 244–58.

Paris. It went on: "Our own pages, which have hitherto undertaken to set forth within the limits of our opportunities, the higher average of contemporary design, are proofs too often of our need of educated perceptions and of that true strength of the artist which is best expressed in its reserve. We pray that this historical record may be speedily improved for the sake of our good name." The watchword is "first correctness, then boldness," said the *American Architect*.[38] To suppose that correctness, as established by schools, might reduce the very boldness and invention which had been American architecture's strength in the midcentury was a proposition which did not occur to the *American Architect*. In September of 1877 it cited in this connection a statement by Auguste Bartholdi, the sculptor of the Statue of Liberty and of the excellent frieze of angels on the tower of Richardson's Brattle Square Church. Bartholdi, who had been a member of the international jury at the Centennial, was quoted as saying that Americans were remarkably inventive and would one day accomplish great things. The *Architect* felt it necessary to append the reservation that if Americans had more schools they would be even better, because more learned.[39] Ware, the editor, seemed to have discovered a cause worth fighting for.

Much of this respect for schools on the part of Ware and the *American Architect* arose from the desire, already noted, to raise the standing of the architectural profession, to draw a sharp line between builders and architects, and to make it clear to the world that the architect was an educated gentleman. This preoccupation was further indicated by a vicious attack upon the informally educated architect which appeared in 1877 and was venomously entitled "Self-made Architects." [40] In this movement toward professional isolation the *American Architect* was the spokesman for the American Institute of Architects, which was, from the late 60's on, the most influential architectural organization in the country.[41]

The end to which these ideals might lead—and of course eventually did lead—was prophetically indicated in an article which came out in the *American Architect* on December 22, 1877. This was a reprint of a criticism of American architecture appearing originally in the *Revue générale de l'architecture,* by several French architects who had visited the Centennial. Among some very shrewd statements there is this comment: "neither do we find anything of what with us is so appropriately termed 'projects.' This last deficiency arises from a very simple cause. Taste is not yet sufficiently developed [in

38. *Am. Arch.*, 2 (1877), 270–1.
39. *Ibid.*, pp. 277–8.
40. *Ibid.*, p. 395.
41. See Ch. 2, n. 10.

America] to permit the purely utilitarian side of questions to be forgotten, nor disinterested enough to lead one to make drawings for a scheme which he is not almost sure in advance of carrying out." [42] An awareness of the average American's incapacity for disinterested contemplation was probably as valid in 1877 as it might be today. Nevertheless, much of the latent irresponsibility of the Beaux-Arts at its worst was contained in this statement by the French architects.

An important problem for Americans was soon to arise from their ideas. On the one hand the *projet* system of the Beaux-Arts theoretically kept alive during a materialistic age the important fact that architecture had always been concerned with the most embracing human ceremonials, with pageantry, with grandeur, and with personal fulfillment alone and in large group projects. Theoretically it inculcated a sense of large formal order, and indeed it would seem to have had this effect upon Richardson in the 60's (though not upon Hunt in the 50's) and upon Sullivan in the early 70's.[43] But in the later 70's the Beaux-Arts was changing. The School of the Fine Arts at Marseilles, by Esperandieu, 1877, is a sobering example of its productions as published in America during these years.[44] In practice the projet was apparently moving away from any connection with fact or with genuine ceremonial invention. The American who yearned toward ceremony in the later 19th century— feeling, perhaps naively, a lack of it in his American past—would eventually be faced only with an artificial and flatulent ceremonial, involving summer palaces for exiled monarchs, monumental gateways, mausoleums, and terrifying memorials. This occurred when "the purely utilitarian side of questions" was forgotten and when the drawing with its gold *poché* was too obviously for a scheme which one never expected to carry out. By the later 70's the American was to have available only the Beaux-Arts in its late phase, when the picture on paper had ceased to have much connection with architecture, or the "monumental" conception with either "utilitarian" or spiritual realities.[45]

42. 2, 408–9.

43. Sullivan attended the École des Beaux-Arts in Paris during 1874–75. Louis H. Sullivan, *The Autobiography of an Idea* (New York, 1949), p. 213 and ch. 12. Actually he felt that M. Clopet, his tutor in mathematics, had more effect upon him than did the Beaux-Arts itself, of which he was not fond. Clopet set him to thinking of the "demonstration [which] shall be so broad as to admit of *no exception!*" *Ibid.*, p. 221.

44. *Am. Arch.*, 2, Oct. 6, 1877.

45. This is not to say that projects have not played a part in modern architectural advance or that the architect should be limited in imagination to what can actually be built at a specific moment in building conditions. It is understood that most of Le Corbusier and much of Wright exists only in project form. But there is a difference in intent between their projects and the Beaux-Arts projet. Founded upon evaluations of the nature of society ac-

Although the *American Architect* made little comment on the French criticisms, it was plain that it took seriously what the Frenchmen had to say. Did they not speak for the Beaux-Arts? By the late 80's, from this still weak and partly secret longing in America for the vaguely monumental and the "non-utilitarian," sanctified by Beaux-Arts example, a real craving for grandeur, opulence, and architectural display was to develop. In 1877 the evidence of such longing was scattered, but it was there, and was, by the late 80's and afterward, to be amply fulfilled.[46]

cording to the architect's lights, the projects of Wright and Le Corbusier yearn toward building and have a final three-dimensional purpose—there is nothing "artificial" about them—whereas the Beaux-Arts projet was eminently artificial, consciously and purposely so; it was the latter which began to dominate American architecture by the 1890's.

46. In line with its policy of pushing the ideas of the Beaux-Arts where possible, the *American Architect* during 1877 published several designs emanating from that source: in the September 15 issue a two-page interior view of the Grand Staircase of the Opéra, Paris, by Charles Garnier; in the September 22 issue two pages of competition drawings for memorials around Paris by various architects; in the October 6 issue the façade of the School of the Fine Arts at Marseilles by Esperandieu; and in the October 13 issue details of the same. These few examples are the forerunners of the flood of European classicistic material which overwhelmed the pages of the *American Architect* in the later 80's.

4. Experiments in Design by 1877.
Theoretical Synthesis to 1883

By the end of 1877 a solid body of Queen Anne and colonial theory had been laid down, and most of the philosophical and design problems which were to engross the attention of the new generation of architects and critics had been exposed and considered. Moreover, during 1877 the architectural development itself accelerated the general movement toward an Americanized Queen Anne and began to explore, much more than it had in 1876, the possibilities and problems of the new design.

Of all the houses published in the *American Architect* of that year perhaps the most interesting, if not the most advanced, was A. F. Oakey's Dorr House at Mount Desert, Maine.[1] This fantasy (Fig. 21) is of the usual stick style turned Tudor—or perhaps here more specifically Jacobean—which was typical of Oakey's work. High and angular, it abounds in stick work which in this example, proliferating around high-piled Tudor window bays, seems more like decorative half-timbering than did the occasionally similar stick work of the earlier stick style itself. A wide veranda, its roof supported by heavily turned pseudo-Jacobean posts, surrounds the house and supports various projecting bays, one of which is octagonal on the second story. An open tower with high candle-snuffer roof tops the whole boisterous mass.

The projecting roof and the upper story bays pull the void of the veranda deep into the volume of the house. In this way, and with the increased window area, interior and exterior space tend to penetrate each other. The house reaches out in space and pulls space into it. Here was a peculiarly American

1. *Am. Arch.*, 2, Jan. 20, 1877. No longer in existence. Oakey also produced two city houses in 1877, the Sprague House at Buffalo, a cramped brick box which explodes in Queen Anne gables on its upper story (*ibid.*, July 14, 1877), and the Coxe House, also at Buffalo (*ibid.*, Sept. 8, 1877). Both use halls and galleries and are very English, if wild.

feature of the new architectural development, namely the expansion and integration of the veranda, a space half open and half enclosed and now becoming an integral part of the volumes of the house. The interior reveals the same invention evidenced by the exterior. The plan is very open, with large halls on both first and second floors. The upper hall adjoins a lobby, above which rises the void of the tower. The freedom so fully enjoyed here raises the house above its blatant eclecticism and was to remain one of the strongest aspects of the new domestic growth.[2] Peabody and Stearns, whose Mr. Peabody was the "Georgian" antiquarian, built in that year a much quieter house at Medford, Massachusetts (Fig. 22), in which the shingles of Queen Anne cover a portion of the surface of the upper floors. The undistinguished plan includes a tight hall on axis, with fireplace. Off this open a dining room and a living room, of which the rectangular corner bay shoots out at a forty-five degree angle. This spatial fillip would also become characteristic of some of Peabody and Stearns' later work.[3]

Another aspect of the development is represented in the Bryce Gray House at Long Branch, New Jersey, by the New York firm of Potter and Robertson.[4] This house is stick style vernacular pulled down vertically, stretched out horizontally, and extended by verandas (Fig. 23). These again are not simply adjuncts but are now becoming an integral part of the house, an extension of the interior space. Also to be noted is the great hall which almost completely opens up the interior volume of the house as it flows under an arch, into a tremendous billiard room with fireplace. Directly inside the front door, the effect of this great space with its gigantic billiard table must have overwhelmed Long Branch.[5] In consequence, the keynote of all these houses, and the most important tie which binds them together, is interior space, expanded and freely manipulated.

A structure which does not enter into this class is a small country house at Peekskill-on-Hudson, the Herrick House by Mead.[6] It is partly covered with shingles, tight and awkward, but very quiet in general massing. Its interior

2. Shortly after Oakey's design was published, Carl Pfeiffer, also a New York architect, published a proposed cottage for Long Branch, N.J., very similar in spirit to Oakey's Mount Desert design. The large hall with fireplace alcove recalls Oakey's open interior space, as does the high piled massing capped by an open tower. Pfeiffer uses shingles instead of clapboards and half-timbering. It would appear that he was moved by the wild invention of Oakey more than by Oakey's overt Tudorisms. *Ibid.*, April 7, 1877.

3. *Ibid.*, Feb. 17, 1877.

4. *Ibid.*, May 19, 1877.

5. One will remember the *American Builder*'s wistful hope in 1876 that "the next millionaire" to build at Long Branch would adopt the Queen Anne style. See Ch. 2, p. 20.

6. *Am. Arch.*, 2, June 20, 1877.

space makes no use of the openness to be gained from a unifying living hall with its fireplace (Fig. 24). Like the other work by Mead already discussed, the house is generally undistinguished.

As Mead runs true to type in the Herrick House, so does his partner, Charles Follen McKim, in a house of this year. McKim's work is of extreme importance. The Dunn House at Newport (Fig. 25) obviously represents his idea of a very Shavian manor house.[7] Spread out and rambling, it is typically McKim, doing laboriously and unconvincingly the kind of thing that Stanford White was able to do easily and well. The first floor is stone and the second clapboard, erupting at several places into cratelike half-timbering and heavily ornamented gables. The plan has a large hall with a fireplace and with rooms giving off it, but the space is arbitrarily divided and tight. Clearly McKim and Mead both did well, so far as picturesque design was concerned, when in 1879 they induced Stanford White to become a member of their firm.[8]

There is another point of greater importance here. To McKim, Old English inspiration, as in his Dunn House, does not seem to have been genuinely sympathetic. But McKim knew 18th-century colonial architecture, in an academic way, perhaps better than any other architect at the time. Even Peabody apparently lacked McKim's practice in restorations and correctly imitative colonial building.[9]

It was probably late in 1876 that McKim designed, and in 1877 built, the Moses Taylor House (Fig. 26) on Ocean Avenue in Elberon, New Jersey.[10]

7. *Ibid.*, July 28, 1877. The Dunn House was never built and the Dunns designed a house for themselves on Washington Street in Newport. Later, *ca.* 1899, Angell and Swift of Providence built this same family an excellent, very Japanese, late shingle style pavilion overlooking Squam Lake, Holderness, New Hampshire.

8. Perhaps the best work designed this year by the firm of McKim, Mead, and the self-effacing Bigelow is the small rectory for Christ Church, Rye, New York, built early in 1878. Of stone, with rather Gothic gables and an unobtrusive tudorish porch, it gives at least a sense of stone as laid random ashlar in a wall. Perhaps those drawings of "three stone colonial houses" which McKim promised to the *American Architect* but never produced, had some effect upon this design. More likely, of course, is the fact that Richardson's Trinity Church had just been completed, as had several of his libraries. In any of those buildings the nature of stone, only rarely sympathetic to midcentury America, was there for any to see. *Am. Arch.*, 2, Nov. 10, 1877.

9. One will recall McKim's colonial room in the Robinson House, Washington Street, Newport, 1872. See Ch. 2, n. 17. His trip with his partners in search of the colonial in 1877 should also not be overlooked. Ch. 3, n. 30.

10. Moore (*McKim*, p. 346) lists an H. A. C. Taylor House as built at Elberon in 1878 and lists no other Taylor House there. It has always been assumed, therefore, that Moore was

This house was not published in the *American Architect* or anywhere else, which may partly explain the fact that it seems to have had no direct or immediate influence upon other architects. The plan of this house is interesting insofar as it makes no use of the living hall with fireplace. From the land side a wide entrance hall runs directly through the house and opens through another range of doors to the sea. To the south, through a wide opening, is the drawing room. On the north, behind the wide, open staircases, are the library and dining rooms. The kitchen occupies an ell on the north side of the house. The space is open and expansive, but there is no real living hall.

Most interestingly, all rooms open widely, through extensive fenestration, upon galleries which surround the first and second floors of the house. In these galleries McKim or the client may have been influenced by an older, stick style, semi-Swiss cottage which is just north of the Taylor House on Ocean Avenue. From the exterior the Taylor House is a simple rectangular cube, an object which, approached from its curving entrance drive, appears as much an abstract form set in sharp contrast to the landscape as does, for instance, Le Corbusier's Villa Savoie at Poissy. On the entrance side the house pushes out two gables which are supported upon the posts of the galleries. In this way the voids of the galleries are integrated fairly well with the main volume of the house. The larger gable is also partly opened by a loggia. The entrance side, though not absolutely symmetrical, gives that impression. The south side of the house is completely symmetrical. It is significant of McKim's true design preferences that the asymmetrical seaside front is much less successful. A few enframed areas of decorative shingling appear in the gables and around the sides of the service ell, but the main body of the house is clapboarded. Most of the decorative details are classical in inspiration, more or less Georgian, but much like those of Shaw's Lowther

---

really referring to the Moses Taylor House and that this, consequently, was the only Taylor House at Elberon and that its date was 1878. See Henry-Russell Hitchcock, "Frank Lloyd Wright and the Academic Tradition," *Journal of the Warburg and Courtauld Institutes,* 7 (1944), 51. This, however, is not correct. There are actually two Taylor houses at Elberon, the Moses Taylor House with which we are concerned at the moment, and the house which Moses Taylor, a year later (1878), built for his son, H. A. C. Taylor. Moses Taylor was a spectacularly successful tycoon and was financially able to build two houses within such a short space of time. During the panic of 1857 he bought control of the Delaware, Lackawanna, and Western Railroad at four dollars a share, worth two hundred and forty dollars seven years later. He was chairman of the banker's committee which made the first war loan in 1861 and upon his death in 1882 left forty million dollars. *Dictionary of American Biography, 18, 338.*

Lodge (Fig. 20) of 1875.[11] The porch posts are treated as pilasters, thin and linear in profile. A decorative motif in the smaller gable of the entrance side and an oculus in the main gable recall 18th-century, Adamesque features.

The whole aspect of the house is dry, precise, a little papery. It is basically two-dimensional in conception, worked in elevation rather than in perspective, not really plastic but flat. At the same time it has order, clarity, and a sense of geometry which is some years ahead of its time. Also, the house is now—and so far as I can determine always was—light in color, a metallic gray, with yellow trim. More than any house up to that time, or for some time later, the Moses Taylor House took direct inspiration, at least in detail and general feeling, from 18th-century prototypes. Unique in McKim's work at this period, it shows clearly his deeply-rooted 18th-century predilections. These, however, were about to go underground, not to reappear until the Appleton House of 1882–83 at Lenox, Massachusetts.[12]

Significant of the temporary submergence of the 18th century in McKim's design was the house which he built at Elberon in 1878 for H. A. C. Taylor.[13] This shows his attempt to create the looser, more picturesque kind of design which represented the main current of the later 70's. Yet the H. A. C. Taylor House seems less successful than the one built for Moses Taylor; its massing is awkward, its details crude. It demonstrates clearly that McKim's real desire —although he was for some years to work in a freer manner—was for a more controlled, more classic kind of form. Therefore, in the re-creative colonial revival of the 70's which saw the colonial through picturesque eyes, McKim stood somewhat apart. He seems to have seen in elevation rather than in perspective, in linear rather than in painterly details, in volumetric rather than in picturesque compositions. The free masterpieces of McKim, Mead, and White in the early 80's, while they certainly owe much to McKim's sense of order and clarity, must be considered as demonstrating the temporary ascendency of White's free, spatial and painterly vision over the tighter habits of McKim.

More typical of the general architectural development in 1877 than the Moses Taylor House was a house by Bruce Price. This was a cottage at Pittston, Pennsylvania, covered with thin slates (not shingles) on the upper stories

11. Lowther Lodge, 1873, published in *Building News* in 1875. See also the flat pilaster decoration of the many English designs which copied Lowther Lodge and which began to be published copiously in *Building News* in 1876.

12. See Ch. 8, pp. 143–5.

13. Dated 1878 in the gable, it was built for H. A. C. Taylor and would certainly appear to be the house listed by Moore. See n. 10 above. If this house represents a return to freer design in the 70's, another house for H. A. C. Taylor, that at Newport of 1885–86, was to be McKim's first completely Palladian design.

but in general resembling the stick style work of E. C. Gardner of the middle
70's more than it does the Queen Anne (Fig. 27). The plan as well shows little
of Price's later invention except that the fireplaces of hall and living room are
carefully lined up opposite each other, suggesting a cross axis not otherwise
developed.[14] From Chicago came also what must be considered a "project" by
F. M. Whitehouse, a semi-Queen Anne pastiche which was probably never
built.[15] Within its tight and insensitive plan it proudly inserts a huge but
meaningless hall with a large fireplace inglenook. The awkwardness of the
whole is a direct indication of the fact that Chicago was, at this particular moment, much less advanced than the East in the new design.

The year 1877 saw also the publication of a reconstruction project at
Milton, Massachusetts, by William Ralph Emerson, of Boston. This large
rambling edifice was an extensive addition to a small colonial house.[16] The
plan as it finally emerged is awkward, since the immovable central chimney
mass made a hall difficult to obtain. The project itself is extremely interesting
because it shows quite clearly that in 1877 (a) an architect was quite prepared
to remodel a colonial house, and (b) when it was remodeled, the result was
usually Queen Anne.[17]

In consequence a growing revival, half colonial and half Queen Anne,
was in the making and had so far, in spite of whatever heredity of academicism and antiquarianism it bore, remained generally creative. If relapse was to
be inevitable, the ground work of an original synthesis had also been laid.
The revival was obviously making a serious attempt to evaluate colonial
architecture, and to understand the Queen Anne.

The climax of this process and the fulfillment of its capacity to inspire
new growth came in the years 1878–83. By that time the new architecture
had been formed, and the creative energies of the early 80's were given
over to an extension and enrichment of its forms. To all intents and purposes

14. *Am. Arch.*, 2, Sept. 8, 1877. Bruce Price was born in Cumberland, Md., in 1845. He
studied architecture in Baltimore and abroad and began practicing in Baltimore in 1869.
In 1872 he moved to Wilkes-Barre, where he practiced until 1877. After this date his office
was in New York. Some of Price's later works, which will not be mentioned in this book,
include the American Surety Building and the St. James Building in New York, Hotchkiss
Preparatory School in Lakeville, Conn., Georgian Court in Lakewood, N.J., Château
Frontenac, Quebec, the railroad stations at Windsor Street and East End in Montreal, and
the Royal Victoria Academy in the same city. Also the Osborne Memorial (destroyed) and
Welch Dormitory at Yale College, New Haven, Conn., and the Colonial Historical Building
at New Haven. Price died in 1903. See also: Russell Sturgis, "The Works of Bruce Price,"
Supplement to the Architectural Record, 9 (1889), 1–65.

15. *Am. Arch.*, 2, Sept. 29, 1877.

16. *Ibid.*, Dec. 22, 1877.

17. Only McKim so far had engaged in academic "colonialistic" practices. See n. 9 above.

the colonial revival had done its work and was over. When it returned as Palladian academicism and sometimes as abject antiquarianism in the later 80's it was no longer the colonial revival as the late 70's had known it. Instead, it was the curious offspring of forces glimpsed in 1877: the sense of cultural inferiority to Europe, the respect for schools which would stress correctness over originality, and the rejection of difficult principles of growth in favor of easily disseminated principles of taste.

Not yet, however, from 1878 to 1883, was the delusion of the "traditional" sufficiently powerful to confuse a continuing development which might in time become a true tradition. That later process, and the threads of continuing invention which were to survive in it, will require study later. At present it is the culmination of the intellectual process, completing the first phase of revival in the years 1878 to 1883, which must be considered.

The pattern of intellectual activity relating to the assimilation of Queen Anne and colonial influences continued after 1878 and reached a synthesis before 1883. In 1878 Peabody produced another paper, signed this time, "R. S. Peabody," not "Georgian." The success of his first venture had emboldened him, and he was even more openly antiquarian than he had been before. Significantly enough, he concentrated upon colonial details, not plans or general massing. He says: "The chief beauties of the detail in colonial work arise from its disciplined and almost universal refinement and dignity, as well as the absence of vulgarity and eccentricity even when display is attempted. These virtues, not too common in our days, lend an added charm to it for us." [18] He then mentions books which he has "discovered" and which the colonists used: "Gibbs' work, published in 1739, including the engravings of St. Martin's Church in London . . . Batty and Thomas Langley . . . 1739 . . . Ware's, 1756, Chippendale's, 1762 . . . Swan's, 1768, Paine, 1783 . . . and the third edition . . . of the correct and elegant Sir William Chambers . . . 1791." [19] All these are based on the classic orders, says Peabody, and therefore correct. While his attitude seems tightly academic, it should be noted that Peabody's interest at this point was only in details. The antiquarianism which stimulated his research was eventually to exert a decisive influence upon American architecture as a whole. In the immediate future the love for comparatively simple colonial wood detailing was to

18. R. S. Peabody, "The Georgian Homes of New England," *Am. Arch., 3* (1878), 54–5.

19. Peabody's discovery of the books so obviously re-creates the original course of American colonial architecture as to indicate an interesting historical process. A generally utilitarian and "organic" 17th-century medieval architecture becomes enclosed in a Palladian shell during the 18th century, through the influence of the English books. Peabody, involved first in a picturesque appreciation of colonial qualities arising from just those utilitarian and "organic" bases, rediscovered the books and set the stage for his own eventual Palladianism.

have only the effect of simplifying wood details in general and lightening
their scale—probably a not undesirable outcome after the previous heavy and
complicated Eastlakian tendencies. On the other hand, there began to be re-
established the restricting habit of going to books for classical details, and a
certain limitation to invention began at least to be implied.

A consciously escapist nostalgia, which was another rather ominous aspect
of the revival, appeared in a letter from England in August, 1878. The
correspondent asserts that the revival in England—which he claims, somewhat exaggeratedly, had now become overtly 18th-century—very nearly has
the women in hoops and the men in "Addisonian bagwigs." The "power of
histrionic architecture," he feels, is literally making all the world a stage
" 'and all the men and women merely players.' "

> This is a new function of architecture. Perhaps it needs only a little
> more pushing of the "Old Colonial" derivative in this country, on the
> part of our clever young architects, to bring about some corresponding
> form of revival here. Who knows what stately virtues of the Province
> may follow on the reintroduction of slender orders and broken pedi-
> ments, urns and festoons, heavy sashes, small panes, and delicate mold-
> ings; what fine manners may come back in front of tiled chimney-pieces,
> and panelled wainscots, and under the wooden modillions and dentils
> of the parlor cornice.[20]

Again, the "classical" details.

Yet in 1878 there was still strong resistance both to academicism and to
escapism. A symptom of that resistance was a talk by A. F. Oakey, of the
exuberant Queen Anne projects. It was given at the eleventh annual convention of the American Institute of Architects and was entitled "The Possibility of a New Style in Architecture." Interestingly enough, Oakey's hold on
invention seems to come from a sense of vernacular frame structure. He
denies the hypothesis that a new style will develop from a study of Italian
Renaissance and states that such losses of heart seem to be all too common
among architects. He feels that "a system embodying the 'Tensile,' together
with a generalized imitation of nature, is the goal we seek." The "generalized
imitation of nature" is part of the romantic derivation of principle from the
structures of nature which was typical of the midcentury, and Oakey makes
it clear that when he talks about the tensile he has light frame construction
specifically in mind.[21]

20. *Am. Arch., 4* (1878), 48.
21. A. F. Oakey, "The Possibility of a New Style in Architecture," *Am. Arch., 3* (1878),
22. See also my "Romantic Rationalism," pp. 135–42.

To offset these archaeological reversions (of architects) we have the provincial builder with his jig-saw and his balloon frame; and we find ourselves admiring the prowess of the engineer as the only worker in the field who has thought for himself, accepted the limitations to his problems and met them with ingenuity; only his lack of artistic training enables us to find a living in our practice, unless we are called upon to minister to the unnecessary and luxurious evidences of civilization, and to take no part in the development that will go on, whether we move with it or not.

It seems to me that Mr. Garbett is nearer the truth with his development of the Tensile system, than Mr. Ferguson with his Italian Renaissance; for this principle already shows its influence strongly in all our utilitarian work—i.e. work in which the requirements must be met without regard to expression; and does not the expression follow inevitably? . . . Why have we not the courage to think for ourselves, and when we are asked in what style we have expressed our thoughts, to answer that we do not think it necessary to classify and ticket everything, to name in one word an ever-varying system that eludes such an attempt.[22]

The statement indicates the nature of the best of the domestic architecture which was to follow. The willingness to experiment and to create confidently are wedded in Oakey's statement (though not, unfortunately, in his later work) not only to a sense of social responsibility but also to that understanding of the reality of technique as a creative process which had inspired the vernacular of the midcentury. Oakey here sums up the most vital elements of the past. His attitude indicates the freedom and the sense of reality which were to create the immediate future and which may be felt to look forward to the architecture of Wright. Oakey's talk marks a sincere attempt to evaluate the nature of creative building. Its preoccupation with the vernacular is echoed by the *American Architect*. When Holly's *Modern Dwellings in Town and Country* appeared in 1878, the *American Architect* praised it as an extension of vernacular traditions. It stated:

Our methods of wooden construction, our verandas, our smooth, workmanlike roofs are all retained . . . and with them are combined the

22. Edward Lacy Garbett was a midcentury English engineer and architectural theorist. His theory of the "tensile" was an important early indication of an aesthetic awareness of the new architectural energies of metal frame construction. The theory was stated in his book, *Elementary Principles of Design*, Weale's Series, London, 1850. For a biographical entry see *Journal of the Royal Institute of British Architects, 19, 651*.

galleries, the great chimneys, the balustered porches, the panellings and the conventional sun-flowers attributed to the earlier Georgian era. . . . The plans are nearly all ingenious. . . . Large habitable halls well opened into the adjoining living rooms, stairs almost always very carefully contrived with embayed and orielled landings, dining rooms in every case connected with the kitchens by a direct passage through the butler's pantry.

Only, says the *American Architect,* not enough indication is given by Holly of the "points of the compass as an indication of proposed orientation for sun and view." [23] Vernacular techniques and expression and their extension by the new living space developed through the Queen Anne and colonial revivals (Figs. 28, 29) are here seen by the *American Architect* as forming the basis of the new architecture. In line with such awareness the *Architect* published a review of A. J. Bicknell, *Specimen Book of One Hundred Architectural Designs.*[24] The reviewer feels that the designs are crude and vulgar, as they surely are. But he states also that they show "the unity of our vernacular," which we must "make . . . better, not by masquerading with foreign shapes," but by developing "our own natural and proper heritage." And the journal does not use the term "colonial," but instead asks that we respect the "vernacular" forms.[25]

If in the next few years scattered evidences of antiquarianism and certain academic attitudes persisted, nevertheless the foundation of thinking remained as indicated above.[26] An original development was shaping upon the basis of the following leads: the idea of architecture as rooted in an organic and improved vernacular; the use of local techniques; the expansion of space through opening the plan, grouping the windows, and extending the verandas; and the clarification of details through a creative appreciation of the crispness of colonial woodworking. To this must be added continuing tech-

23. *Am. Arch., 3* (1878), 198–9.

24. New York, 1878.

25. *Am. Arch., 4* (1878), 5.

26. The antiquarian tendencies indeed become temporarily recessive after 1882, as if choked off by the original power of the new modern architecture. An example of the occasional academic reasoning which appears is a review of Jacob von Falke, *Art in the House,* trans. with notes by Charles C. Perkins, Boston, 1879. This book is excellent, says the reviewer, because it emphasizes the Renaissance. His reasoning: (1) The Queen Anne uses debased archaeological classical details; (2) this is bad because Viollet-le-Duc says that only in pure types can one find the energy for a long career; (3) consequently, let us get back to the Renaissance itself, where the details are not debased as in the Queen Anne, but pure. *Am. Arch., 5,* Feb. 8, 1879. Again, a search for archetypes seems to be diverted toward the specific details of a single style.

nological experimentation and the improvement of heating and ventilation.[27] Queen Anne and colonial as such, although they were occasionally still argued about or praised, had a tendency to recede from the main arena of attention.

To encourage original research in space and expression the *American Architect* ran a series of competitions throughout 1878 and 1879, first a series of designs for halls and stairways and then a series for fireplaces. These gave way in the early 80's to competitions for summer hotel halls, small cottages, low-priced houses, and complete summer hotels. As case studies in the new sense of space and shelter, they contrast strongly with the competitions for monuments and mausoleums which began to appear in the later 80's.[28] The early competitions, running constantly from 1878 to 1884, give an excellent indication of the building types which most preoccupied architects of the period. Small houses, cottages, and summer hotels—resort and suburban architecture—reflected a sincerely romantic and rational concern with simple building types. They express, perhaps, a kind of comfortable escapism, but they were genuine architectural problems, concerned directly with a simplified life. They were without pretension or concern with monumentality. When in 1885 projects for monuments began to appear, a different set of values emerged.

By 1880 the passion for Queen Anne and colonial had become partially objectified and synthesized into a creative basis for design. Architectural progress was now firmly in the hands of architects who felt themselves necessarily superior to the vernacular builder but who still sensed his qualities and who were aware of their own responsibilities in developing further the possibilities of a native art. In that desire they were not yet, on the whole, antiquarian, although they had passed through antiquarian moments.[29] It might

27. These items continued through the period. Moreover, the sense of contemporary technology in structure remained strong, although occasionally challenged. When the *American Architect* (*10,* July 30, 1881) hinted that balloon frame houses had withstood the hurricane of 1881 at Winona, Minn., less well than "the substantial structures of our ancestral homes" would have done, it was attacked immediately by eye witnesses and others who claimed the superior resistance of the flexible frame over either mortice and tenon or brick construction (*ibid.,* p. 79).

28. *Am. Arch.,* 1878–84, *passim.* The later competitions for monuments, mainly military in nature, began in 1885.

29. Interest in the colonial remained always to some extent antiquarian, although, as we have already indicated and will discuss later, it seems to have been distinguished from design. In February, 1879, the Rhode Island chapter of A.I.A. began a competition for the best drawing of a colonial building in the state, in order to build up "a record of such ancient buildings, especially those built in colonial times, as may be worthy of notice." *Am. Arch., 5,* Feb. 22, 1879. In May of that year the Boston chapter announced a similar competi-

be said that this new architectural thinking had escaped all dangers but one,
although touched by many, and that danger was the architect's pride of place
and position. They took pride in themselves as educated men and therefore
exhibited a growing respect for European precedents, methods, and schools,
and for the knowledge whereby they could distinguish themselves from the
crowd. Such an attitude may have had many virtues. Certainly much later
creation would have been impossible without it. As a corrective to mediocrity
and "conformism" it might have been expected to serve a useful purpose in
American culture. Yet the attitudes surrounding this new and rather syn-
thetic élite had much of conformism in them. An article in the *American
Architect* of 1878 shows how, when once launched on the subject of the educated architect, the men of these years lost all sense of the very qualities of
originality and growth in which they otherwise professed to believe and
which their work itself expressed in this period. The article decides that
there are two architectures in America, that of the vernacular and that of
the educated architect. The vernacular "is as innocent of archaeology as the
Romanesque work of the tenth century, or as any architecture can be. In
fact it is the modern example of an architecture practised . . . by men who
work without regard for precedent or rule, using forms which they know
only by tradition and example, and with a simple adaptation to the wants of
a people, to the materials and mechanical processes at their command." If
it seems ugly, we must look through "to its vigorous independence, and have
confidence that time will develop an artistic sense to chasten and shape it.
It is, however, distinct and coherent; in spite of many local differences in
mechanical expedients, it is the same thing from Maine to California, and it
is unlike anything else in the world." So far so good. Now, in addition to this
vernacular there is the

> art of the educated profession. . . . Out of their fusion or confusion
> must come the future of American architecture . . . it is clear from
> the present tendencies of society that the prevailing force must be the
> educated one. . . . The vigorous independence of our vernacular archi-
> tects is their birthright; being their only possession it should not be
> taken away from them, and it cannot. But the eclecticism of the edu-
> cated ones is to our mind far too lawless. . . . A study of style close

---

tion for all New England, in order to keep "the inheritance of good work from being forgotten," and they announced concerning the drawings: "If artistic sense and professional
knowledge are present it is a great gain, but the essential thing is intelligent exactitude."
Ibid., p. 153. "Intelligent exactitude" with regard to colonial was at this time not applied
to creative work, but the time was to arrive when it would be.

enough to satisfy archaeology is the best corrective that we know for this fault. For this reason we have urged the study of individual styles as the necessary means of training in architectural schools. For the same reason . . . such archaeological study as our country gives opportunity for,— from the inclination to revive what we call "colonial architecture". But we have been disappointed to see how in most cases the irrepressible American instinct has turned the repose of this into fussiness, its quiet order into lawlessness.[30]

A paradox then: the *American Architect* praised the vitality of the vernacular but in order that it might be improved insisted upon archaeology and had, indeed, used colonial enthusiasm to that end. Yet that enthusiasm, once kindled, had been too creative and had escaped the very discipline which the *Architect* had desired from it. It is possible that the journal was well advised in wishing at that time for a new discipline of design, but it was apparently ill advised if it believed that such discipline could be other than a deeply reasoned growth. Especially was it ill advised in believing that its schools might presently supply it. As a matter of fact, it soon unconsciously stated the nature of the schools of its period. In reply to a request from a prospective aspirant concerning how best to get along at the Beaux-Arts, it replied: "In the examination in architectural design it is safest to avoid anything bizarre; accurate mediocrity will answer every purpose, and the time that can be saved by not seeking for striking combinations of plan or elevation can be to good purpose spent on the renderings of the drawings." [31] This is an excellent exposition of the nature of the Beaux-Arts as it existed in the late 19th century in France and eventually in America.

It was probably inevitable that the thinking of the later 70's and 80's should turn in the end to the schools. A belief in the power of formal education to solve all problems was deeply rooted in 19th-century thought and nowhere more so than in democratic America. The modern world has had reason to look more deeply into this question, but for the early 80's it represented the most advanced idealism. Later, for instance, the *American Architect* again praised freely developing American architecture:

So far as there is anything of real interest in the novelties of American architecture it has come by mere provision for practical needs or mechanical convenience, and this has been the way of all worthy architectural progress. The wooden architecture of our houses, slight as they are;

30. "Archaeology and American Architecture," *Am. Arch., 4* (1878), 114–15.
31. "L'École des Beaux-Arts," *op. cit.,* p. 119.

their plans, which have developed distinct types both for city and country unknown elsewhere; our manner of using iron in architectural construction,—these are examples.

But then the journal felt compelled to note that the Beaux-Arts would discipline and improve all this.[32]

The respect for schools, especially as they were represented by the École des
Beaux-Arts, remained a characteristic of the thinking of these years and
filled the pages of the *American Architect* with classicistic material, eventually
in photographic form. However, another, more intrinsic discipline was to
grow up parallel to, partially influenced by, but mainly in reaction against
the imposed classicistic discipline of the late 19th-century Beaux-Arts system.
This discipline was to evolve out of researches into form by individual architects, working freely to arrive at a personal expression. In 1880 that freedom
was still alive in America, nourished at new and dangerous streams but full
of power. In 1879, when Viollet-le-Duc died, the *American Architect* quoted
a statement of his which may serve to indicate the kind of strength which
infused the domestic growth of the late 70's and early 80's and which was to
be the most important continuing factor in the work of the years immediately
following:

> My conclusions shall not be lengthy. There are but two modes of exist-
> ence for art: hieraticism and liberty. Hieraticism tends fatally towards
> irremediable decadence. Liberty may have its excesses, its moments of
> splendor and eclipse; but however low it may fall it always springs up
> again with new youth and vigor.[33]

32. "American Architecture—with Precedent and without," *op. cit.*, pp. 138–40.

33. *Am. Arch.*, *6* (1879), 97, quoted from Viollet-le-Duc's "Decoration Applied to Buildings in the periodical *L'Art*. It may be interesting to note that Peter Wight, who built
Street Hall at Yale, when he wrote in 1880 about the new commercial architecture of Chicago
saw, as early as this, the beginnings of their great qualities and spoke of them in words
which Viollet-le-Duc himself might have used. Wight said that of all the buildings of the
West the commercial structures of Chicago were the most original, the strongest, and the
simplest, and in them "In strength made evident to the senses we find the first dawn of
architecture." P. B. Wight, "The Condition of Architecture in the Western States," *Am.
Arch.*, *7* (1880), 107–8. There is another point concerning Wight which may be of some
interest. In an unsigned article entitled "New Haven Revisited" the writer states that Yale
had seemed for a while on the point of falling into "an architectural rut," namely, "the
Tudor style." However, then the Art Building (Street Hall, built by Peter Wight in the
1860's) came along, and the University realized that here was a new department of study,
with its own special requirements, and that it was "natural, therefore, that it should result
in a new architecture." *Am. Arch.*, *4* (1878), 155–6.

By 1881 this basic romantic rationalism, enriched by the sources of experience opened up by colonial and Queen Anne enthusiasms, had reached a point where the whole progress of the new architecture as part of a revival could be summed up percipiently and objectively. In 1881 the American Institute of Architects appointed a committee to investigate the "Practise of American Architects and Builders during the Colonial Period and the First Fifty Years of Our Independence." [34] In an article illustrated by many picturesque and textural sketches of colonial houses, the committee reported:

> Your committee have thought it best to preface their report . . . with a brief account of the rise of so-called Queen Anne or Free Classic architecture; together with the causes which have led architects to apply to modern buildings the details and principles of construction employed by their predecessors of the last century. It, moreover, seems necessary, in order to understand the principles involved, to study the analogy, if any, between the thoughts and manners of life of the two periods, and thus be prepared to judge how much of the revival is due to our honest convictions of the superior excellencies of colonial building, and how much to an affected longing for novelty and sensational effects.

The article then shows how colonial had become related to Queen Anne through the enthusiasms of the centennial year and how the architectural development since then had been a Queen Anne development, based on English sources and invoking a colonial past.[35] It decides further that much of the new enthusiasm had been based upon a desire to retreat into the 18th century. This attitude toward the colonial past the committee cannot condone:

> All this is poetical and delightful; we take it in, sigh for the days departed, and straightway attempt to remodel our houses of today upon the plans of yesterday. We partially succeed, but only partially. Alas, in the lapse of a hundred years, three generations have come and gone;

---

34. *Am. Arch., 10* (1881), 71–4. The sketches are by George Mason and are all of Newport.

35. It is important and indicative of their intelligent awareness of what had actually occurred that they should have seen what after all had been stated by everybody, namely that Queen Anne and colonial had developed together. By 1886 and 1887, if one judges by certain statements made at that time, such knowledge had been lost. Pure colonial was assumed to be the only real revival, Queen Anne a fashionable and baseless eclecticism. See Ch. 2, pp. 31–3. With that untrue distinction the stage was set for the later colonial and classicistic academicians' use of "Queen Anne" as a term of reproach for the free, picturesque architecture, and "colonial" as a benison for Palladian academicism. See Joy Wheeler Dow, *American Renaissance* (New York, 1904), ch. 9, "Fashion in Architecture," pp. 118–31.

the world has moved on and men have changed. We . . . cannot bring ourselves back to the ways of life and modes of thought familiar to our ancestors, and our habitations must necessarily reflect our tastes.[36]

What is necessary, says the committee, is an intelligent study by architects, aware that their age is different from the 18th century but willing to enrich themselves by a greater understanding of their past.

> If not absolute copyists, we may however learn much from the past; the youngest are ever the oldest, in that they have at their command all the knowledge and hard-won experience of their predecessors. Let us therefore study the principles that shaped and guided the architecture of the colonial period . . . study the material resources and appliances of the times, and thus elicit data which when brought together and well sifted will reward us with an insight into the causes which led to the adoption of forms of construction which we now admire, and the necessities which forced upon the early settlers systems of building which should be avoided in an age better supplied with materials and appliances.[37]

The restricted historicity, concentrated upon one period of architecture, which is advocated here was eventually, in later years, to exert a certain stifling effect upon creation. Still, the attitude toward colonial architecture in the early 80's, at the height of the genuine colonial revival and as demonstrated by the architects' committee, was clearly not dominated by a desire to impose colonialism upon the modern world. The intention instead was to create new forms, enriched by a genuinely creative experience of the past.

How much that experience in the early 80's owed to picturesque sensibility is shown in the impressive gelatine print of the old "Fairbanks House" at Dedham, Massachusetts (Fig. 30), published in the *American Architect*, November 26, 1881. This was the first colonial house to be chosen for photographic reproduction in that magazine. The house is seen nestling among its vines and its trees. An asymmetrical combination of textured masses, it hugs the ground and stretches out along the inequalities of its site. Picturesque, powerful in the expression of rough masonry and weathered shingles, it is similar to the best of the original houses of the early 80's themselves. As a colonial house it plays a rich part in a counterpoint of vision and influence into which academic rigidity does not enter. An antiquarian love of colonial

36. *Am. Arch., 10* (1881), 73.

37. This article concludes in the next issue (*ibid.*, pp. 83–5) with a further historical investigation of early Newport architecture.

things has been transformed by free imagination into an original architectural synthesis.[38]

Thus invention was the aesthetic order of the day by 1883, with the colonial as a picturesque aid to be used rather than copied. Consequently, in 1882 when a certain Mr. Cook in an article entitled "American Architecture" slipped into an antiquarian and academic point of view concerning the colonial, he was pounced upon by everybody. Colonial architecture, claimed Cook, was honest building, while modern architecture was a sorry mess.[39] The nature of the attacks on Cook's conclusions can sum up the temper of the period. It was pointed out to him (1) that he was living in the 19th century and that it was therefore impossible for him to return to his "rude Yankee forebears"; [40] (2) that such an attempt would result in a childish architectural masquerade, a simplification of modern life beyond reason; [41] and (3) that modern architecture had simplified itself already, partly under the influence of the colonial but mainly according to the necessities and possibilities of its own time. Since that was the case, he, Cook, had better get away from his books, look around, and appreciate some living architects.[42]

Having considered the whole critical background of the new architecture up to 1883, one can only concur with the proposition of the *American Architect*. By 1883 the real Queen Anne and colonial revival had, to all intents and purposes, run its course.

38. The apotheosis of the picturesque which this represents is seen also in innumerable sketches of textured details and painterly nooks which flooded the *American Architect* during these years. It will be noted that the Fairbanks House at Dedham was the first building cited by Peabody in his first "Georgian" article. The illustrations of old houses in the books by Edwin Whitefield which began to appear in 1879 are also indicative of the freely picturesque way in which colonial architecture was seen by most people at this time. The drawing is sketchy, the views oblique and in perspective. No one could copy a colonial house from these drawings, but one captures a rich sense of loose masses nestling in their landscape. Edwin Whitefield, *The Homes of Our Forefathers . . . in Massachusetts*, Boston, 1879. Other Whitefield books appeared in 1882 (Rhode Island and Connecticut), 1886 (Maine, New Hampshire, and Vermont), and 1889 (Boston, England, and Boston, New England).

39. Clarence Cook's article appeared in the *North American Review*, 1882. It was answered by the *American Architect* in a series of short but pointed articles, each one entitled, viciously, "Mr. Cook on American Architecture." *Am. Arch., 12* (1882), 95, 153, 193, 205, 213.

40. *Ibid.*, p. 193.

41. *Ibid.*, p. 153.

42. *Ibid.*, p. 205.

5. Formation of the Shingle Style

The architects of the generation of the late 1870's faced certain possibilities and problems in the design of new domestic buildings: how to develop most fully the spatial possibilities of the living hall, the large areas of glass, and the veranda; how to expand the use of shingles so that their possibilities for continuity could most completely express the continuities now possible in interior space; how to transpose into creative forms—as was being done in theory—the influences of colonial and Queen Anne; and most of all how to discipline the picturesque without falling into the trap of academicism. The various experiments and solutions along these and related lines will be the subject of this and the following chapters.

Among the architects who experimented with Queen Anne space and materials at an early date were some who failed to develop into mature practitioners of the new architecture. In this group must be placed Alexander F. Oakey of New York, who had come under Shavian influence as early as had Richardson and whose early work had been so promising.[1] Oakey, however, never really passed beyond that early phase. On the whole, his architecture remained at once excessively English and eclectic, while exhibiting the technical dominance of the old stick style. It may be that his strong Gothic revival sentiments and his admiration for the "tensile" as revealed in frame construction combined to keep him enamored of English medieval forms and at the same time interested in the skeletal energies of the stick.[2] Certainly as late as 1882, in the J. Griffiths Masten House, Everett Place, Newport, Rhode Island (Fig. 31), he was still combining Tudor forms with strong stick expression.[3] This house, hollowed out by a two-storied hall with a gallery on

1. This refers specifically to Oakey's Dorr House at Mount Desert, published in *Am. Arch., 2,* Jan. 20, 1877. See Ch. 4, p. 54.

2. See Ch. 4, pp. 61–2.

3. *Am. Arch., 13,* April 21, 1883. This house is impossible to find in Newport at the present time. It has been either torn down or altered beyond recognition. No records have as yet been found to settle the problem.

the second level, was nevertheless rather backward for its date. The brick lower story was partly half-timbered to skeletonize the wall. The second story was shingled, with the gable divided into decorative half-timber panels, and the windows of many small panes were arranged in long Queen Anne banks. The real verticality, however, in addition to the skeletal effect of the studlike half-timbering of the first story, identified the house as midcentury American stud and board building, masquerading in Old English forms.

Similarly, a house of 1883–84 on Prospect Avenue, Milwaukee, Wisconsin (Fig. 32), shows a continuation of the old vernacular with a few added eclectic elements.[4] A first story of stone supports a shingled second story of which the walls are stripped here and there to indicate the skeleton inside. The curving brackets which support the gables and the scroll work ornament in the gables themselves are English elements, as are the brutally profiled "Jacobean" posts of the second story porch. High and angular, the house as a whole recalls the midcentury, although Oakey was obviously attempting an effect of volume by bringing his roofs down low. But the effect is spoiled by the heavy, scalloped tiles of the roof, which are as out of scale with the rest of the house as are the ponderous Jacobean posts. Oakey never seems to have moved through Queen Anne influences, or beyond his earlier experiments, into the current of originality of the early 80's. At its best his work remained angular and excited in the midcentury manner and at its worst excessively burdened with English-inspired details which were usually out of scale.[5]

Perhaps his best work was the Jewett House at Montclair, New Jersey, 1884.[6] Here the shingled roof comes down in a great sweep, opened at the second story by a porch and enclosing a veranda around two sides of the lower story (Fig. 33). The plan is tight and unimaginative, but the house as a whole has a cohesion which Oakey's work usually lacks. Again, Jacobean posts on both porches sound a jarring note. It is interesting to observe, however, that in the gables Oakey reverted to a projecting type of stick work which recalls the midcentury much more than it does the Queen Anne.

In sum, Oakey's work rapidly loses interest. A stone mansion on the Hudson which he projected in 1884 was so eclectically François Premier as to remove it from our immediate zone of attention.[7] Oakey represents, therefore,

4. *Am. Arch., 16,* Nov. 15, 1884.

5. The very fact that Oakey never succumbed to American colonial may have kept his detailing heavy. Certainly, as already mentioned, the main effect of the colonial at this period was to lighten and simplify wood details and reduce their scale.

6. *Am. Arch., 15,* July 26, 1884.

7. *Ibid.,* June 14, 1884. See nn. 24 and 36 for further mention of the François Premier in the early 80's.

an architect whose technical instincts remained rooted in midcentury skeletal expression and who progressed very little after his first enthusiastic splurge in the Queen Anne. Of all his houses, none again achieved the interest of the early extravaganza of 1877 at Mount Desert (Fig. 21).[8]

Another architect who came early to the Queen Anne but who did not develop very far or ever become very original was Henry Hudson Holly. His articles on the Queen Anne began in 1876 and appeared amplified as a book in 1878.[9] The *American Architect* noted in its review of this book that Holly's design relied upon a use of the new open living hall with its fireplace and of Queen Anne shingle, scroll-work, or sunflower patterns grafted onto the traditional stick style frame. Three houses built by Holly at Montclair, New Jersey, in 1879 (Fig. 34) are excellent examples of this type.[10] Their plans are somewhat, though not radically, more open than those of the midcentury houses; there is perhaps a greater flow between rooms; and the halls, now with fireplaces, are more dominant features of the interior. A fairly direct passage leads between kitchen and dining room, and the whole makes a very workable, fairly open and quite free plan. Yet the living hall in a house of this size presents a peculiar problem. When space is limited, the hall can take over the living room in one large and spatially unified living area. If, on the other hand, it is desired to have a circulation area free of the living space, the hall can be reduced to a circulatory function, as in the midcentury houses, and the living room made as large as possible. Holly, however, and many Queen Anne builders and architects after him, desired both a living hall and a living room or parlor. Both usually contained fireplaces; neither was very large, and the hall especially became neither fish nor fowl, too big for a circulation area, too small for a living space. In this way the hall, instead of liberating the space, as in the best of the original planning, rather unhappily chops it up.[11] It is therefore no accident that the best planning of the 80's is found usually in large country houses, where it was possible to have both a good-sized hall and a living room as well, or in summer cottages where it was easier for the architect and his client to make the judgment of value involved and to decide upon simplicity and informality in the shape of one large and open living area, both hall and living room. There was undoubtedly a prob-

8. See n. 1 above. Oakey brought out a small book in the early 80's which also reproduced drawings of the Mount Desert house and of other houses similar to those we have discussed. A. F. Oakey, *Building a Home,* New York, 1881.

9. Holly, *Modern Dwellings.* See Ch. 4, n. 23.

10. *Am. Arch.,* 7, Feb. 21, 1880.

11. This can be seen in such books as Louis H. Gibson, *Convenient Houses with Fifty Plans for the Housekeeper,* New York, 1889. See also Ch. 6, n. 23.

lem of heating involved as well. The summer cottages were not heated, and
the owners of large country houses could afford the expense of heating open
areas. Holly, in his vernacular designs, probably wished to make it possible
for the owners to close off separate areas, as in the English houses noted
earlier.[12] For houses of all types the solution to this problem was to come only
later with the mature planning of Wright and, one might add, with improved
systems of heating.

At any rate, Holly's type of plan became the basis for most vernacular
planning until the early 20th century, especially for narrow city lots.[13] The
elements of Holly's exteriors were echoed in many of the less expensive vernacular houses for many years. They are basically midcentury stick style structures with high, squeezed masses and jagged silhouettes. Thin clapboarded
sides and occasional stripping indicate the frame beneath. In gables or down
the side of projecting bays, decorative patterns of variously cut shingles may
appear. Over windows or in the peaks of gables may erupt a lean wooden
pediment, a sunflower, or a scroll. These are their classical details. Many one-
and two-family houses built by anonymous builders in New Haven, Connecticut, in the 80's and later are of this type.[14] Holly, consequently, is of im-

12. See Ch. 3, n. 32.

13. The houses by David Russell Brown and Ferdinand von Beren in New Haven,
Connecticut, are typical of this kind of planning. Brown and Von Beren, *Architecture.
A few types of houses and other buildings exemplifying the tendency of modern architecture,*
New Haven, n.d. [*ca.* 1912]. Note especially the plans of the Greist and Hotchkiss houses,
dated *ca.* 1900–05. This firm has built a vast number of buildings in New Haven, including
stores, police stations, firehouses and innumerable residences. Brown had worked for Henry
Austin and is responsible for the later additions to Austin's City Hall. The firm name continues to be Brown and Von Beren, 295 Sherman Avenue, New Haven.

14. A house at 459 Prospect Street, dating from the 80's is one of the more elaborate Holly
types; a simpler type at 385 Whalley Avenue, dating from the 90's, is only one of scores of
vernacular examples. See "Pictorial New Haven, Old and New, its homes, institutions, activities . . . ," compiled and edited by Arnold Guyot Dana, 145 vols. This fascinating
grab-bag of maps, photographs, documents, newspaper clippings, and hearsay is deposited
in the New Haven Historical Society. It should be noted also that E. C. Gardner, whose
writings were important at the culmination of stick style theory (see my "Romantic Rationalism," p. 141), never passed much beyond his early phase of skeletal expression. His
Rumrill House at New London, Conn., is an example of the general tendencies continued
in his work. *Am. Arch.,* 5, Jan. 25, 1879. Similarly, his book, *The House that Jill Built* (New
York, 1882), really continues the method already developed by him in the middle 70's. The
plan of Jill's house, however, if efficiently organized, is somewhat rigid and the hall is badly
lighted, but the whole reflects the new open planning. It is used by Giedion as a typical
American 19th-century house plan, whereas it is in reality only a rather pale reflection of
the specifically new planning developments of the late 70's and early 80's. Giedion, *Space,
Time and Architecture,* pp. 288–90, fig. 168.

portance only in that he set the type for a good bit of later vernacular building. He himself did not progress beyond that point.

In a similar way, the firm of Potter and Robertson, of New York, whose Bryce Gray House at Long Branch had shown a shift toward Queen Anne space and massing, developed little in the new architecture and never reached a point of originality.[15] Although they came to the Queen Anne early and grew with it, their growth was apparently over by 1881, and they did not pass on into the later and more original phase. In 1877–78 Potter and Robertson built the C. H. Baldwin House at Newport, Rhode Island (Figs. 35, 36).[16] It is a tumultuous pastiche of the Watts Sherman House. Its plan differs insofar as its hall is not really developed as a living area. This hall is a large cube of space two stories high, with a gallery at the second story level. It opens widely into dining, drawing, and (largest of all) billiard rooms; but the doors from the hall into these other rooms are of different heights; the stairs intrude awkwardly, and there is little sense of true spatial continuity, although the hall itself is a dramatic shaft of space. The exterior erupts into a confusion of Queen Anne gables which bump into each other at awkward angles and oppose each to the other their hurly-burly of sunflowers and half-timbering. The southern end of the house makes use of a design which becomes quite common in much later building: the exterior chimney mass pierces the second story gable which projects to receive it. This passage of a vertical mass through a projected horizontal volume achieves that strong interpenetration of elements which becomes important in later events. A sense of the interlocking of units is created. Elements do not merely touch but pass through and overlap each other.

Potter and Robertson's Adam House at Oyster Bay, New York, 1878, is simpler and more coherent than the Baldwin House.[17] The hall is smaller, though more awkwardly shaped, and contains a fireplace. On the whole the plan is undistinguished—as are most of Potter and Robertson's plans—but from the exterior the Adam House presents a fairly unified appearance. The gables are fewer and more integrated than in the Baldwin House, and their sunflowers and half-timbering are less obtrusive. The windows are more simply arranged and, especially in the library bay and the chamber above, are allowed a really expressive continuity. The long void of the piazza is also

15. See Ch. 4, n. 4. This is E. T. Potter, W. A. Potter having been an architect of the previous generation. The Samuel Clemens (Mark Twain) House at Hartford, 1872, an example of the developed stick style, was a work of E. T. Potter while in partnership with Thorp.

16. *Am. Arch., 3,* Mar. 23, 1878.

17. *Am. Arch., 4,* Nov. 2, 1878.

a unifying element. Whereas the Baldwin House used a brick first story and a
shingled second in a pronouncedly Queen Anne way, the Adam House uses
clapboards instead of brick for its lower story.

During this period Potter and Robertson never reached the point of shingling the whole house. Their houses of 1879, one at Oyster Bay, one at New
Brunswick, New Jersey, and one at Newport, represent very little advance
over the Adam House.[18] The plans of all are confused; the halls contain no
fireplaces and buried in the middle of the house are neither large enough nor
well enough lighted to be living halls. Yet as circulation areas they are sufficiently large to be rather wasteful and pretentious. The formal vocabulary
of these houses remains a Queen Anne massing, with half-timbering, and
with Queen Anne and semi-Palladian details; the materials are brick, shingles, and stucco.

Probably Potter and Robertson's best house, and their last of any importance in this connection, is the Van Ingen House at Washington, Connecticut, 1879–80.[19] Here again the large hall contains no fireplace (Fig. 37),
but it is better lighted and the stairs are more subtly arranged in connection
with it than in the earlier houses. Because the plan is simpler, the brick and
shingle mass of the house stretches out more easily in a horizontal extension
which is continued by the projection of the piazzas. The Van Ingen House
represents Potter and Robertson's best, a fairly integrated development from
colonial and Queen Anne influences, but still somewhat confused and eclectic
in its mixture of materials and its touches of half-timber and Palladian details. Potter and Robertson's design reflects quite well that inchoate quality
which was characteristic of some of the Queen Anne and colonial thinking
of these same years.

An architect who in an interesting way represents a different phase of the
process of assimilation is William A. Bates of New York. Bates modeled his
rendering style upon Shaw's and published freely, but he evidently built
little until the 80's. In general his work remained very English, some of it
extraordinarily smooth and integrated but obviously dependent upon the
English Queen Anne of Shaw for its formal vocabulary. Excellent examples
of this are various projects for country houses and one outstanding project
for a city house published in the *American Architect* in the late 70's and early

18. Oyster Bay, *ibid.*, Dec. 21, 1878. Carpender House, New Brunswick, New Jersey: 5,
May 17, 1879. T. B. Potter House, Newport, R.I.: 7, Jan. 24, 1880.

19. It should be noted further that Potter and Robertson's project for the Union League
Club in New York, published in *Am. Arch.*, 5 (May 31, 1879), reveals on their part a close
study of Shaw's Lowther Lodge, published in *Building News* in 1875.

80's. In this vein also is a house at Longwood, Massachusetts, built in 1883 and one at Cheyenne, Wyoming, in 1883–84.[20] The house at Cheyenne (Fig. 38) is especially important because it represents the spread of the new design to far western areas, where it was shortly to spring up at the sites most favored by eastern visitors, such as Colorado Springs.

In the years 1878–80, however, other architects working in the east were leading toward a new synthesis beyond the point attained by Oakey, Holly, Potter and Robertson, and Bates. Among these must be counted that elegant gentleman and erratic genius Bruce Price. In 1878–79 Price built an extensive addition to the West End Hotel at Bar Harbor, Mount Desert, Maine.[21] This large wooden summer hotel (Fig. 39) was encircled by a deep veranda and capped by a high, shingled roof. Clapboards sheathed the first three and one-half stories and shingles finished the top story and a half. The note accompanying the publication of this building in the *American Architect* referred to its roof as "French," and part of it was certainly a true mansard. The main portion, however, might better be described as the type called "berm," wherein the steep slope from the ridge flattens out near the plane of the wall below and extends horizontally as a deep overhang, supported by brackets. The roof thereby becomes a mountain of shingles, reaching out over the building below, and in the shingles of the upper stories seeming to drip its rich texture down over the surface of the walls. Each window has its little individual overhang, also shingled, as is the shed roof of the stick-work piazza. The building consequently takes on the character of a stick style structure from whose mountainous roof a rich, wild, and naturalistic surface of shingles spills down its walls, splashes on its overhangs, and overruns its porch. Price's hotel made use of no overt colonial or Queen Anne details. It was a great barn, rough, boisterous and warm in its colors of "Indian red, brown, and olive green." [22] Awkward and disarming, its qualities arose from the hearty exploitation of its rough materials. Crudeness and wildness were its strength.

20. Examples of the published projects by Bates are a Country House published in *Am. Arch., 7*, Feb. 21, 1880; and a city house published in the same year. The house at Longwood, for George H. Wright, was also published: *Am. Arch., 14*, Dec. 22, 1883. The Sturgis House at Cheyenne, Wyoming was published in the same vol., Dec. 22, 1883. Not all Bates' work remained English in spirit during the 80's, but he is far behind other men in the Americanization of the Queen Anne, although he handled the English elements with great skill.

21. *Am. Arch., 5*, Jan. 25, 1879. The building no longer exists.

22. *Ibid.*, p. 29. Colors of this nature are typical of the cottage architecture of the early 80's.

A comparable strength appears in "The Craigs" (Fig. 40), a large cottage by Price at Mount Desert, built in 1879–80.[23] Unlike the West End Hotel, this cottage contains many stylistically derivative elements, such as a partially half-timbered tower, Queen Anne plaster panels, sundials, barge boards with crude carving, and violently turned posts. Although supposedly a cottage it seems a kind of fantastic feudal castle, a hodge-podge of picturesque bits and romantic skylines, an exacerbation of the industrialist's dream of the picturesque.

Price develops the space in a free and imaginative way. One enters under a porte-cochère, through a piazza, into a vestibule, and, beyond, into a huge hall. From this hall a large dining room with a round bay opens widely straight ahead. To the left, up a few stairs, is the ubiquitous billiard room, and to the right, down several short and twisted flights of stairs, are the garden and music rooms. Shapes of rooms are greatly varied, and the whole wild plan tumbles down the hill in a cascade of interrelated spaces. Price's love of spatial movement, variety, and tumult is echoed in external massing by his love of shapes—by the round towers of the Valley of the Loire with pigeon cotes in their high roofs and by the variety of gables and piazzas.[24] Again, as in the West End Hotel, the crudity of "The Craigs" is the key to its vitality. Price's design at this period is without discipline, and it is hearty, violent, and free. His sense of tumultuous open space and his love of texture and variety represented in 1880 some of the vitality which marked the new summer hotel and cottage architecture.[25]

If Bruce Price during these years demonstrated a sense of freedom, Peabody and Stearns represented a different aspect of the new development, namely that dichotomy between Palladian detail and picturesque vision which was discussed above in connection with the intellectual and aesthetic side of the Queen Anne and colonial revival. In Peabody and Stearns' domestic architecture before 1880 a sense of discipline conflicted with their longing

23. *Am. Arch., 6,* Dec. 27, 1879. Burned in the great fire of 1947, which destroyed almost all of the many houses of the 70's and 80's at Mount Desert.

24. The round towers especially have that Loire Valley look which, in the cities, was soon to sprout into the François Premier of the early 80's. The developed shingle style of this period was to absorb such towers and make them part of itself, their eclectic background lost and transformed in the flow of wooden shingled structure. See n. 36.

25. The extraordinary discipline of some of Price's later planning must really be based upon this early vitality, however crude. Interesting in this connection is the fact that Price's daughter, Mrs. Emily Post, published in 1930 a book entitled, *The Personality of a House, The Blue Book of Home Design,* New York, 1930; 2d ed. New York, 1948. Her aesthetic judgments are based upon a preference for colonial eclecticism typical of her generation, but not of her father's in its youthful days.

for the picturesque; but by 1879 they had resolved their difficulties into an easier and less self-conscious domestic design. Enamored of Peabody's Georgian details, as early as 1877–78 the firm built, on Brush Hill near Boston, Massachusetts, a house (Fig. 41) of which all the details were strictly Georgian in derivation, if not in scale.[26] The plan is excellent and very simple, perhaps remotely Palladian in intent. A central hall with fireplace opens widely right and left to parlor and dining room. A long piazza, reached by a door from the hall, shelters the rear of the house. The clapboarded exterior sports a tremendous Palladian window over the stairs. The massing is irregular and picturesque. Colossal pilasters appear at the corners, and one of them is embraced by the shingled roof of an octagonal bay sprouting from a corner of the living room. In this manner the house as a whole is slightly confused, as if the architects were unsure of their purpose, but the plan has a clarity unusual for its period.

In public architecture Peabody and Stearns soon rationalized that confusion between picturesque vision and Georgian details into a rather stricter Palladianism. Their Dickinson School at Deerfield, 1878, may be said to correspond roughly to Norman Shaw's Lowther Lodge. A basically medieval massing was composed from an authentic 18th-century vocabulary of forms, with pilasters, more or less Palladian windows, and generally classical detail. The Dickinson School happily combined these two design influences and remained a very pleasant building until its destruction in the early 1930's to make way for a larger but hardly more successful structure.[27] In Peabody and Stearns' Hemenway Gymnasium at Harvard (1879–80), the whole massing, however, was treated in a much more Palladian manner. Though still irregular and asymmetrical, the elements were pulled closer together and their brick walls were decorated with white stone trim. The intent was definitely Georgian but as yet academic in detail only.[28]

If in public architecture Messrs. Peabody and Stearns moved more or less steadily toward Georgian classicism, in domestic architecture they progressed irregularly toward a less derivative kind of building. The confusion attendant upon this move was apparent in the Pierre Lorillard House, Newport, 1878.[29]

26. *Am. Arch., 3,* Feb. 16, 1878.

27. The Dickinson School, Deerfield, *ibid.,* April 27, 1878. (This issue included also sketches of colonial Deerfield by Peabody.) The new school, academically classical in conception, was designed by Charles Platt.

28. *Am. Arch., 8,* Dec. 25, 1880.

29. *Am. Arch., 4,* July 6, 1878. The Lorillard House is also illustrated and discussed in George William Sheldon, *Artistic Country Seats: types of recent American villas and cottage architecture, with instances of country club-houses,* 2 vols. in 5 parts, New York, 1886–87. 50 illus. and 50 pls. This book is by far the most important single source for illustrations

Here the plan (Fig. 42) was as monumentally symmetrical as the firm could make it. The central hall, huge in size, was spatially static. A grand double stairway rose over the entrance in an awkward relationship to the large fireplace at one end of the hall. To the right a drawing room opened on axis, with morning room and library on either side. The library and the dining room at the other side of the hall both projected into those insistent rectangular corner bays of which Peabody and Stearns had always been inordinately fond. A billiard room was tucked away opposite the library behind the hall toilet. If the plan was symmetrical and formal in intent, the massing of the house was merely confused (Fig. 43). An evident desire for symmetry appeared in the flanking gables which balanced each other, but these were set upon by so many subsidiary masses that the result was a jagged series of relationships. A pictorial tower rose at the right of the entrance, concealing a private stairway and capped by a Renaissance arcade on dwarf columns. Palladian windows and little pediments appeared suddenly in odd places, and most of the detail, inside and out, was doggedly Georgian. All in all, the Lorillard House revealed conflict but not coherent design. Still, it was not without qualities of vitality and gaiety, and perhaps in all its confusion exerted a certain charm. Its scale was comparatively gentle for a large house, and it was much less overbearing upon its semisuburban site than the Hunt palazzo which succeeded it.

In the E. S. Barrett House at Concord, 1878–79, Peabody and Stearns arrived at a simpler and more coherent kind of design.[30] Built of stone and shingles, with a little half-timbering, one Georgian oculus in the gables, and turned posts on the porches, this house showed considerable advance over the Lorillard mansion. The plan was uninspired but pleasant: an open, medium-sized central hall (no fireplace), a large living room with window bays and fireplace alcove, library and dining rooms, and a service wing at an oblique angle to the main mass of the house. While the Barrett House was by no

---

and contemporary aesthetic comment concerning the country houses of the early 8o's. Sheldon lists this house, "The Breakers," under the name of Cornelius Vanderbilt, to whom Pierre Lorillard sold it for four thousand dollars. It burned in 1891 and Vanderbilt then built the new "Breakers," the well-known palazzo by R. M. Hunt. Peabody and Stearns' original house was evidently well out of style by 1886. Sheldon mentions the house as little as possible, saying only that the architects "have depended principally for effect upon the towers and the enormous gables." He quotes Downing at length, however, concerning the beauties of a good lawn, a point not without interest, as it indicates Downing's continuing influence—probably by this time mainly in landscape gardening. Sheldon, *Country Seats, 1,* 143–6.

30. *Am. Arch., 4,* Nov. 23, 1878. Another similar Peabody and Stearns project is the "Sketch for a Summer Hotel," *Am. Arch., 7,* Jan. 31, 1880.

means unusual or especially advanced, it represents a temporary settlement of Peabody and Stearns' minds in relation to domestic architecture. The Palladianisms tend to recede. Simple materials and structure and an easy manipulation of related spaces begin to take over the design. There is also something in the fact that the Barrett House was undeniably a simple country house and the Lorillard House was a mansion, exerting a disruptive influence upon the architects' approach to their problem. Grandiosity and monumental design, foreign to the most inventive American work since Downing's day, seemed to exert a malevolent effect upon domestic work, unless burlesqued and made playful as in "The Craigs." Even in Lorillard's "Breakers" the monumental design turned into a kind of burlesque through confused intentions.

Peabody and Stearns' Barrett House was about at the same scale as Stanford White's James Cheney project, published in a two-page spread in the *American Architect*, May 25, 1878 (Fig. 44), presumably about the time Peabody and Stearns were designing the Barrett House.[31] The Cheney project was almost the last work turned out by White while in Richardson's employ, and it was never built. Stone below and shingles above, it used much of the plaster ornament, half-timber, and spindle work that flowed so easily from White's pencil. The plan of the Cheney project was awkward, with a badly lit hall. In sum, the project was a decorative continuation of the line initiated by the Watts Sherman House. The Cheney House contained little which need excite our interest, but it marked the end of one phase of the career of Stanford White.

In 1878 White left Richardson, went to Europe, and spent the best part of a year there. He looked at many things with benefit—especially the chateaux of the Loire. Upon his return he joined McKim and Mead as a partner, and the firm of McKim, Mead, and White came auspiciously into being.[32] The domestic work of that firm can best be discussed later, for most of the more important examples fell after 1880 and led to the last phase in the cycle of development.

31. *Am. Arch., 3,* May 25, 1878.
32. Mead states of White's joining the firm:
> In these years [1872–78, while with Richardson] he was our close neighbour and became our very intimate friend. In 1878 he left Mr. Richardson for an extended trip in Europe with, I think, the intention of returning to him. Naturally he was ambitious to go into business for himself, and on his return in 1879, on the retirement of Mr. Bigelow, we offered Mr. White a partnership which he accepted with great enthusiasm. . . . White had been brought up in Richardson's office, and his whole early influence had carried him towards the Romanesque, in which he certainly was an adept.

Baldwin, *Stanford White,* pp. 112–13.

One house by the firm of McKim, Mead, and Bigelow during this period should, nevertheless, be discussed. This is the Mrs. A. C. Alden House, Fort Hill, Lloyd's Neck, Long Island (1879–80).[33] Above a stone foundation this house is sheathed with clapboards on its first story and shingles on its second (Fig. 45). The house is simple and quiet, despite its small-paned windows, the touches of plaster decoration in the gables, the one or two small Palladian pediments over windows, and the screen of turned posts at the entrance. The plan is also simple and well organized. At the level of the entrance a moderate hall opens fully onto a long and extended piazza by the water. A library to the left has a parlor behind it. Up a few steps to the right the dining room gives off the staircase hall, and beyond that stretches a long, thin service wing. The mass is extended horizontally in a serene way, anchored by the unobtrusive staircase tower and the easy gable of the main wing. The turrets of the chateaux of the Loire—probably White's, although technically he was not yet part of the firm—are pulled into an over-all unity through an axial scheme, probably by McKim. Moreover, one feels in the Alden House a crisp and clean expression of the light wooden frame. The Alden House is one of the simplest and most coherent of any of the country houses built in America in the period before 1880. With all its variety, it still has sweep and order.

One architect in the late 70's probably contributed more to the development of the new architecture—except in some aspects of planning—than any designer discussed so far. William Ralph Emerson, of Boston, not only combined in his own work many of the new characteristics already noted in the work of other architects but also developed from these a type of synthesis beyond which Richardson's own synthesis of the early 80's had only to advance one short step. Emerson began to practice in the early 70's, publishing late stick style and early Queen Anne domestic projects by the middle 70's.[34] Among his early works is the barn which he remodeled and enlarged as a workshop for William Morris Hunt in 1877: "The Hulk," Magnolia, Mas-

33. *Am. Arch., 6,* Aug. 30, 1879. Already noted: McKim's two Taylor Houses at Elberon of 1877 and 1878. Other pertinent buildings finished in 1880 by McKim, Mead, and White include the Elberon Hotel and Cottages, and the Fahnestock, Garland, and Wood Houses, all at Elberon, N.J., and the Brokaw House, Long Branch, L.I. One of the Elberon houses was a simple, low-gabled rectangle, surrounded by porches, somewhat like the Moses Taylor House but with plain wooden detailing rather than pilasters. See Moore, *McKim,* appendix 3, for a list of his work.

34. Emerson created at least one extremely sensitive masterpiece in the midcentury stick style, namely the Forbes House at Milton, Mass., published in the *New York Architectural Sketch Book, 3,* 1876. William Ralph Emerson was born in Illinois in 1833; his family moved to Boston when he was young, and he studied architecture with Jonathan Preston (Boston Theater). He was a promoter of both the Boston Architectural Society and the Boston Art Club (*Herringshaw's National Library of American Biography, 2,* Chicago, 1909). Emerson died in 1918.

sachusetts.[35] A simple structure with a projecting roof over a second-story porch, a stick-work balcony, and a general air of studied casualness, "The Hulk" was at least an indication of Emerson's sensitivity to simple materials and his ability to handle small problems lightly and with a sense of scale. One may well shudder at the thought of such a project in the hands of the painter-client's heavy-handed brother, Richard Morris Hunt.[36]

Yet a house of 1878 by Emerson at Milton, Massachusetts, was much less sensitively handled. One wonders whether the original barn from which "The Hulk" was made was not responsible for its final delicacy.[37] The Milton house of this year was a harsh box, undistinguished in plan and overloaded with heavy projecting gables, using both shingles and half-timber and supported by particularly unsuccessful examples of the ubiquitous turned post. The gables and the partial shingle work were perhaps added to an older structure, like the strange shingled canopy and porch added to the Dr. Francis House at Brookline at this same period.[38]

At any rate it is pleasant to turn from these houses to the one at Mount Desert which Emerson built "for a Boston gentleman" in 1879.[39] This house has perhaps the most distinguished plan to be produced in 1879 (Fig. 46). It

35. *Am. Arch., 3,* Feb. 23, 1878. The *Architect* (p. 66) says of this building:
"The Hulk," so called from its fancied resemblance to an old stranded ship, with its ropes for lifting the gangway stairs, its davits for raising the doors of the carriage-house, and the employment of whole ribs and vertebrae for braces, railings, and ornamental features, was built by adding an old barn and carpenter's shop together at Mr. Hunt's suggestion, and affords accommodation for horses, carriages, sleeping-quarters, and a large painting-room.

36. It is characteristic of Richard Morris Hunt that, generally, while others were building cottages, he was building palazzi. His 1872 remodeling of the Wetmore House in Newport, originally built in 1852, is an excellent example of Hunt's taste for the grand. See Downing and Scully, pp. 139, 147. Hunt's eclecticism during this period is also to be observed in his Vanderbilt House, New York, 1879. This is important as being one of the first of the many François Premier city mansions which formed the urban and less original counterpart to the suburban shingle style of the early 80's. An excellent example is McKim, Mead, and White's Whittier House on the water side of Beacon Street, Boston, 1882–83. See Hitchcock, *Richardson,* pl. 123. (The building of a house which sounds almost like the Whittier House and which was also on the water side of Beacon was described with considerable architectural sensitivity by William Dean Howells, *The Rise of Silas Lapham,* Boston, 1886.)

37. *Am. Arch., 4,* Nov. 9, 1878.

38. *Am. Arch., 5,* Feb. 8, 1879.

39. *Ibid.,* p. 93. [In 1970: My note here that this house had probably been destroyed in the fire of 1947 was incorrect. The welcome short monograph on Emerson by Cynthia Zaitzevsky and Myron Miller (cf. *The Architecture of William Ralph Emerson, 1833–1917;* an exhibition presented by the Fogg Art Museum in collaboration with the Carpenter Center for the Visual Arts, Harvard University, Cambridge, 1969, pp. 8–9, 41, fig. 1, pls. 8–10) shows it to be the C. J. Morrill House and still extant.]

is conceived as an envelope for varied human movement in space. Its boundaries swell and contract around pools and rivers of spatial rest or direction. One enters under a projection of the second story and emerges into a large hall. To the right opens a parlor and to the left, through a narrow door under the staircase, is the dining room. Directly facing the entrance, four steps rise to a large living hall from which a great bay of continuous fenestration overlooks the sea. From this hall it is possible to look down into the parlor through an arched opening protected by a rail, or to move out through a door to a covered octagonal pavilion which echoes the shape of the window bay of the hall. From the hall, partially two storied, the stairs continue to the second floor. The variety of levels and closed and open spaces is handled easily and without strain. Light is manipulated here as by a painter—dark in the quiet dining room, flooded with sun in the open hall, diffused and mingled in the partially sheltered parlor. The enclosing skins of wall are shingled on both the first and second stories, giving that continuity of surface which had apparently been striven for since 1872 but which was fully attained here for the first time.

This is the first house in the whole development to be completely shingled. The windows are set in the shingled surface with precise wooden trim, expressing thin frame structure. The corner windows of the parlor are noteworthy in this respect, and the slight projection of the wall above them increases the sense of surface continuity retained by the windows and expressive of the volume within. A few eclectic details still appear in the house, and it has a remotely English look. The chimneys are a Queen Anne type, there is some half-timber work in the gables, and the arched window of the parlor with a seat in front of it is definitely a Shavian touch. The clapboarding under the windows of the hall bay, an attempt to express the different level of that area, is perhaps not very successful. Nevertheless, the shingled surface of the house as a whole is richly expressive of its interior volumes, as for example over the rear porch, where the movement in space down the stairs from the hall and toward the pavilion is echoed in the flow of wall into roof above it. In sum, this house by Emerson at Mount Desert, 1879, may be said to be the first fully developed monument of the new shingle style.

Emerson's production at this period was still uneven, and his T. R. Glover House at Milton, also 1879 (Fig. 47), marks a retreat from the advanced point reached in the Mount Desert House.[40] The plan of the Glover House is considerably less interesting. The hall is awkward and tight in shape; there are too many rooms in plan, and the kitchen is an excessive distance from the dining room, as in an English house. On the exterior Emerson reverts to

40. *Am. Arch., 6,* Aug. 2, 1879.

a clapboarded first story, with shingles above, and he continues the use of heavy clapboarding under the parlor bay window. The covered portion of the piazza surrounding three sides of the house is supported on bulbous turned posts, and much half-timbering is used in some of the gables. Although all this represents a kind of reversion, the mountainous sweep of the shingled roof, adjusting itself from gable to gable and then gliding down like a deeply sheltering wing over the piazza, must be considered an important and advanced feature of the house. Through its continuous adjustment all the subsidiary masses are pulled together into one plastic and richly surfaced mass, various but coherent, indicative of plastic volumes within, and expressive of shelter. This development of the plastic continuity of roof and wall was peculiarly Emerson's own. Where it is most successful—as in that portion of the Glover House where the wall above the piazza slopes down into the piazza roof, which has itself flowed irregularly from the highest gable— the roof seems to take over the walls, so that the volume of space within is molded totally from ridge to ground by the continuous and three-dimensional movement of its thin shell.[41]

Although Emerson still continued to use clapboards on the first story, the cottages he built in 1880 for J. Greenough at Jamaica Plain, Massachusetts, developed further the plastic continuity of the shingled mass.[42] The plans are less interesting, with too many rooms on the main floor and a long trek necessary to reach the kitchen; but on the exterior, gable flows to gable and wall to piazza roof in a very expressive way. In these smaller houses the half-timbering has disappeared, and the wooden trim, exact and quiet, is only remotely colonial or Queen Anne.

Two drawings by Emerson in 1880 are interesting because they show the sketch technique he developed as a means of catching very quickly that flow of painterly surfaces toward which he was tending in his designs.[43] These sketches, one for a stable and lodge (Fig. 48), the other for a country house, are made up of fast, coarse pencil lines like brush strokes, creating not an architectonic effect of precise outlines and structural solidity but rather an impression of the mass as revealed in light. The outlines blur, and solid form tends to dissolve in the patches of light on the shingled surface. This tech-

41. Emerson's earlier, stick style Forbes House at Milton should be noted in this respect. There also he had shown concern for a deeply pitching roof, extended in order to increase a sense of shelter. It differs from the T. R. Glover roof in being of a single plane from gable to porch. See n. 34.

42. *Am. Arch., 7,* Jan. 31, 1880. Emerson also used a rough stone chimney mass in one of these houses, a further development of the sense of natural materials and sensuous surface. The influence of Richardson is certainly of importance here at this date.

43. *Am. Arch., 8,* Aug. 21, 1880; Oct. 9, 1880.

nique was eventually to develop into a burlesque in the Beaux-Arts *esquisse-esquisse,* where the whole architecture dissolved into a mass impression and stayed there. In Emerson's hands it was a real tool toward the creation of his shingled masses.[44]

Pictorial vision, as already indicated, was implicit in the whole shift to shingles and in the new sense of space and light. As such, Emerson's technique relates to that of Stanford White, as in the latter's interior perspective of the Watts Sherman hall (Fig. 12).[45] It relates also to Richardson's own sketch technique at this period, as seen in his drawing of 1880 for the Crane Memorial Library at Quincy, Massachusetts.[46] Richardson's drawing, however, is at once firmer and more delicate. Less concerned with surface variation, although indicating it warmly enough with a few touches, he never loses the sense—however sketchy the drawing—of the precision of the outlines, the solidity of the mass. His drawing was always specifically architectural. To say further that White's and Emerson's vision of forms dissolving in light may be related to the technique of the French Impressionist painters, maturing through these same years, does not seem too far-fetched.[47] Certainly a sense of the dissolution of precise outlines into splinters of light forms a common bond between the shingle style, its sketch technique, and Impressionist painting.

The last phase of Emerson's activity may be seen in two buildings of 1880 and 1881: the Church of St. Sylvia on Mount Desert and a house at Beverly Farms, Massachusetts.[48] The church is probably the more interesting; it so completely continues the trend of Emerson's design in so domestic a scale that it may certainly be mentioned here (Fig. 49). Plastic and flowing in mass,

44. The difference between Emerson's rendering as a painterly tool and the Beaux-Arts *esquisse-esquisse* can perhaps be made clearer by referring to Ch. 3, p. 52, above, where the Beaux-Arts projet in general is discussed. That Emerson's approach, and that of shingle style architects in general, was basically a pictorial one is seen quite clearly in a statement made to me in personal conversation in August, 1948, by Mr. Von Beren of New Haven (see n. 13). He stated concerning his design method in houses of this type: "I'd get the picture and then work on the plan." It should be noted also that Wright felt sometimes that his first master, Silsbee, a shingle style architect, "was just making pictures." Frank Lloyd Wright, *An Autobiography* (New York, 1943), p. 71. That Wright admired Silsbee's sketch technique, however, is shown in his comment (p. 91) concerning Silsbee's drawing: "Silsbee's way was magnificent, his strokes were like standing corn in the field waving in the breeze."

45. See Ch. 1, n. 52.

46. Hitchcock, *Richardson,* fig. 75.

47. The same necessity to acquire a technique wherein the momentary effects of light might be re-created quickly worked in both.

48. Both were published in the *Am. Arch., 9,* No. 287, June 25, 1881.

with a tower which is firmly if awkwardly wedded to its gable, this church was shingled, as the *American Architect* put it, "both within and without." [49] Totally shingled, completely flowing and all painterly, the Church of St. Sylvia was an exercise in that continuity of flow and surface toward which Emerson had been experimenting. Even the posts which support the roof over the entrance porch and the cupola on the tower submit to the inexorable flow of surface and receive their shingles.

Perhaps less interesting is the house at Beverly Farms of the same period (Fig. 50). Unlike the earlier Mount Desert House, it is not completely shingled but uses a brick first story. Similarly, its plan is less coherent and fluid, with too many rooms, too many spaces (as in much of Emerson's work), and here a rather awkward if deeply sheltering hall. Still, it is a fairly good plan, with some flow between hall, parlor, and dining room, and with that variety of light which Emerson occasionally handled so well. Set deep back in the hall is a dark inglenook with fireplace. Near it rise the stairs, lighted at the landing. Across the back of the house a large piazza opens toward the sea, and on the other side the service wing shoots off at a diagonal. The route between dining room and kitchen is again circuitous. A Palladian window appears in one of the gables, and the detail of the entrance and the staircase window has a definitely Georgian look. There is no half-timbering, and the mass of the house stretches out, easy and horizontal, coherent and assured.

How original and specifically American this house was—even though perhaps less advanced than some of Emerson's earlier work—may be demonstrated by comparing it to a house at Sunninghill, England, by Richard Norman Shaw, republished from *Building News* by the *American Architect* in September, 1880.[50] The Shaw house (Fig. 51) uses purely decorative and rather heavy half-timbering on the gables of the entrance side and on the whole of the second story of the garden front. The mass is more broken up than in the American house, and each gable asserts itself as a picturesque element. The American house is lighter. The skin of its upper stories is expressed as shingle sheathing upon a light wood frame. In comparison with the American house, Sunninghill seems assertively Old English, doggedly quaint. If it exerts a more dramatic impact than the American house—a power peculiarly Shavian—it is also more self-conscious. Altogether, when seen with the Emerson house it looks very English, a fact which emphasizes

49. *Ibid.*, p. 306. It is worthy of note that the churches of the early 80's tended in general toward a certain domesticity of scale, a fact which emphasizes the importance of domestic architecture in the period as a whole. See Richard Newman, "Yankee Gothic," unpublished dissertation, Yale University, 1949.

50. *Am. Arch., 8*, Sept. 25, 1880. 2 pls., entrance and garden views.

how far the American work had traveled by 1880 from its original Queen
Anne inspirations. The plans especially are different in important ways. In
the English plan each room is a separate entity, an inviolable cube of space
closed off by a narrow door, while in Emerson's house the plan is open and
the veranda is an extension of it. If the route to the kitchen in the Emerson
house is more circuitous than in most American planning, the English route
by comparison is a marathon, even though it is more direct in Sunninghill
than in many of Shaw's houses. All these contrasts are even more striking
when one looks at Emerson's Mount Desert House of 1879 (Fig. 46).

In sum, the American house had now undergone a variety of changes
adapting it to American conditions, functional requirements, and materials,
which separate it, as an original style, from Norman Shaw's Queen Anne.
The openness and flow of its space are American. So are the sheltering void
of the piazza, the lightly scaled woodwork, and the rough shingles. By 1880
the American domestic development was clearly, for the time being, at least,
on its own. It had assimilated its influences and according to the necessities of
its own nature passed beyond them. American architects by 1880 had nothing more to learn from Norman Shaw.[51] Although some of them continued to
build Tudor mansions complete with half-timber, the original development
continued to grow in its own right. One must recognize, therefore, a mode
of building, approaching maturity around 1880, which was specifically American. That it should be called American has nothing to do with chauvinistic
enthusiasms or with that piety of place which has corroded some historical
studies, especially of the colonial.[52] The term signifies a sensitive adjustment
of materials, techniques, and sense of space to specific and newly evaluated
conditions of American living. The insistent suburban evocation of a lost
agrarian simplicity remained a constant factor, directly related to the simplified life of the shore or the country suburb. In this development the role
of the simplest and least pretentious buildings cannot be overestimated. It
is natural that some of the most significant aspects of the new architecture
should be found in the smallest cottages.

Not the simplest or the smallest of these was a house of 1880 at Kennebunkport, Maine, by Henry Paston Clark of Boston.[53] This confused structure
with a few Queen Anne details was totally shingled. Its entrance drive divides

51. See Fred Symonds Eaton, "Design for a Country House," *Am. Arch., 8,* Dec. 31, 1880.
This was obviously inspired by Sunninghill and is an excellent example of the kind of
Tudor manor-house eclecticism which persisted but which the new domestic architecture
of the early 80's definitely was *not.*

52. Perhaps appropriately, the eclectic critics of the early 20th century combined a
cultural dependence upon European academicism with this same chauvinism. See, particularly, Dow, *American Renaissance,* as an example of this.

53. *Am. Arch., 8,* May 1, 1880.

the house into two halves, bridged by the second story. It is significant that the design includes a gigantic bowling alley and two servant's rooms, but only one large room for living and dining. The informality of vacation life was sufficiently appreciated to allow the combination of these functions into one room. Such a step indicates a basic evaluation of what was necessary in a house for informal living and a willingness to follow the logic of the analysis to its conclusion, without regard for convention.

These qualities are probably more apparent in a much smaller cottage by Clark (no bowling alley), also at Kennebunkport and of the same year.[54] The picturesque jumble of flowing shingled surfaces (Fig. 52) is capped by a tiny tower looking out to sea and is surrounded on two sides by a large veranda. This is partially covered by a projection of the second story, supported on thin and simple posts. Here again there is only one room with a large ingle-nook for living and dining. The cottage serves its simple function simply but with imagination. Clark combines warm textures, the support of volumes on slender posts, corner windows, and light balconies with semicolonial and semi-Japanese details.[55] Picturesque and playful, the combination is founded upon an awareness of the architectural possibilities of the program's limitations. The shingle style, consequently, did not destroy but enhanced and grew upon vernacular building. This was a very important part of the original American development, and its influence was at work equally in the open spaces and natural materials of the larger houses as well.

Although its date, 1882, should properly place it in a later phase of development, Clark's Sprague Cottage at Kennebunkport (Fig. 53) must also be mentioned in this connection.[56] Here is a simple L-shaped plan organized around a central chimney mass. Entrance is directly into the living hall from which the stairs rise. Behind and to the left of the fireplace is a dining area and to the right the kitchen. A wide veranda forms a clear void around the living hall. The gambrel roof of the house and its gable wall continue down in one long, serene slope to form the veranda roof, supported on slender posts. The whole mass is decisive and compact, its quality arising from its natural shingles and the large amplitude of its simple shapes.

In this connection one should mention as well "Redcote" by William H. Dabney of Boston (Fig. 54), a small cottage at York Harbor, Maine, also 1882.[57] Less coherent than the Sprague Cottage, it nevertheless expresses a casual and

54. *Ibid.,* July 3, 1880.

55. Clay Lancaster has reproduced this house, stressing its Japanese feeling. "Japanese Buildings in the United States," *Art Bulletin, 35* (1954), 217–24, pl. 4.

56. *Am. Arch., 13,* Nov. 4, 1882. This house was built in partnership with Ion Lewis of Boston, as was the Nanepashemet Hotel, Great Neck, Marblehead, 1882. The latter was published in the *Am. Arch., 12,* July 15, 1882.

57. *Ibid.,* Sept. 16, 1882.

appealing adjustment to function. Windows appear as needed; one sprouts a
steep colonial pediment, and the light scale of the detailing gives way only in
the heavy posts of the porch. A hall with stairs and fireplace adjoins a kitchen
with two alcoves (one labeled "Servant"). Upstairs are three bedrooms in a
row. There is a toilet in the shed, as in the Sprague House, but, also as in the
Sprague House, there are no other sanitary gadgets. Built for the simplest kind
of living, and with complete freedom, these cottages, as already noted, were
thought important enough by the architects of the day to be published as full-
page illustrations in the *American Architect*. Certainly the simplicity and
experiment which they represented played an important part in the growth of
the new domestic architecture.

6. Richardson and the Mature Shingle Style

At this creative moment in the early 80's the influence of Henry Hobson Richardson began once more to make itself felt in suburban and country house architecture. Hitchcock has already covered Richardson's domestic work of the period at some length.[1] Only those features of Richardson's houses which had the most important effect upon domestic design as a whole need be of concern here. For this purpose the principal Richardsonian works of the early 80's are the F. L. Ames Gate Lodge, North Easton, Massachusetts, 1880–81; the Dr. John Bryant House, Cohasset, Massachusetts, 1880; the Percy Brown House, Marion, Massachusetts, 1881; the M. F. Stoughton House, Cambridge, Massachusetts, 1882–83; the Walter Channing House, Brookline, Massachusetts, 1883–84; the R. T. Paine House, Waltham, Massachusetts, 1884; and the F. L. Ames Gardener's Cottage, North Easton, Massachusetts, also 1884.[2]

The Ames Gate Lodge is important because it was a demonstration and an object lesson in the nature of rough stone (Fig. 55). The American development in domestic architecture since 1840 had been primarily based upon wood techniques. Its effects had grown from the varying natures of framing wood as stud skeleton and sheathing wood as rough shingles. The occasional Queen Anne brick or stone first stories of the houses before 1880—including Richardson's Watts Sherman House—had been generally less expressive than the shingles above them, and when the shingles had finally covered most of

1. Hitchcock, *Richardson,* pp. 197–290, *passim.*

2. All are mentioned and illustrated by Hitchcock. See n. 1 above. Trinity Church Rectory, Boston, 1879–81 (Hitchcock, pl. 69), although certainly of great quality, will not be discussed here because it is a specifically urban residence of brick with stone trim and of little influence upon the development of cottage architecture as a whole.

the surface it was usually to the benefit of the design.[3] But throughout the 70's, especially in Trinity Church and his libraries, Richardson had been building magnificent masonry structures, tending more and more toward powerful sculptural expression based upon the solemn pressures and textures of stone.[4] The cyclopean rubble of the Ames Gate Lodge culminated this development and brought violently to the attention of American architects the expressive possibilities inherent in construction with rough stone, up to boulder size.[5] Although the Ames Gate Lodge was not published until 1885,[6] it was certainly well known before that time. The great masonry arch, for example, was much imitated in masonry and even in wood construction by other architects. Other elements in the Lodge, although they exerted a continually growing influence, remained for some time peculiarly Richardson's own. These were the order and cohesion of the plan and massing. In plan (Fig. 56), the movement is up a curving stair from the entrance, down a corridor past guest rooms, and around a fireplace into the bachelor's hall, from which, on a cross axis, a passage moves out to a covered well. The fireplace stands solidly as a core around which the space changes, and in all the loose and asymmetrical freedom of the plan there is at the same time a unifying order of direction. Similarly, the massing of the building, while free and asymmetrical, is at once extended and contained. The larger mass of the living quarters is stabilized by the lower mass on the other side of the drive, the two flowing solidly together in the great arch. The continuity of the windows in the smaller portion of the building is decisive and calm, and the void of these windows detaches the plane of the roof from the stone mass below. This clear void between massive wall and sheltering roof makes palpable the volume within. This serene order in three dimensions, so powerful in Richardson's work, was also to have its effect upon the domestic development in general.

3. The Emersonian development to 1880 is an example of this. Note especially his house of 1879 at Mount Desert, discussed above, pp. 83 ff. It should be noted, however, that Emerson, also, was using rough stone chimney masses as early as 1880, as in the Greenough Houses at Jamaica Plain. See Ch. 5, n. 42.

4. Hitchcock, *Richardson*, pls. 59, 66. The Ames Memorial Library of 1877–79 and the Ames Monument, Sherman, Wyoming, 1879.

5. He "seemed to be seeking his inspiration back in the time before architecture took form." Hitchcock, p. 203. It will be remembered also that Viollet-le-Duc had remarked that only in primitive sources could one find the basis for a long career. In a poetic sense the Ames Gate Lodge represents an investigation into the primitive nature of a material. It is thus also concerned in the search for archetypes characteristic of its period.

6. The Ames Gate Lodge was published in *Am. Arch., 18,* Dec. 26, 1885. Its plan was reproduced on p. 204 of the same issue but has not been published since.

If the Ames Gate Lodge was a statement in stone, the Dr. John Bryant House of 1880 was the most complete statement so far of the nature of wooden frame construction covered with shingles.[7] In this house the shingles cover the entire surface; there is no ornament of any kind, and the total continuity of shingled surface is retained by the small paned windows with their simple and inconspicuous wood details. Since the Bryant House is described at length by Hitchcock, there is little need to discuss it completely here.[8] Of special note is the service wing, placed at a diagonal angle to the main part of the house, which straddles a deep ravine. The main entrance to the house is from the ravine, so that one mounts a flight of stairs to the living area, coming first to a wide landing from which one can look up into the living hall and then moving up another half flight behind the fireplace mass, around which one passes into the living hall itself. Hitchcock has criticized the great area given to the stairs, although it was that very movement in space, up and around the fireplace, which formed the spatial core of the house and was to remain an important feature in many of the houses of the 80's. Equally important for later developments was the absence of Queen Anne or colonial details on the exterior of the Bryant House. The successful use of harmonizing window trim with stained shingles indicated forcibly to other domestic architects that the Queen Anne or colonial details which they occasionally used were by no means a necessary adjunct to the new architecture. Sitting decisively on its water table, its shell all wood and its chimney rough stone, the Bryant House stated firmly the premises of the new design: natural and indigenous materials, simple construction, free adjustment of space to function and expression, and amplitude without pretension.[9]

7. Hitchcock, pls. 72, 73.

8. *Ibid.*, p. 206.

9. The point concerning the use of a "water table" is, I think, of some importance. In much frame construction the studs are set forward on the sill, resting on the top of the foundation, so that the sheathing of the walls projects farther forward than the foundation and is continued down over it for a little way. The wall then, visually, seems to "bleed" down over the foundation and the effect is indecisive; there is no sense of the foundation as a solid base for the decidedly different light frame structure of the house above it. With a water table, however, the sheathing stops at the foundation—which now projects farther forward than the wall above—and rests upon a slanting strip of wood or stone which sheds the water at that point and is, consequently, if a little inaccurately, called a "water table." With this method the house, visually, sits decisively upon its foundation. The visual base is like a low platform. Richardson seems always to have used this in his wood houses. He even made use of a comparable effect in his masonry work, as in the Crane Memorial Library, Quincy, Mass., of 1880–83, for instance, where the whole seems set upon a base. A further development of this was made by Wright in his early houses and continues to be used by him. The studs are set well back upon the foundations, which then project even

In these connections the Percy Brown House of 1881 was equally important, and perhaps even more significant in being a smaller and simpler
house. Since the house has been described and illustrated by Hitchcock, it
may be more desirable here to emphasize the nature of its impact upon
contemporaries. Thus Mrs. Schuyler Van Rensselaer, whose biography of
Richardson appeared in 1888: [10]

> It is one of the smallest structures that Richardson ever built, and I
> believe, the least expensive; yet in its way it is a very great success. It
> stands on the crest of a short but steep slope overlooking a road on the
> outskirts of the village, beyond which lie flat meadows and the not dis-
> tant sea. It is very low and comparatively very long, with many windows
> in broad groups, a loggia in the center of the front, a piazza at one end
> and across a portion of the back, small dormers, and low but massive
> chimneys. Its foundations follow with delightful frankness the variations
> of the ground upon which it stands, while its good proportions and the
> harmonious arrangement of its roof-lines gives it that truly architectural
> character in which dignity may lie for even the most modest building.
> It is so appropriate to its surroundings that it seems to have grown out
> of them by some process of nature, and it is equally appropriate to its
> purpose. It explains itself at once as a gentleman's summer home, but
> with a simplicity which does not put the humble village neighbor out
> of countenance.[11] Inside, the planning gives an unexpected amount of
> comfort and air of space. The doorways are very wide, and are so ar-
> ranged as to afford a diagonal instead of a straight perspective. The
> windows are carefully placed to command every possible point of out-
> look, the rear views toward woods and sunset being as much considered

---

more decisively as a low, firm platform for the house. A typical example is the Ward
Willitts House, Highland Park, Illinois, 1902. H.-R. Hitchcock, *In the Nature of Materials*
(New York, 1942), pl. 73. Almost any other work by Wright will serve as well. Wright him-
self states of his early work: "House walls were now started at the ground on a cement or
stone water-table that looked like a low platform under the building, and usually was."
Wright, *Autobiography*, p. 141.

10. Hitchcock, *Richardson*, pls. 87–9. Mrs. Van Rensselaer's biography of Richardson
appeared in 1888, two years after his premature death. Mrs. Van Rensselaer soon succumbed,
as did everyone else, to the "monumentality" of the late 80's and early 90's, and her continued admiration at this time for Richardson's smallest house is therefore very important.
Mrs. Schuyler Van Rensselaer, *Henry Hobson Richardson and His Works, with a portrait
and illustrations of the architect's designs*, Boston and New York, 1888 (500 copies printed).

11. The difference in intent between this house and such later summer homes as Hunt's
"Ochre Court," 1888–91, or "Breakers," 1892–95, both at Newport, is a significant comment
upon a shift in values.

as those which show the sea. The longer one studies this little house the more one likes it, the more typical it seems of that sort of excellence which the American owner so often craves—artistic [*sic*] treatment combined with cheapness, comfort with small dimensions, beauty with simplicity, refinement without decoration. Outside, the only touch of ornament is given by the varied shaping of the shingles,[12] and inside, pleasant tints alone relieve the plainness of the woodwork, and good outlines the severity of the chimney-pieces. It has sometimes been said that Richardson took so much interest in great problems that he had none left to give to small ones. But no one could have more carefully studied a little house like this, the cost of which, exclusive of foundations, barely exceeded twenty-five hundred dollars.[13]

Awareness of imaginative adjustment to site, simplicity of materials, freedom of space, expression of function, lack of pretension, creation of order—all are present in this statement by Mrs. Van Rensselaer, and the general influence of the Percy Brown House upon other architects had to do with these qualities.

The Stoughton House of 1882–83 (Figs 57, 58) also made a great impression, mainly because of the calm and truly classic order of its design. George Sheldon, in his extremely valuable but now difficult to find book, *Artistic Country Seats*, 1886–87, had this to say of Richardson's Stoughton House:

One of the simplest private residences designed by the late Henry Hobson Richardson is Mrs. Stoughton's cottage, in Cambridge, Massachusetts; and few cottages of equal dimensions were ever planned, in this country or abroad, which show better results in point of convenience, spaciousness, and architectural purity. The architect has used on the external walls, as well as on the roofs, cypress shingles of a size somewhat larger than usual, and has caused them to be painted a deep olive-green. The hall runs through the center of the building, and on the left are the parlor and library, and on the right the dining-room, with kitchen, china-closet, and pantry adjoining. The finishing of the interior is in harmony with the simplicity of the exterior, and the effect is that of a comfortable country-house, without ostentation, and yet at the same time with a pervasive and stimulating sense of the organizing presence of an artist.

12. Richardson cut the shingles to a triangular point over the dormer windows—forming a kind of dotted instead of hard line, which creates a horizontal continuity from gable to gable across the top of the windows.

13. Van Rensselaer, pp. 105–6.

When Mr. Richardson built this house, he set the style, so to speak, for many other country houses; and since its erection, the use of shingles instead of clapboards has greatly increased, while the entire absence of all frivolous ornamentation of scroll-work, and other souvenirs of the "Vernacular" architecture of former years, set hundreds of architects thinking. . . .[14]

Sheldon is historically inaccurate, as he often was, in the importance he assigned to the Stoughton House in the shift to shingles, as well as in his ideas on the origin of the "scroll-work." Still, he sensed the combination of natural freedom and coherent design in the Stoughton House. He clearly indicated that its effect upon architects was enormous.[15] Certainly the Stoughton House, with its spatially expansive living hall and its bulging shingled surfaces was a masterpiece of the new architecture. The order toward which it moved can be seen at a further stage of development in the Walter Channing House at Brookline (1883–84), where the subsidiary masses are fewer and the whole is pulled even more decisively together. The shingle surface seems distended with the volume inside.[16]

Besides discipline of design, the elements of Richardson's architecture which were of importance in suburban and country domestic building are summed up in two very different buildings of 1884: the Paine House and the F. L. Ames Gardener's Cottage.[17] The Paine House can serve as a final il-

14. Sheldon, *Country Seats*, *1*, 157. See Ch. 5, n. 29.

15. An example is a house built as late as 1897 on Lincoln Parkway, Buffalo, N.Y., by Edward Laney, which is an exact reproduction of the Stoughton House. Besides being on an Olmsted Parkway it is next to the Heath House (by Wright), 1905. The relationship between the two is revealing. Both are classically coherent forms, but the Wright house obeys a more inexorable architectural discipline than does the Richardsonian house. The scale is also different. The Richardsonian house is higher, more relaxed; the Wright house is very low to the ground, consciously forcing the scale. The reception of the light is also significantly different. The warm shingled surfaces of the Richardsonian house break it up softly in a painterly way. The hard, red-brick surfaces of the Wright house reflect it sharply and flatly. Beside their Olmsted Parkway, these two houses express the continuity of organically developing American architecture, as well as the important changes in that development between the early 80's and 1900. They also show up sharply in a regional sense, one as eastern, the other as western.

16. Hitchcock, *Richardson*, pl. 102.

17. *Ibid.*, pls. 117–20, 125. The Glessner House (*ibid.*, pls. 128–9) is not included here, since its urban monumentality is somewhat apart from our interest in cottage architecture, as are the other Richardsonian urban mansions. There is another important point concerning Richardson's city houses in masonry. Whatever their own originality, they were seen by their contemporaries in a stylistic way, as a revival of the Romanesque, and their influence was mainly along that line. In domestic architecture the Romanesque revival itself

lustration of Richardson's sense of space and his use of materials. In the dim and quiet living hall the great stairs, which, as Hitchcock describes them, "pour down into the room like a mountain cataract," oppose the energies of their movement to the massive bulk of the fireplace diagonally across the room.[18] There is a pull in space between these two elements, both tense and calm. In this dynamic but serene hall one finds the culmination in Richardson of the long process of living hall design which had begun with the fireplace and stairs of the Codman project of 1869 (Fig. 2). On the exterior of the Paine House the long void of the second story porch is stabilized on either side by rough stone towers. Supported below by clean but massive piers of stone, the shingled wooden structure of the porch butts decisively into the stone of the towers to form an expressive structural intersection of different but equally appropriate materials.[19]

Whereas the Paine House was a large and elaborate residence relying for its effect upon simple architectural elements, the Ames Gardener's Cottage (Fig. 59) was a small shingled structure. It illustrates once more how the principles of the new architecture worked equally well for inexpensive buildings.[20] Because of this the shingle style had become by 1884 a natural way of construction, limited only by the fact that its method extended mainly to one or two family homes, summer clubhouses, or summer hotels. Like the rest of the more original development in America since the 1840's, it was a country and suburban architecture. Its strengths, as well as its limitations, lay in its characteristics as a cottage style. Its energies expanded in the country or by the sea. With the problems of city building it had little to do, and in the city it tended to become absurd. Indeed, its own most positive qualities were basically anti-urban.[21] Notwithstanding all this, the Ames Cottage shows the

---

may not have got fully under way until after Richardson's death in 1886. By this time the peak of the development of the free shingle style had already passed. The Romanesque revival in domestic architecture was much more a part of the psychological landscape of the later 80's and early 90's than it was of the early 80's. See Montgomery Schuyler, "The Romanesque Revival in New York," *Architectural Record, 1* (1891), 7–38; and "The Romanesque Revival in the United States," *op. cit.,* pp. 151–98.

18. Hitchcock, *Richardson,* p. 268.

19. The pseudoregency bay windows which now enclose a portion of the porch are a later and perhaps unfortunate addition.

20. Hitchcock, *Richardson,* pl. 125. See n. 17 above.

21. Wright's project of 1932 for Broadacre City represents the culmination in this whole development. Decentralization reaches such lengths that most families receive a minimum of an acre of ground. The city as such is destroyed—the triumph of the cottage style—and the living units are connected with each other and with the industrial areas by motor transportation. This concept, of course, has been seriously attacked by many competent

possibility in the shingle style for small house building of a high order.

Similar to it, and only slightly larger, is a house at 66 Mansfield Street, New Haven (Fig. 60), of about the same time.[22] Its shingles are stained red, and a little delicately scaled wooden lattice work appears in its gables. This house opposes the round and thinly surfaced volume of its tower to the voids of its porches in a way similar to Richardson's work.[23]

Consequently, Richardson returned to domestic work in the early 80's and created mature masterpieces of which the main characteristics were a rejection of stylistic evocations and the development of a discipline of design which was at once ordered and capable of considerable variation and future growth. He owed much, however, to the work of other men, as, for instance, to Emerson's. These others, who must now be considered, actually carried the new design farther than did Richardson along those lines of spatial invention which led toward the work of Frank Lloyd Wright.

Thus during the early 80's Richardson was by no means alone in the new domestic architecture. This period saw the creation of mature masterpieces by many of the architects already discussed and by others not yet mentioned. If elements appeared in the work of some of these men which may be considered specifically Richardsonian, nevertheless the nature of their design as a whole was, as has already been shown, part of a larger and more general trend. In the work of the early 80's a wide range of design solutions and a

---

critics as inefficient and socially undesirable. See especially Christopher Tunnard, "The American Planning Tradition," *Architectural Review, 98* (1945), 37–42, 126–34. Nevertheless, its basis in Wright's thinking ties it, as we have seen, to deep-seated forces in American architectural growth. The opposite concept to Wright's decentralization has been stated most eloquently in the 20th century by Le Corbusier. This is one of maximum density in a few huge skyscraper apartments, leaving most of the ground free and public. See Le Corbusier (Charles-Edouard Jeanneret), *Œuvres complètes,* 5 vols. Zurich, 1929–53. See especially *idem, La Ville Radieuse,* Boulogne, 1935. Other theorists tend toward a middle view. See Paul and Percival Goodman, *Communitas* (New York, 1947), *passim.*

22. This is the H. W. Mansfield House, which is not in the real estate map of the area of 1879 but is included in that of 1888. Its date is undoubtedly in the middle 80's. Dana, "Pictorial New Haven," *41,* 5. The lattice work on the gable of this house reminds one a little of some of White's work.

23. A lower level, architecturally, of general building is seen in the middle 80's in such pattern books as Shoppell's and Palliser's, now however considerably less important as carriers of growth than they were in the midcentury. See H.-R. Hitchcock, *American Architectural Books. A list of books, portfolios, and pamphlets on architecture and related subjects published in America before 1895* (3d ed. Minneapolis, 1946), pp. 75–6, 96–7, for an investigation into the Palliser and Shoppell bibliographical tangles. Probably most important are George Shoppell, *How to Build a House,* New York [1883?], and George Palliser, *Palliser's New Cottage Homes and Details,* New York, 1887.

variety of experiments emerged. Varieties of materials, light, and adjustment to site—all counted strongly in the shingle style. Above all, its architects developed large, open volumes of interior space. If any trend moved
through this rich diversity it seems to have been one toward design discipline
and order, growing in strength toward 1885. Here, too, space was important.
Design moved toward an interweaving of interior and exterior spaces, bringing to full fruition that sensitivity toward the interweaving of the architectural fabric which had been an important aspect of American work since the
early stick style. The final result of this development need not be of concern
at the moment. Nor should it be necessary to discuss all the work of the architects involved. A selection of works by different architects will demonstrate
the variety of the architecture and the main trends of the period.

   "Kragsyde," the large summer cottage at Manchester-by-the-Sea, built for
G. N. Black by Peabody and Stearns in 1882–84, was this firm's one great masterpiece of the early 80's (Figs. 61, 62, 63).[24] It illustrates the amalgamation
of Richardsonian influence with the more general development. High upon
a rocky crag, its rough stone base supports a loose and rambling wood frame
structure covered with natural shingles. A wide, heavy-headed, shingled
arch at a diagonal to the main mass of the house spans the entrance drive.
Above the arch a "boudoir" is surrounded by a deep porch. This arch illustrates in wood the influence of Richardson's masonry in the Ames Gate
Lodge. Entrance is under the arch, up a contained flight of stairs, through a
vestibule, and into the living hall. The main portion of the hall, up an open
flight of five stairs more, contains a large fireplace with built-in seats around
it. A window wall, almost entirely of glass, extends the hall to an open piazza.
To left and right are living and dining rooms, both widely fenestrated and
extended by covered porches. The ceilings are fairly low, giving a constant
sense of horizontal extension, prolonged by the piazzas.[25] The variety of light
and spatial movement recall Emerson's house of 1879 at Mount Desert (Fig.
46). From the hall the stairs mount a three-quarter level to the diagonal
passage leading to the boudoir with its covered porch. Up another quarter
level are the various bedrooms. Each room provides a view of the sea far
below. Around all these volumes the shingled shell of the house wraps freely,
projecting overhangs in its dormers, sprouting towers, and containing the

24. *Am. Arch., 18,* Mar. 7, 1885. Published in pencil sketches by E. Eldon Deane, the
picturesque sketching specialist whose work appeared frequently in the *American Architect*
throughout the 80's. Kragsyde was also published by Sheldon, *1,* 169–72.
25. Sheldon (p. 170) cites Viollet-le-Duc as an authority for the statement that continuous
low ceilings make space seem horizontally more extended. Note also J. Cleveland Cady's
reaction to the Dutch farmhouses, above, Ch. 3, pp. 48–9.

whole mass with its continuous surface flow. Texture and tone range between the rough, coloristic stone base with flanking walls and the unpainted shingles silvering in the salt sea air. The shingles are like a thin membrane over echoing volumes, as the boom of the surf below reverberates low and deep through the house. Upon its solid base the light and flexible frame structure thus "balloons" with its caves and pavilions of space. Here is an integral unity between technique and expression. Peabody and Stearns never again, to my knowledge, created a house of such quality. One may wonder whether later, as they produced their cool Georgian formulas out of books, they regretted their freer early days.[26]

In the early 80's Peabody and Stearns also built the Elberon Casino (Fig. 64), a loose, picturesque assortment of shingled shapes which flow together in massing like the waves of the sea. The building is awkward, but its formal variety is appropriate for a summer clubhouse. Its variously cut shingles were stained a warm brown. The wood trim, originally more neutral in color, has recently been painted white. The building's greatest quality is its free virtuosity in wood frame construction and the unification of that variety by the continuous shingled surface.[27]

Similar in feeling to Kragsyde and the Elberon Casino, if much less dramatic, is the William Pratt House of the early 80's at Manchester-by-the-Sea, by Arthur Hooper Dodd. Its plan is as open as that of Kragsyde, although spatially less rich in variety of level and extension to the outside. The massing of the house, where the roofs and the thin shingled walls seem to expand and billow with their volumes, relates to that of Kragsyde. The short tower with its railing pushing up from the roof of the house also recalls that feature both in Kragsyde and at Elberon.[28]

26. By the early 90's Peabody and Stearns had become one of the most important and busy architectural firms in the country, the Boston equivalent of McKim, Mead, and White in New York and Burnham in Chicago. Their buildings became as Georgian or as academic as the work of those firms. Among a multitude of other buildings they built Machinery Hall at the Chicago World's Fair of 1893.

27. The Elberon Casino was published by Sheldon, 2, 99–101. The (English) *Builder,* Dec. 25, 1886, published it as McKim, Mead, and White's, probably because so much of the building at Elberon was done by them. However, it is definitely by Peabody and Stearns. Built as a casino for this fashionable summer resort of New York financiers and of various statesmen such as Grant and Garfield (who was buried at Elberon), the Elberon Casino has reversed the usual process and has now become a private residence.

28. Sheldon, *1,* 127–9. Sheldon (p. 129) says of the Pratt House, "There is no sham ornamentation in Mr. Pratt's house—an air of honesty, simplicity and suitableness prevails." Interesting is Sheldon's use of the word "eclectic," which he generally uses as a synonym for the word "original," indicating another of the semantic traps into which architectural

The kind of freedom which Kragsyde and the Elberon Casino exhibit seems to have led some architects of the period toward an exacerbated picturesque design. Their work recalls those "excesses" of which Viollet-le-Duc had spoken and which he had recognized as healthy components in free design.[29] Perhaps most excessive was the firm of Lamb and Rich of New York, much of whose work was done in and around Short Hills, New Jersey.[30] Their planning at first was seldom skillful, but they exhibited an unrestrained love of materials, texture, and color which, though often coarse, may represent that sensuous appreciation of shapes and surfaces which was important in the new design.

Their house for A. B. Rich, D.D., at Short Hills, New Jersey, built in 1881–82 (Fig. 65), excellently exemplifies their qualities.[31] Spatially undistinguished, with a tight hall and awkward parlor, it nevertheless features upstairs "a low arch off the stair landing, through which the studio is seen." More important, "The stairs are of bamboo, while the hall is finished in rough-cast plaster." Japanese influence is obviously involved. In the free massing of the house, where towers echo chimneys and dormers erupt from the roof slope, appear rough stone, brick, lapped siding under the windows, fuzzy shingles, and a rough plaster panel with sea-shells stuck in it. Also, "The exterior is to be stained deep yellow at peak of gable and grade into bronze green and then into deep indian-red at base." [32]

Other houses of the early 80's in New Jersey by Lamb and Rich are more or less of the same type. One at Naversink Park, dating from 1882 (Fig. 66), is representative of the general run.[33] Perched upon a rough stone basement, with a big Richardsonian arch, the shingled upper portion, surrounded by verandas, crouches like a spider. In this house, picturesque enthusiasm seems

---

thinking was slipping during this period. He states (p. 128), "The style of the house is eclectic and modern, although a light colonial feeling in the window-fronts under the gables reminds one of the old Salem Houses." The cost of the Pratt House was $11,000.

29. See Ch. 4, p. 67.

30. Lamb and Rich were a New York firm who played a large part in the development of such New Jersey commuting country suburbs as Short Hills, first laid out in the late 70's. *Am. Arch., 16,* July 12, 1884.

31. *Am. Arch., 11,* Jan. 7, 1882. Sheldon, *2,* 125.

32. *Ibid.,* p. 126. A wide range of autumnal colors is typical of the shingled houses of this period, although few run such a gamut as this. It will be noted that all the colors mentioned are warm and earthy in a continuation of Downing's desire for earthy colors (discussed in my "Romantic Rationalism," pp. 126–7). Such rich color sense contrasts with the uniform and unimaginative use of white or pale yellow developed later after the triumph of a more Palladian colonialism.

33. *Am. Arch., 12,* July 1, 1882.

to infuse materials with a kind of eerie life. Every surface crawls with form.

Better plans appear in Lamb and Rich's Seney House, Bernardsville, New Jersey, 1882, and in another house at Short Hills of the same year.[34] In the Seney House an easy flow leads from the central hall into the dining and living rooms, which are imaginatively varied in shape. A quiet study is tucked in behind the hall fireplace mass. The Short Hills house has a free-standing fireplace which separates from the parlor a small space optimistically labeled "Den." [35] More totally expressive of Lamb and Rich's barbaric power, however, is their house called "Redstone," at Short Hills, published in September, 1882.[36] With a great open well over the massive fireplace of the hall and with all kinds of textures (including cut brass heating registers, "all different"), Redstone amply exemplifies picturesque energy at its fullest.

Perhaps the best house produced by the firm was the S. P. Hinckley House, "Sunset Hall," at Lawrence, Long Island, built in 1883 (Figs. 69, 70, 71, 72). This was long, extended, and comparatively serene. The drawings of its interiors, published in the *American Architect,* illustrate the space and light, the fireplace masses, ornamental ironwork, and comparatively simple colonial and modern furniture which played their part in the new design.[37] The plan is excellent. A flow of space extends loosely along one axis. Horizontal expansion is emphasized by low ceilings everywhere.[38] Thus there developed in the work of Rich, the designer of the firm, a sense of unified space.

34. *Am. Arch., 11,* Feb. 11, 1882: Seney House. *Ibid.,* May 13, 1882: house at Short Hills.

35. This use of an absolutely free-standing fireplace mass to define a space is of course characteristic of modern planning. One of its first and best known examples in the 20th century is Le Corbusier's little weekend house near Paris, 1935. Le Corbusier, *3, 1934–38.*

36. *Am. Arch., 12,* Sept. 2, 1882.

37. *Am. Arch., 15,* Feb. 2, 1884. The interiors are seen as a free scramble of antiques and new furniture. In the flow of their shapes some of the pieces are distant ancestors of much contemporary furniture which exploits the possibilities of plywood. The hall shown in these drawings was reproduced in photograph form in Appleton's publication. See following note.

38. Sheldon (*1,* 139–42) says of this house:

> The purpose was to produce, at a moderate cost, an effect of length and lowness. . . . The finishing of the hall is in pine, stained a light peacock-blue, and paneled to the ceiling, where heavy beams appear. Next to the Dutch doors of the south side are seen transomed English basement windows, which completely fill the remaining space of the wall. The fireplace on the west side has an opening six feet six inches wide, and over the mantel, eleven feet wide, a large hood is supported by four brackets whose three intervening spaces show each a lion rampant in relief . . . on each side a door leads into the parlor.

He notes also that this hall was reproduced in Appleton's *Artistic Houses, being a series of interior views of a number of the most beautiful and celebrated homes in the United*

The Mallory House of Port Chester, New York, by Arthur Rich working alone (Figs. 67, 68), is another excellent indication of the trend.[39] Here the space clusters around fireplace masses in a way which later appears in the remarkable plans by Bruce Price, at Tuxedo Park, New York.[40] The exterior of the Mallory House also expresses concentration and intensity in design. The voids of the surrounding porches, with some posts shingled, play a counterpoint against the solids of projecting gables, splashed with plaster between the windows. The mass of the house projects and recedes in space, draws space into its piazzas and projects its gables into space as if pushing boldly against a palpable substance.

The design of Lamb and Rich, in sum, was utterly picturesque, coarse in its treatment of materials, and always bold. Their sense of interior space, at first undeveloped, became more and more intense as the early 80's progressed, until by 1883–85 it was capable of concentrating powerful nodes of spatial energy. If Lamb and Rich were often blatant they were always free, and the wildest energies of their time were expressed in their work. In such an atmosphere of free experiment all kinds of formal invention flourished.[41] Above all a feeling for the possibilities of architectural space gave vitality and direction to the new design.

States, with a description of the art treasures contained therein . . . , 2 vols. in 4, New York, 1883–84 (500 copies). This book, like Sheldon's, was a publication prepared especially for subscribers. It unfortunately confines itself mostly to city house interiors. However, it includes some country houses. The quotation from Sheldon above is lifted almost entirely from Appleton, 2, Pt. 1, 91–2, which further states (p. 92) of the Hinckley House that the "second story is colored an old gold, the base courses an Indian-red, and the roof allowed to obtain a foxy tone from the weather." Sheldon may have anonymously written the Appleton text.

39. Sheldon, *1*, 218–20. Sheldon makes an interesting comment (p. 220) in relation to this house: "One of the most inspiriting facts revealed by the present collection of 'Artistic Country Seats' is the disappearance of the Queen Anne craze as a potent influence in American suburban architecture." By 1886, when Sheldon was writing, the phrase "Queen Anne" had become synonymous with "fashion," a word which was to represent the nadir of the transitory and the disreputable for the later classicistic, colonialistic, and eclectic critics. Sheldon, it must be remembered, was past the critical date of 1885, and if his feeling against Queen Anne shows that American domestic architecture had progressed far into an originality of its own from its first English inspirations, it was also approaching an academic phase, for whose proponents "Queen Anne," as a disreputable fashion, would eventually come to mean the whole free domestic style. See Dow, *American Renaissance*, ch. 9, pp. 118–31.

40. Discussed below, in Ch. 7, pp. 126–9.

41. For the wildest of extravaganzas see the Trask House, Saratoga Springs, by A. Page Brown. Sheldon, *2*, 163.

Perhaps no one in these years manipulated space more dramatically than Arthur Little, of Boston.[42] This is all the more remarkable since Little's houses of the period often, though not always, have an avowedly colonial look, tending eventually toward the Palladian. He became one of the first architects to follow the later lead of McKim, Mead, and White toward Palladian academic planning.[43] Yet in the early 80's a feeling for space in three dimensions dominated his design. As in Peabody and Stearns' Kragsyde, it was the space of open interior volume. His house called, "Shingleside," at Swampscott, Massachusetts, 1881 (Fig. 73), is a case in point.[44] The shingled surface of the exterior does not flow, as in most of the houses already considered. Instead it is contained rigorously at each change of plane by wooden stripping. Except for a projecting bay, also stripped at each intersection, the main mass of the house is severely rectilinear, like a gigantic colonial farmhouse of the salt-box type. Within that rectangle the space of the living hall is hollowed out to form a great two-storied volume. The house is built against the side of a hill at second-story level. From the entrance hall one ascends to the bedrooms. To the left is the dining room, with the kitchen behind it in an ell. To the right, across an open gallery, is the parlor. From the gallery an open stair descends to the floor of the two-storied living hall. From the parlor a balcony overlooks this hall, as does a small bay window from the upper staircase. Under the stairs a low, deep inglenook with built-in seats surrounds a tremendous fireplace. The whole seaside of the hall opens by a two-storied and slightly bayed window, set far enough back in plan to be crisply contained within the rectangle of the house.[45] The large-scaled

42. Little brought out a book of colonial details and spatial studies in 1878. Arthur Little, *Early Colonial Interiors . . . Salem, Marblehead, Portsmouth and Kittery,* Boston, 1878.

43. As in his George D. Howe House, Manchester-by-the-Sea, 1886, discussed on p. 152.

44. This house was published, interestingly enough, in the English *Building News,* April 28, 1882, one of the first of the better American houses to be so published and thus one of the first to begin to exert some influence upon events in England and on the continent.

45. One is reminded of Le Corbusier's two-storied living rooms in the 20th century, great spatial hollows within an enigmatic and rectangular exterior surface. Balconies also project from upper rooms at second story level. One two-storied wall is also all of glass. See especially Le Corbusier's Maison Citrohan, 1920. *Œuvres, 1,* 31. More advanced examples would be the Maison Cook, Boulogne-sur-Seine, 1926 (*ibid.,* pp. 130–5), or the Citrohan type at the Weissenhof Exhibition, Stuttgart, 1927 (pp. 150–4). There are, of course, numerous other examples, such a spatial sense being basic in Le Corbusier's work. Its formation may have been begun by Adolf Loos, who visited America in the 'nineties. Thus, the solution of Shingleside becomes, curiously, the solution of the apartment units in the "Unité d'Habitation" (*Œuvres 5,* 189–223). Much earlier in date and also with two-storied living rooms are such early works by Wright as the *Ladies' Home Journal* project of 1901, the Hillside Home School of 1902, or the Isabel Roberts House of 1908. Hitchcock, *In the Nature of Materials,* pls. 58, 81, 156.

colonial details of the interior do not spoil its effect, and indeed the twisted colonial balusters of the stairs—a common cliché in the 80's—here splinter the light from the great window and serve to increase the sense of diagonal and vertical motion within the space.[46] Analogies to later architectural developments (to Le Corbusier's work in particular) are heightened by a study of the exterior, where much of the lower two stories is voided by deep piazzas, and simple columns support the crisp but not weighty mass of the house overhead.[47]

Little's house for Mrs. James L. Little at Swampscott, Massachusetts, built in 1882 (Fig. 74), has less interesting spaces.[48] "Grasshead" is lower and more horizontal than Shingleside, with most of its lower story brick and the rest shingled. The shingles are again contained at the intersections, except over the doorway, where a bulbous shingled roof serves as an entrance shelter. In general massing the house is like a reorganized colonial salt box, with entrance facade and gabled side stretched out together in a single plane. A six-sided tower connects with the main portion of the house through a door onto the piazza. It serves as smoking room on the ground floor and as observation tower or what-you-will in the lantern above. The upper level connects with the house by a variety of open decks and stairs. The use of tree trunks, with short stubs of branches left on as posts for the main piazza, is a fairly unusual feature during this period and not a particularly happy one. The elliptical oculi of house and tower are more or less Georgian forms, as are the small broken pediments of the dormers, which are connected by busy stick-work railings. The interior space is chopped up, but there is good circulation from the entrance, and a deep curving inglenook with fireplace opens off the parlor. Although less dynamic than Shingleside, there is in this house again a variety of light, of spaces, and of movement in space.

Three houses of 1882–84, by Little at Manchester-by-the-Sea, Massachusetts, the so-called "Barn," "River," and "Fort" houses (Figs. 75, 76), are more freely flowing shingle masses than either Shingleside or Grasshead.[49] They have all the vitality of Lamb and Rich's productions combined with a developed spatial sense and a more coherent design. The plans of all are interesting; that of the Fort House, moving up and down in various dramatic

46. Another house (*ca.* 1883) where twisted colonial balusters serve the same purpose in a somewhat similar space is the John A. Gardner House, Boston, Mass., by John Sturgis of Boston. Appleton, 2, Pt. 2, 185.

47. As in, for instance, Le Corbusier's Villa Savoie, 1929. *Œuvres*, 2, 31.

48. *Am. Arch., 12,* Aug. 19, 1882. Sheldon, 2, 147.

49. The "Barn" and "River" houses: *Am. Arch., 16,* Nov. 1, 1884. The "Fort" house: *17,* Jan. 10, 1885. All these are pencil sketches by the indefatigable and picturesque E. Eldon Deane.

changes of level within the main volume, is the most exciting. Like the best of Peabody and Stearns' work and like Little's Shingleside, these houses are designed in section. They are felt as unified volumes in which vertical space is seldom entirely interrupted by the various floors. These instead are used as pierced planes providing vertical as well as horizontal vistas and changes of level within one space. Stabilized upon rough stone foundations, all three houses, like Peabody and Stearns' Kragsyde, are hollow and mountainous masses of weathered shingle, touched occasionally with bright warm colors and loosely adjusted to their sites. Full of knick-knacks, "cottagey," and strewn with a variety of new and old furniture, all of it comparatively rough, simple, and light, they are nevertheless not oppressively quaint. They give a sense of life enjoyed, in touch with its traditions but not dominated by them, a slightly irresponsible life, consciously on holiday. As such—except for their size, which in most cases is that of a bygone building economy— they remind one strongly of the best of modern Swedish cottage architecture.[50] Both have a relaxed adjustment to function and a casual scale. Both barely skirt quaintness and are filled with miscellaneous objects of all kinds and from all periods. Both are expressions of the creative possibilities of simple and indigenous materials and techniques.

The holiday spirit of the American cottages was enhanced by the homely-romantic names they were given, as here, for example: "Barn," "River," and "Fort." Sometimes in the 80's such playful romanticism became rather forced and sentimental. A house in point is the one for E. C. Stedman on Newcastle Island, Portsmouth Harbor, Maine, by E. M. Wheelwright, completed in 1883 [51] (Figs. 77, 78). Set close to the sea, this house has somewhat the appearance of a stone lighthouse tower, to the landward side of which nestles a shingled cottage.[52] Loving care went into the laying of every stone in the house. Sheldon states:

50. Swedish cottage architecture can be seen in such books as *Trettiotalets Byggnadskonst I Sverige,* ed. Svenska Arkitekturs Riksförbund, Stockholm, 1943. See especially pp. 55–9. See also *Ny Svensk Arkitektur,* Svenska Arkitekturs Riksförbund, n.d., pp. 42–3, 46–7.

51. The Stedman House was published in the *Am. Arch., 16,* Dec. 27, 1884. Also: Sheldon, *1,* 31–4. Other works by Wheelwright, a member of the class of 1876 at Harvard, include the Wells House at Brookline, Mass., not completed until 1887 (Sheldon, *2,* 151) and a cottage at Interlaken, Florida, *Am. Arch., 19,* Feb. 20, 1886. He also later produced a book on the building of schools, Edmund March Wheelwright, *School Architecture,* Boston, 1901.

52. Of the tower Sheldon states (p. 32): "The most characteristic feature of the exterior is the grand tower, about thirty-five feet high by fifteen feet thick at the base and eighteen inches thick at the top. On each of three sides the tower swells slightly, and the scheme is that of an old lanterne on the French coast; so much so, indeed, that one almost misses an iron brace run out from the tower to hold a lantern." In the next line Sheldon adds

The trap-rock of different colors, looking like quartz, but not quartz, with blackish spots staining it, bears some resemblance to lava . . . but the effect has been varied by the introduction of white, dark, or yellow boulders, picked up on the sea-coast by Mr. Stedman. Occasionally, handsome stones project from the surface, and small circles of stone appear in the rubble-work, while many of the lower stones are arranged in the form of garlands or wreaths. Mr. Stedman and his architect gave the Yankee masons various points during the erection of these walls, and he has great faith in their artistic capacity. In fact, he says that they are the equals of the Japanese. . . . The roof-shingles were dipped in oil and in lamp-black before being used, and the other exterior woodwork was oiled and stained a Venetian-red, so that the house, though finished in 1883, looks at least one hundred years old.[53]

The plan of this new one-hundred-year-old lighthouse cottage is interesting even if, like the mass of the house itself, somewhat awkward and cut up. The hall with massive fireplace inglenook off the loggia connects by a narrow door with a dining room. Up a half flight of stairs is a small study tucked into the mass of the tower. If the romance of the site is felt in this house, it is perhaps felt to be not quite true; there is something here of the specious sentimentality always lurking behind the escape of the 80's to the country and the sea. Something is wrong with the scale; the loggia wall is too high, and the cottage is forced awkwardly in its relation to the tower, as the stone itself was forced into "garlands or wreaths." Thus the dangers inherent in a cottage style are illustrated: playfulness turning self-conscious and becoming play-acting, the love of rough and simple materials developing into crafty

---

wildly: "The *loggia* is Italian, and the house itself, the walls of which are back-plastered, New England colonial."

53. In connection with the hundred-year-old aspect of the house it should be noted that much of Newcastle's popularity as a summer resort revolved around its old colonial associations.

> Newcastle is becoming a summer resort of considerable celebrity. On the old estate of George Jaffey—one of the colonial Governors—the farmhouse containing his original council-chamber, and owned by Mr. John Albee, is distant only twenty rods from Mr. Stedman's house. In the rear, on the hill, is the cottage of Professor George Bartlett, of Cambridge. Mr. Jacob Wendell, of New York, has erected a large villa. . . . The famous Lord Wentworth House, which has fifty rooms, is half a mile back on the mainland, and has just been bought by Mr. Coolidge, the Boston artist, a son-in-law of Mr. Francis Parkman, who is restoring it in strict colonial style. It still contains the old spinnets and portraits of the last generation.

Ibid., pp. 33–4.

foolery.[54] The Stedman House is like the *American Architect* of these years: full though it is of excellent work, there are somehow too many picturesque sketches crawling over the pages.[55]

Yet the picturesque in its late phase was one of the most important bases for the cottage work of the early 80's, concerned as this was with the pictorial qualities of architecture, seen in a changing light, in a painter's landscape. Quite naturally, considering the nature of his sketch technique, William Ralph Emerson's houses of the period were rich embodiments of these qualities.[56] In a series of houses built in Maine and Massachusetts between 1881 and 1884 he continued with easy assurance to develop the solutions of his earlier years. During this period Albert Winslow Cobb, who became in 1886 the partner of the Portland architect, John Calvin Stevens, was in Emerson's employ and evidently acted as his chief renderer. His style reproduced quite faithfully Emerson's own.

A house of 1884 at Bar Harbor, published in the *American Architect* in that year, as well as one at Petersham, Massachusetts, published early in 1886,

54. The kind of girlish excitement, although coupled with a real feeling for nature and materials, which this sort of thing seems sometimes to have aroused in the 80's can be observed in the description of the Stedman House, quoted by Sheldon (p. 31), which appeared in the novel, *Mrs. Peixada,* by Sidney Luska:

> Beacon Rock rose before us. For a while we did—could do—nothing but race around the outside of the house, and attempt, by eloquent attitudes, frantic gestures, ecstatic monosyllables, to express something of the admiration it inspired. It falls in perfectly with the nature round about it. It is indigenous—as thoroughly so as the sea-weed, the stone-walls, the apple trees. . . . Fancy a square tower, built of untrimmed stone. . . . This solemn, sturdy tower, is pierced at its base by divers sinister-looking portholes, which suggest cannon and ambushed warriors, but which, in point of fact, perform no more bellicose function than that of admitting daylight into the cellar. . . . The tower faces the sea and defies it. Behind the tower, and sheltered by it, nestles the cottage proper, a most picturesque, gabled, rambling structure of wood. . . . The interior simply carried us away. Imagine the extreme of aestheticism combined with the extreme of comfort. There are broad, open fireplaces, deep chimney corners, luxurious Turkish rugs, antique chairs and tables, beautiful pictures, interesting books, and everything else a fellow's heart could desire. We can sight several lighthouses from the tower windows; and a mile out at sea, in everlasting restlessness, floats a deep-voiced, melancholy bell-buoy.

55. These appear everywhere throughout the early 80's. One drowns in textures. It becomes possible sometimes to feel the picturesque, in its exaggerated form, as a disease which feeds like a parasite upon the body architectural, consuming it with a spreading and fuzzy malady, an exaggerated case of shingles.

56. See above, Ch. 5, pp. 85-6, for a discussion of Emerson's sketch technique.

were presented in drawings signed by Cobb.[57] The pictorial qualities of Emerson's houses also made them favorite subjects for the pencil of E. Eldon Deane, the *American Architect*'s itinerant sketcher. The Hemenway and Loring Houses at Manchester-by-the-Sea, and the Stevenson House at Readville, Massachusetts, were all published in this way.[58] Across Emerson's work the light is always in motion, changing on the rough stone and warmly varied on the shingles. With his sense of splintered light Emerson loved the dotted rather than the hard line, to which end he sometimes scalloped his shingles, as over the stone first story of the Hemenway House, or multiplied his thin twisted balusters, as in Colonel Stevenson's House and stables. He loved also the picturesque nook, as in the bedroom of the Stevenson House, as well as the picturesque intersection of a variety of different elements, as in the gables, dormers and chimneys which multiply near the side door of the Hemenway House (Figs. 79, 80).

This house has a strange plan with a narrow, dark central hall running through it which isolates the living room. It is unusual in Emerson's work and in the period as a whole. One can only regard it as a feature insisted upon by a noise-hating client who—new-fangled open plan notwithstanding—demanded a living room entirely closed off and private. More typical of Emerson is the exterior of the house with massive stone first floor, shingled work over the rear porches, light balcony, and the rich yet delicate combination of varying materials and textures.[59] The louvered clerestory over the ter-

57. House at Bar Harbor: *Am. Arch., 15,* June 28, 1884. House at Petersham: *19,* Jan. 23, 1886. For a discussion of the book Cobb wrote in conjunction with Stevens, see Ch. 7, pp. 113–17.

58. Hemenway House (erroneously spelled "Hemingway" by Deane): *Am. Arch., 16,* Sept. 27, 1884. Loring House: Oct. 4, 1884. Stevenson House: Nov. 8, 1884.

59. Sheldon, *1,* 213–16. Sheldon made some important comments (pp. 213–14) about this house. He called it characteristic of a certain phase of architecture, by which he made it abundantly plain he meant an original American cottage style. He admired its adjustment to site and to its water view, and he noted the moss-covered stones, gathered on the site, which form its walls. He felt that its nonstylistic approach was its strength, although there were colonial details in the interior. Most significantly, he quoted from W. M. Woollett (*Old Homes Made New,* New York, 1878) to the effect that modern American architecture was of little interest and that "it is only in the houses of colonial times that we find much to interest." (This of course was a part of that late 70's aesthetic controversy which was discussed earlier.) Sheldon, however, says he cannot agree with Woollett and makes this statement (pp. 215–16):

> Although the examples of current architecture in the present portfolio contain some specimens of colonial architecture that are notable for artistic feeling, and for adaptation to their owners' comfort, enough has been shown to demonstrate the fact that the

race is especially worthy of note. Since E. Eldon Deane obviously loved these things, they have been preserved in his sketches with the vision of the early 80's.

Emerson also retained a weakness for light colonial details, the twisted balusters, the Palladian windows in gables, and sometimes a little plaster ornament of vaguely Queen Anne derivation. Such embellishments can be seen near the front entrance of the Stevenson House, used with Emerson's characteristic lightness. If his details were colonial they were at any rate slender in section at this period, and his porches showed a feeling for thin wood members, airy voids, and the delicate play of light. However pictur-esque his houses may have been—and some, like the Loring House (Fig. 81), were wildly so—they were never forced, as the Stedman House was. The plan of the Loring House, for instance, opens easily; there is a sense of gracious expansion and of a flood of space through the house and to the outside. The house is a pavilion to which surrounding nature is very close. The twisted-post porches which sprout and the seat with its shelter which sweeps suddenly from the outside wall remain playful elements, giving a pleasant sense of hav-ing been casually knocked together and possibly to be taken down tomorrow. The canopy over the service entrance is of this type, crudely shaped of wooden boards and with a rough ropelike design worked in it which is disingenuous enough not to be offensively quaint. Such looseness was Emerson's most characteristic quality during these years, and in a way it was a great quality. It justified the picturesque: it expressed the best aspects of summer resort living and romantic pictorial vision.

With the Loring House, perhaps Emerson's best house was the W. B. Howard House on Mount Desert (Figs. 82, 83).[60] High on one of the wooded hills of that island, it echoed with its light, shingled masses and pointed gables the forms of the mountains and pine trees around it. Eminently pictorial, it

---

present very interesting epoch of American architecture in country-seats is not depend-ent upon the imitation of colonial architecture, or indeed of any other architecture whatsoever, but has strong and striking original features of its own which have com-mended it to the good will of even the foreign architects.

This is, of course, all true, but one should not take Sheldon's protestations in any direction too seriously. His perception is acute enough but he has no really solid body of principle, a general characteristic of thinking after the early 80's—a development traced in Chs. 3–4. Furthermore, he was writing for the subscribers and felt it necessary to praise each house. He praised the Appleton House, for instance, for its colonialisms. This is part of that pe-culiar spiritual bankruptcy which overwhelmed the later 80's and which eventually withered the very perceptions which enabled Sheldon at least to make the comments noted above.

60. Sheldon, 2, 4. Burned in 1947.

was a 19th-century romantic landscape painter's ideal of an upland dwelling, perched lightly above misty valleys, its rough texture and warm colors in harmony with the colors and textures of its terrain. Like the Loring House, its plan was open and loose, a great cave of space: a large hall, a fireplace ingle-nook with a gallery above it, a parlor opening widely from the hall and connected with a piazza, a dining room off at the other side of the house on a decisive diagonal, a billiard room across the entrance drive. If less permeated by exterior space than the Loring House, its views nevertheless pulled the great sweep of the surrounding terrain visually into the house, accepting the mountains and the sea. As in many of the best houses under consideration, there was a great sense of openness to the vista, of a plunge into the voids of space. In this the Howard House is similar to Peabody and Stearns' Kragsyde, but looser, less Richardsonian. It is playful in such features as the porch above the billiard room section, covered by an open gable roof supported on shingled piers and with lattice work in the open gable. The undercurrent of influence from Japanese frame construction, which had been present ever since the midcentury, gave this porch a vaguely Oriental aspect.[61]

Emerson's importance in the picturesque cottage architecture of the early 80's lay in the imagination and freedom of his formal invention. It was never coarse—as that of Lamb and Rich, for example, often was. Yet it was always free, spontaneous, and expressive of light wooden structure and shingled surfaces. These and Emerson's sense of space and light, with a feeling for the casual type of architecture he was designing, created a shingled achitec-ture which was always authentically picturesque, often daring in its invention.[62]

61. The Japanese Building at the Philadelphia Centennial of 1876 made use of similar lattice work. "A lattice of lath-work covers the lower story, so that the inmates may open all the shutters within, and yet not be exposed to the public gaze." *Am. Arch., 1* (1876), 136.

62. It should be noted that this opinion of Emerson was shared by the *Journal of the American Institute of Architects, 1* (1918), 89, in the obituary it published after Emerson's death in 1918. It states:

> Mr. Emerson was a native product of New England, delighting in ingenious con-trivances and original inventions, filled with enthusiasms for whatever was spontaneous and natural, and abhorring conventions of any sort. He was the creator of the shingle country house of the New England coast [this is a slight exaggeration] and taught his generation how to use local materials without apology, but rather with pride in their rough and homespun character. He was keenly alive to the picturesque in nature and art, and sketched unceasingly, in the most charming way, often with strange tools and methods of his own devising. To his friends and pupils he was a source of inspiration, a unique personality, not shaped in the schools, a lover of artistic freedom. . . . Only they can justly estimate the great value of his influence in liberating architectural de-sign from artificiality and in making simple and natural means artistically effective.

An example of such formal daring can be seen in a sketch of a summer residence which Emerson submitted to the *Builder* in 1886 (Fig. 84).[63] It has a fat round tower surrounded by the sweeping circular planes of porches. Again, as in the Stedman House, a lighthouse is apparently being evoked. If the relationship of this feature to the rest of the house is awkward, it at least demonstrates the invention of the early 80's, through which powerful abstract forms were occasionally produced. One of the most dramatic of these forms is the circular corner tower of the Bayview Hotel on Jamestown Island, Rhode Island, which looks across the bay toward Newport. A great round shingled volume capped by a fantastic high roof sprinkled with dormers, it is encircled by the voids of porches in a way that recalls the Emerson project. Dating from the middle 80's, it was joined about 1890 by the Hotel Thorndike a little way down the street.[64] These two mountains of shingles (Fig. 85), each in its own way a dynamic architectural form, created by the shore at Jamestown a vision of the kind of monumentality which was possible in the shingled style: a monumentality of inspired impermanence.[65] Such buildings represent the qualities of abstract formal organization which were not without importance in the last phase of the domestic development of the early 80's.

63. *Builder,* Dec. 25, 1886. The English *Builder* puts Bar Harbor in Massachusetts. Again one should note that after 1880 American houses began to appear frequently in English publications. Their possible influence upon Voysey and others has not yet been adequately investigated. [In 1970: This was "Thirlstane," the R. B. Scott House, of 1881. Cf. Zaitzevsky and Miller, *The Architecture of William Ralph Emerson,* pp. 15–16, fig. 4, pls. 16–17.]

64. This hotel burned in 1912. Neither of these buildings was published during its period.

65. The whole attitude behind these shingled structures differs markedly from the later monumental preoccupations of the eclectic architects. Burnham's desire to provide every important town with a monumental mall and ceremonial center was an excellent example of their passion for permanence. See Christopher Tunnard: "The American Planning Tradition," *Architectural Review, 98,* Pt. 2 (1945), 126–34. (Above, n. 21.) The work of the eclectics in Washington was, of course, the most striking example. See Moore, *McKim,* ch. 15, "The Senate Park Commission Plan for Washington," pp. 182–203.

7. Order and Archetype, 1885

In the movement toward geometric and spatial discipline in design, the work of John Calvin Stevens, of Portland, Maine, is of critical importance. Stevens in some ways may be considered a disciple of William Ralph Emerson. In 1880 he was running the Boston branch of the office of Francis H. Fassett, an architect of Portland. Emerson, already a noted architect, was practicing in the same building, 5 Pemberton Square. The influence of Emerson upon Stevens was probably intensified after Albert Winslow Cobb, who had actually worked with Emerson, joined him as a partner in 1886.[1] In 1889, when the partners published a book on domestic architecture, they spoke of Emerson in terms which Wright, for instance, reserves for Sullivan.[2] They say of Emerson:

1. John Calvin Stevens' son and grandson, still practicing architects in Portland, Maine, are of the opinion that Cobb was much more Emersonian than Stevens was and that the sentiments expressed in the partners' joint book belong to Cobb rather than to Stevens. Stevens was born in Boston in 1855. He graduated from the Portland High School, Portland, Maine, in 1873 and in that year entered as an office boy the architectural office of F. H. Fassett, of Boston. He was a junior partner in the firm, Fassett and Stevens, from 1880 to 1884, and a partner of A. W. Cobb from 1885 to 1891. Stevens' son, John H. Stevens, joined him in 1906. Stevens died in 1940. (*Who's Who*, 1940)

2. John Calvin Stevens and Albert Winslow Cobb, *Examples of American Domestic Architecture,* New York, 1889. Roger Hale Newton, in "Our Summer Resort Architecture— An American Phenomenon and Social Document" *Art Quarterly* (Autumn, 1941), pp. 297– 318, wherein he touches upon the cottage architecture of the early 80's, states (p. 312) of Stevens, "But that genius of Portland, John Calvin Stevens, evolved an idiom of wooden shingles owing allegiance to no previous style. He inspired Emerson, Henry Paston Clark and Ion Lewis, and a host of others everywhere to do the same." Newton's statement here is hardly correct. The influence was in the opposite direction, as can be seen from a simple comparison of dates, as well as from Stevens' and Cobb's statements. Stevens' work in the free cottage style did not begin to appear until well into the early 80's, whereas Emerson was carrying on advanced experiments in the second half of the 70's. However, the Newton article deserves credit as one of the few modern ones to consider the cottage building of the early 80's. Cf. Newton, pp. 308–12. (The article was based upon an exhibition arranged in 1941 by

There is an architect in this country, whose beautiful domestic work, scattered over a wide area from Mount Desert to Colorado Springs, is a delight to all who know it. There are some few favored men who have been by him year after year, who have seen him daily at work—and who know the process of his creation. They have seen him, drawing-board before him and pencil in hand, his face aglow with earnestness as he rapidly sketches his conception of a design, explaining as he goes, so that all is a vivid picture of what the Home he is planning will be. Here is a Dining-room with broad, cushion-seated window to let in the morning sunlight; here a Library with cosy reading-nooks to nestle in; here a Parlor, with a generous chimney-piece and with windows arranged to command this or that charming view, which is graphically described while the pencil flies unceasingly.[3]

This gives an excellent idea of Emerson's pictorial technique in design, a sketching of elements which eventually develop into an architectural scheme for the whole.[4] Stevens and Cobb then go on to say that Emerson's work is good because it is domestic work concerned with simple needs and pandering to no expression of megalomania or power:

Now this man's work is lovely because there is instilled into it the power of a chivalrous, joyous nature, revering everything pure and brave and holy in his fellow-creatures; while scorning all that is extravagant, meretricious. The virtue which another of his line instils through his philosophy, he himself instils in American life through his Art. And, be it repeated, only as the Architect possesses a heart that thus beats in sympathy with the righteousness in society about him, can his work tend to ennoble that society.[5]

Such a conception of the relationship of the architect to society, with its roots deep in Gothic revival theory,[6] clearly forms the basis for the later,

---

Talbot Hamlin at the Avery Architectural Library, Columbia University, entitled "A Century of Summer Resort Architecture in the United States." *Ibid.*, p. 297.)

3. Stevens and Cobb, p. 29.

4. For a discussion of the pictorial method and the reaction of a disciplined architectural mind to it see Ch. 5, n. 44.

5. Stevens, p. 30. Stevens, of course, refers to Ralph Waldo Emerson, who was apparently only very distantly related to William Ralph Emerson. See n. 7 below.

6. For Sullivan it was democracy which made architecture flourish, even as it was what he called "feudalism" which killed it. For Sullivan the architect bears a precious responsibility to that democracy and must enhance it by his work. This point of view links his philosophy with that of Stevens, as it links it also to the general social consciousness of the midcentury

1. H. H. Richardson House, Arrochar,
Staten Island, by H. H. Richardson.
1868. (Wayne Andrews)

2. Project for Richard Codman House,
by H. H. Richardson.
1869-71. (Hitchcock, *Richardson*)

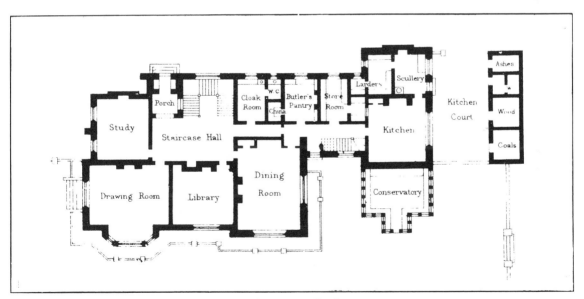

3. Hinderton, Cheshire, by Alfred Waterhouse. Plan. 1859. (Kerr)

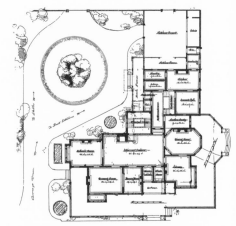

4 *and* 5. **F. W. Andrews House, Newport, R.I., by H. H. Richardson. Elevation and plan. 1872. (Hitchcock, *Richardso***

6. Leyes Wood, Sussex, by Richard Norman Shaw. Bird's-eye view. 1868. (*Building News,* 1871)

7. New Zealand Chambers, Leadenhall Street, London,
by Richard Norman Shaw. 1871-72. (*Building News*, 1873)

8. "Hopedene," Surrey, by Richard Norman Shaw.
1873. (*Building News*, 1874)

9. W. Watts Sherman House, Newport, R.I., by H. H. Richardson. 1874

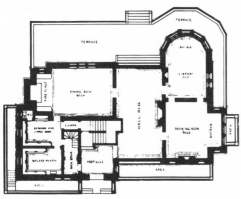

10. W. Watts Sherman House. Plan

12. W. Watts Sherman House. Sketch of living hall looking toward rear of house. Probably by Stanford White

11. W. Watts Sherman House. Living hall. (William King Covell)

13. Library, Watts Sherman House. Decorated by Stanford White before 1880. (William King Covell)

14. British executive commissioner and delegates residence and staff office, Centennial International Exhibition, Fairmount Park, Philadelphia, by Thomas Harris, 1876. (*American Builder*)

15. Bishop Berkeley House, Newport. 1728.
(*New York Sketch Book*, 1874)

16. Dennis House (now St. John's Rectory), Newport, R.I.
Living hall by Charles Follen McKim. 1876. (William King Covell)

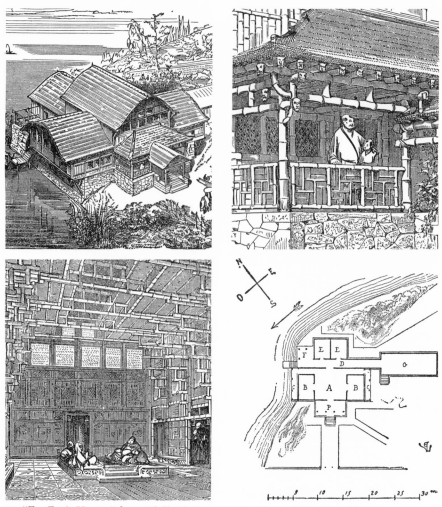

17. "Fat Fau's House," from Viollet-le-Duc, *Habitations of Man in All Ages.*
(Reprinted in *American Architect, 1,* 1876)

18. T. G. Appleton House, Newport, R.I.,
by Richard Morris Hunt. 1875-76.
(*American Architect,* 1876)

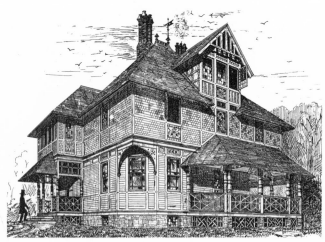

19. House at Lenox, Massachusetts,
by Alexander F. Oakey. 1876.
(*American Architect,* 1876)

20. Lowther Lodge, Kensington, by Richard Norman Shaw. 1875. (*Building News*, 1874-75)

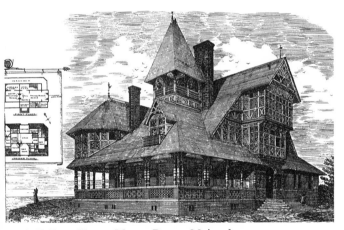

21. C. F. Dorr House, Mount Desert, Maine, by
Alexander F. Oakey. 1876-77. (*American Architect*, 1877)

22. House at Medford, Massachusetts, by Peabody
and Stearns. 1877. (*American Architect*, 1877)

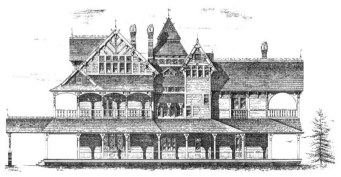

23. Bryce Gray House, Long Branch, New Jersey,
by Potter and Robertson. 1877.
(*American Architect*, 1877)

24. Dwight S. Herrick House, Peekskill-
on-Hudson, New York, by William Mead. 1877.
(*American Architect*, 1877)

26. Moses Taylor House, Elberon, N.J., by Charles Follen McKim. Entrance front. Probably 1876-77   (Wayne Andrews

25. Design for Thomas Dunn House, Newport, R.I., by Charles Follen McKim. 1877. (*American Architect*, 1877)

27. Sketch for a cottage at Pittston, Pa., by Bruce Price. 1877. (*American Architect*, 1877)

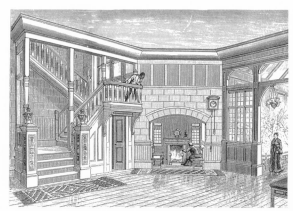

28 *and* 29. Design 18, staircase hall and Design 22, grand staircase, from Holly's *Modern Dwellings*. 1878

30. "Fairbanks House," Dedham, Massachusetts, 1636. Shown with later additions. (*American Architect*, 1881)

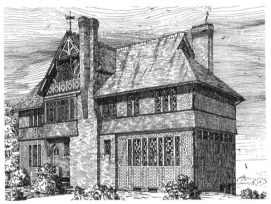

31. J. Griffiths Masten House, Newport, R.I., by Alexander F. Oakey. 1882. (*American Architect*, 1883)

32. House on Prospect Avenue, Milwaukee, Wisconsin, by Alexander F. Oakey. 1883-84. (*American Architect*, 1884)

33. Jewett House, Montclair, New Jersey, by Alexander F. Oakey. 1884. (*American Architect*, 1884)

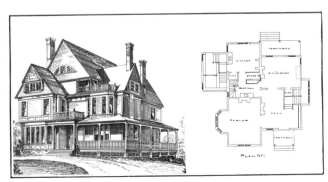

34. One of three houses at Montclair, New Jersey, with plan of another house, by Henry Hudson Holly. 1879. (*American Architect*, 1880)

35 *and* 36. C. H. Baldwin House, Newport, R.I., by Potter and Robertson, 1877-78. Exterior. (Stanhope Collection, Newport) Hall. (William King Covell)

37. F. H. Van Ingen House, Washington, Connecticut, by Potter and Robertson. 1879-80. (*American Architect*, 1880)

38. William Sturgis House, Cheyenne, Wyoming, by W. A. Bates, 1884. (*American Architect*, 1884)

39. West End Hotel, Bar Harbor, Mount Desert, Maine, by Bruce Price. 1878-79. (*American Architect*, 1879)

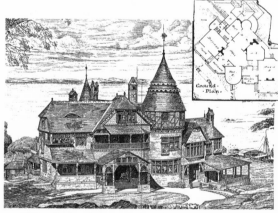

40. "The Craigs," Mount Desert, Maine, by Bruce Price. 1879-80. (*American Architect*, 1879)

41. House on Brush Hill, by Peabody and Stearns. 1877-78. (*American Architect*, 1878)

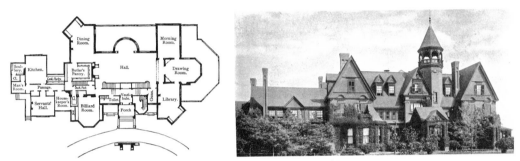

42 *and* 43. Pierre Lorillard House, Newport, R.I., by Peabody and Stearns.
Plan and entrance front. 1878. (Sheldon)

44. Project for a house for James Cheney, by Gambrill and Richardson,
designed by Stanford White. 1878. (*American Architect*, 1878)

45. Mrs. A. C. Alden House, Fort Hill, Lloyd's Neck, Long Island, by McKim, Mead,
and Bigelow. 1879-80. (*American Architect*, 1879)

46. House at Mount Desert, Maine, by William Ralph Emerson. 1879. (*American Architect,* 1879)

47. T. R. Glover House, Milton, Mass. by William Ralph Emerson. 1879. (*American Architect,* 1879)

48. Sketch for a stable and lodge, by William Ralph Emerson. (*American Architect,* 1880)

49. Church of St. Sylvia, Mount Desert, Maine, by William Ralph Emerson. 1880-81. (*American Architect,* 1881)

50. House at Beverly Farms, by William Ralph Emerson. 1881. (*American Architect,* 1881)

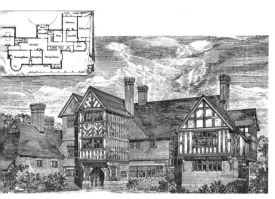

. House at Sunninghill, England,
 Richard Norman Shaw. Entrance front.
 79. (*American Architect,* 1880)

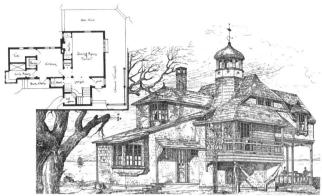

52. Design for a small summer house,
Kennebunkport, Maine, by Henry Paston Clark.
1880. (*American Architect,* 1880)

3. F. W. Sprague House, Kennebunkport, Maine,
y Henry Paston Clark and Ion Lewis. 1882.
American Architect, 1882)

54. "Redcote," York Harbor, Maine, by William
H. Dabney, Jr. 1882. (*American Architect,* 1882)

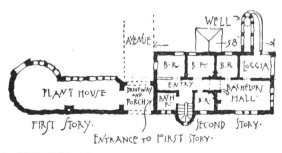

55 *and* 56. Ames Gate Lodge, North Easton, Massachusetts, by H. H. Richardson. 1880-81.
Exterior. (Hitchcock, *Richardson*) Plan. (*American Architect,* 1885)

57 *and* 58. M. F. Stoughton House, Cambridge, Massachusetts, by H. H. Richardson. *Below left,* plan. 1882-83. (Hitchcock, *Richardson*) *Above,* exterior. (Sheldon)

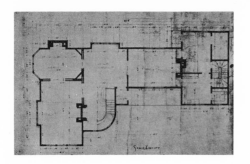

59. (*Above*) F. L. Ames Gardener's Cottage, North Easton, Mass., by H. H. Richardson. 1884. (Hitchcock, *Richardson*)

60. (*Left*) H. W. Mansfield House, 66 Mansfield Street, New Haven, Conn. *c.* 1885. (Norman Ives)

61, 62, *and* 63. "Kragsyde"" (G.N. Black House), Manchester-by-the-Sea, Mass., by Peabody and Stearns, *c.* 1882

to 84. Exterior. (Sheldon) Plan. (*American Architect*, 1885) Sketches by Eldon Deane. (*American Architect*, 1885)

64. Elberon Casino, Elberon, New Jersey, by Peabody and Stearns. *c.* 1885. (Sheldon)

65. A. B. Rich House, Short Hills, New Jersey, by Lamb and Rich. 1881-82. (Sheldon)

66. House at Navesink Park, New Jersey, by Lamb and Rich. 1882. (*American Architect*, 1882)

67 *and* 68. Mallory House,

Port Chester, New York,

by Arthur Rich. *c.* 1885. (Sheldon)

Plan. (Sheldon)

69 *and* 70. "Sunset Hall" (S. P. Hinckley House), Lawrence, Long Island, by Lamb and Rich. Exterior. 1883. (Sheldon) Plan. (Sheldon)

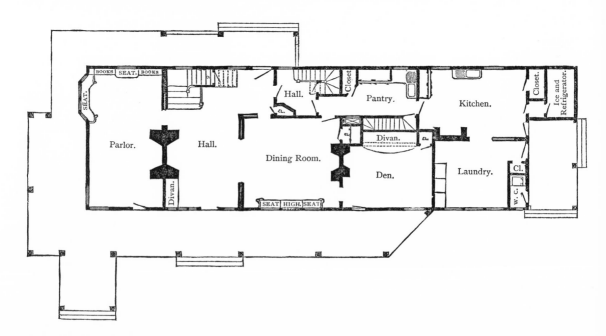

71 *and* 72. "Sunset Hall." Sketches of the interior. (*American Architect*, 1884) Living hall. (Appleton)

Piazza   Entrance

Gallery

Parlour
22 × 18.

Outer
Hall

Sta

Balcony

Upper part
of Hall

Piazza

Coats

Plan of first Storey

Furnace

Stairs

Lobby

Closet

Piazza

Hall

Seat

Ingle
Nook

Seat

Plan showing Lower Hall

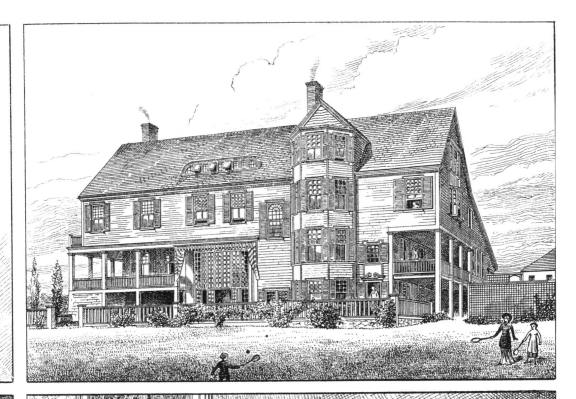

73. "Shingleside," Swampscott, Massachusetts, by Arthur Little, 1880-81. (*Building News*, 1882)

74. "Grasshead." Mrs. James L. Little House, Swampscott, Mass., by Arthur Little. 1882. (Sheldon)

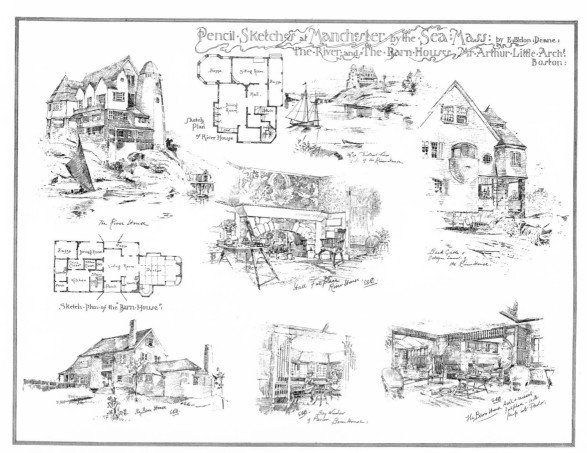

75. "Barn" and "River" Houses, Manchester-by-the-Sea, Massachusetts, by Arthur Little. *c.* 1883.
Pencil sketches by E. Eldon Deane. (*American Architect,* 1884)

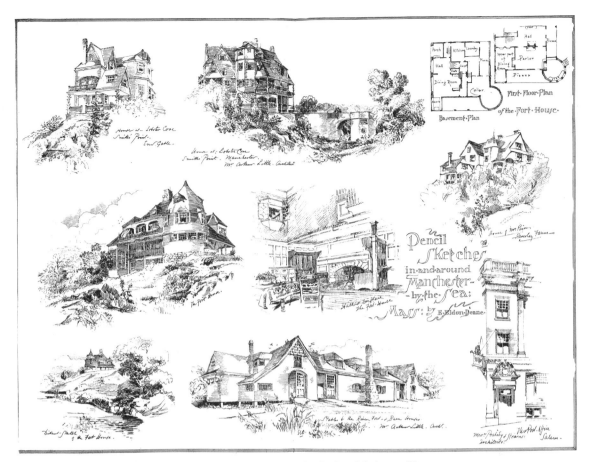

76. "Fort" House, Manchester-by-the-Sea, Massachusetts, by Arthur Little. *c.* 1883.
Pencil sketches by E. Eldon Deane. (*American Architect,* 1885)

77. E. C. Stedman House, Newcastle Island, Portsmouth Harbor,
Maine, by E. M. Wheelwright. 1882-83. (Sheldon)

78. E. C. Stedman House.
Plan. (Sheldon)

79 *and* 80. Hemenway House, Manchester-by-the-Sea, Massachusetts, by William Ralph Emerson. *c.* 1883. *Below left,* plan. (Sheldon) *Above,* exterior. (Sheldon)

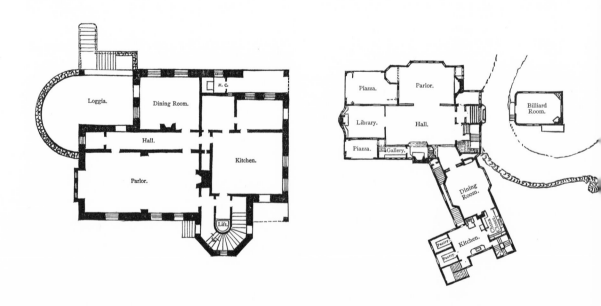

Plan of Principal Floor

Pencil Sketches in & around Manchester by the Sea, Mass.
House of Gen! Chas. G. Loring.
Mr W.R. Emerson, Archt. Pride's Crossing.
by E. Eldon Deane.

81. General Charles G. Loring House, Manchester-by-the-Sea, Massachusetts, by William Ralph Emerson. *c.* 1883. Sketches by E. Eldon Deane. (*American Architect*, 1884)

82 *and* 83. W. B. Howard House, Mount Desert, Maine, by William Ralph Emerson. *c.* 1883-84 *Above*, exterior. (Sheldon) *Opposite page*, plan. (Sheldon)

84. Summer Residence, Bar Harbor, Maine, by William Ralph Emerson. *c.* 1885. (*Builder*, 1886)

85. Hotel Thorndike, Jamestown, R.I. *c.* 1885. (Stanhope Collection, Newport)

86. Stevens House, Portland Maine, by John Calvin Stevens. 1883.
(Stevens and Cobb, *Examples of American Domestic Architecture*)

87 and 88. James Hopkins Smith House, Falmouth Foreside, near Portland, Maine, by John Calvin Stevens. 1885. Exterior and plan. (Sheldon)

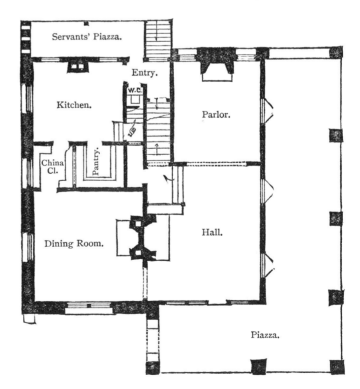

89 *and* 90. C. A. Brown House, Delano Park, by John Calvin Stevens. 1885-86. Exterior and detail. (James McNeely)

THE SEA;

91 *and* 92. Project for a "House by the Sea," by John Calvin Stevens. 1885. Exterior, plans, section, and details. (Stevens and Cobb, *Examples of American Domestic Architecture*)

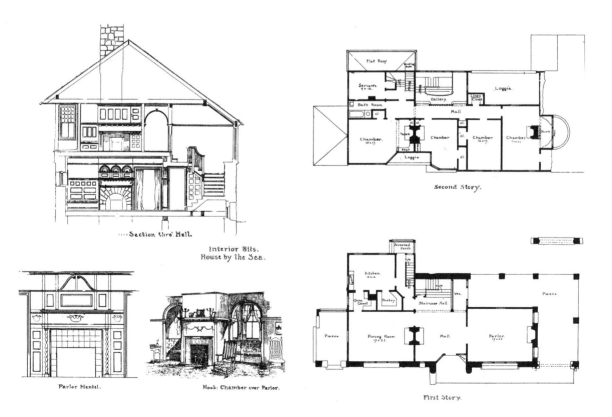

····Section thro' Hall.

Interior Bits.
House by the Sea.

Parlor Mantel.

Nook: Chamber over Parlor.

Second Story.

First Story.

93 *and* 94. Lyman C. Joseph House, Newport, R.I., by Clarence S. Luce. 1882-83. Exterior and plan. (Sheldon)

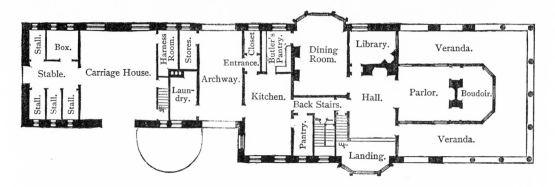

95 *and* 96. Charles A. Newhall House, Chestnut Hill, Pa., by Wilson Eyre. *c.* 1881. Exterior and plan. (Sheldon)

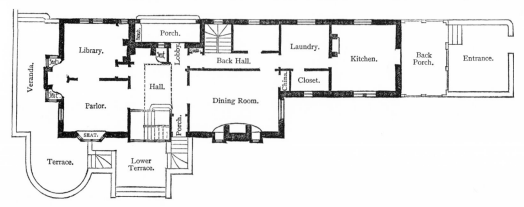

97 *and* 98. Charles A. Potter House, Chestnut Hill, Pa., by Wilson Eyre. *c.* 1881-82. Exterior and plan. (Sheldon)

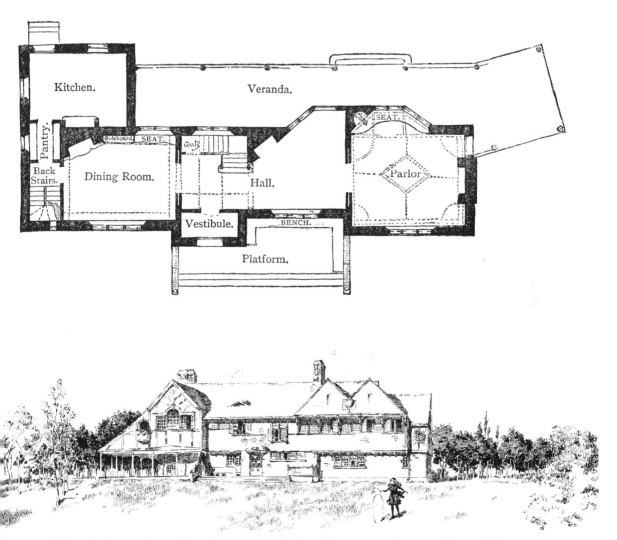

9. House in Downingtown, Chester County, Pennsylvania, by Wilson Eyre. 1883. (*American Architect,* 1883)

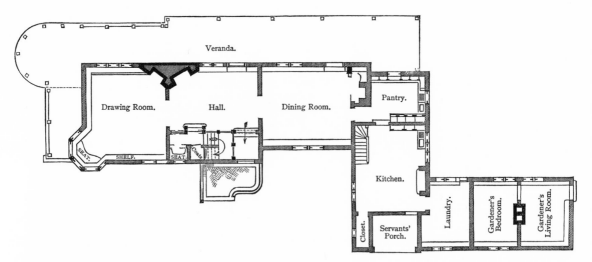

100 *and* 101. Richard L. Ashurst House, Overbrook, Pennsylvania, by Wilson Eyre. *c.* 1885. Exterior and plan. (Sheldon

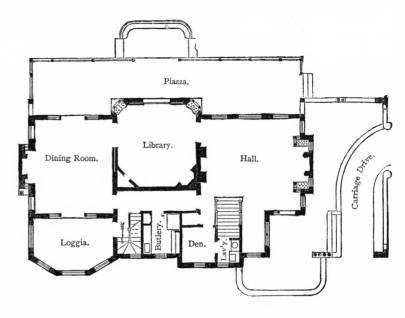

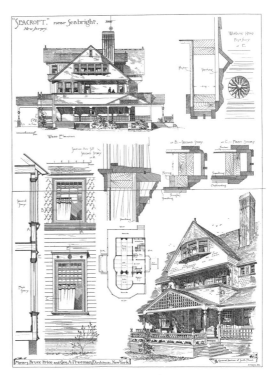

102. Dr. C. G. Thomas House,
600 Madison Avenue, New York,
by Bruce Price. 1885.
(*American Architect*, 1886)

103. "Seacroft," near Seabright, N.J.,
by Bruce Price and George A. Freeman.
Plan and details. 1882.
(*American Architect,* 1883)

104 *and* 105. George F. Baker House, Seabright, New Jersey, by Bruce Price.
Opposite page, plan. *c.* 1884. *Above*, exterior. (Sheldon)

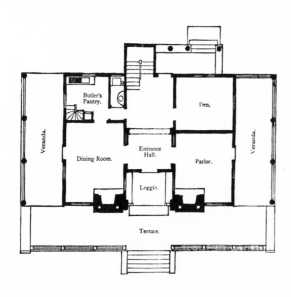

106 *and* 107. Pierre Lorillard House,
Tuxedo Park, New York,
by Bruce Price. 1885.
Exterior and plan. (Sheldon)

108 *and* 109. William Kent House, Tower Hill, Tuxedo Park, New York,
by Bruce Price. 1885. Exterior and, *below left*, plan. (Sheldon)

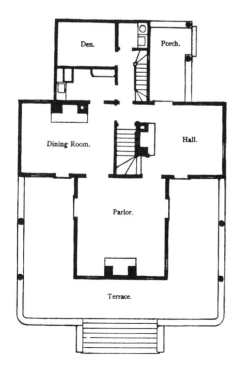

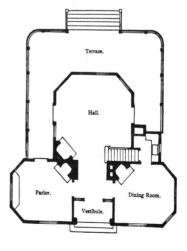

GROUND PLAN.

110. Travis C. Van Buren House,
Tuxedo Park, N.Y., by Bruce Price.
Plan. 1885. (Sheldon)

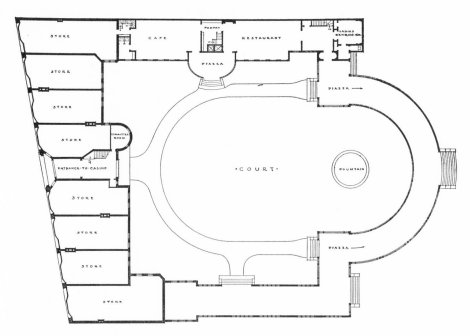

111. Casino at Newport, R.I., by McKim, Mead, and White. 1879-81. Plan. (*A Monograph of . . . McKim, Mead, and Whi*

112. Newport Casino. Street facade. (Harvey Weber) See also the drawing on title page.

113. Newport Casino. Court with tower. (Stanhope Collection, Newport)

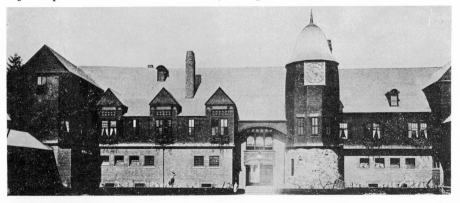

114 *and* 115. Newport Casino. Fountain and piazzas. (Stanhope Collection, Newport)

116. Short Hills Casino, N.J., by McKim, Mead and White. 1882-83. Exterior. (Sheldon)

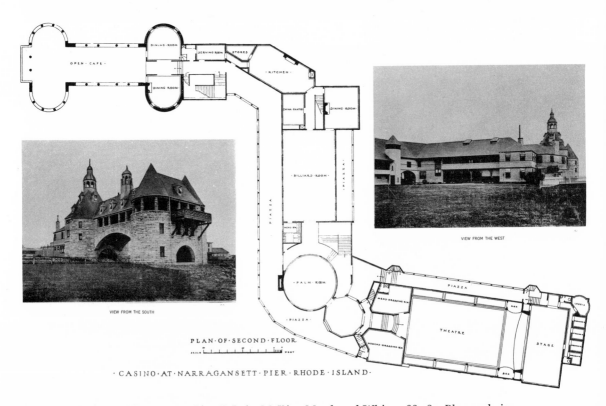

VIEW FROM THE WEST

VIEW FROM THE SOUTH

· PLAN · OF · SECOND · FLOOR ·

· CASINO · AT · NARRAGANSETT · PIER · RHODE · ISLAND ·

117 *and* 118. Casino at Narragansett Pier, R.I., by McKim, Mead, and White. 1881-84. Plan and views.

119 *and* 120. Victor Newcomb House, Elberon, New Jersey, by McKim, Mead and White. 1880-81. Exterior and plan. (Sheldon)

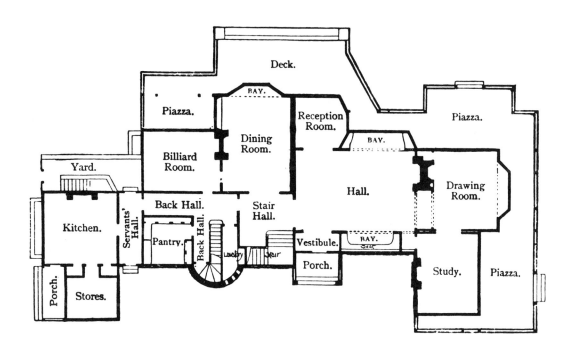

121. Victor Newcomb House, Elberon, New Jersey, by McKim, Mead, and White. 1880-81.
Living Hall. (Appleton)

122. Cyrus McCormick House, Richfield Springs, New York, by McKim, Mead, and White. Angle view. 1880-81

123. "Kingscote," Newport, R.I. Dining room by Stanford White, 1880-81. (William King Covell)

124. Nakamura Villa, Nara, Japan. Tokonoma with round and square windows.
(Harada, *The Lesson of Japanese Architecture*)

125. Tilton House, Newport, R.I., by McKim, Mead, and White. 1881-82. Hall. (William King Covell)

"Southside"

126, 127, *and* 128. Robert Goelet House, Newport, R.I., by McKim, Mead, and White. Seaside. 1882-83. Exterior and plan. (Sheldon) Living hall showing fireplace. (Appleton)

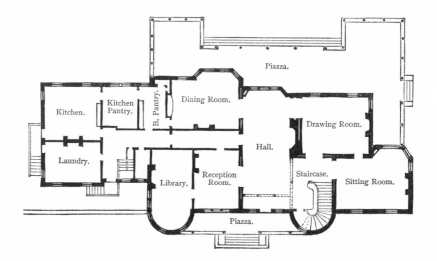

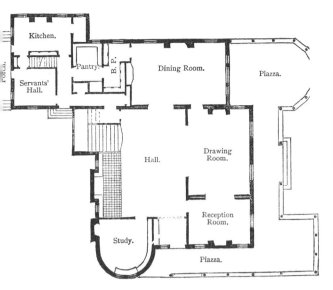

129, 130, *and* 131. Isaac Bell House, Newport, R.I., by McKim, Mead, and White.
Plan. 1882-83. (Sheldon) Living hall. (William King Covell)

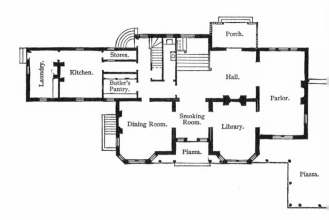

132 *and* 133. Samuel Colman House, Newport, R.I., by McKim, Mead, and White. 1882-83. Exterior and plan. (Sheldon)

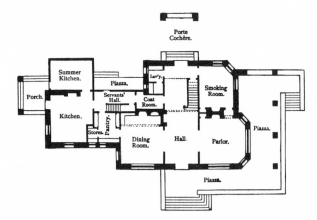

134 *and* 135. Cresson House, Narragansett Pier, R.I., by McKim, Mead, and White. 1883-84. Exterior and plan. (Sheldon)

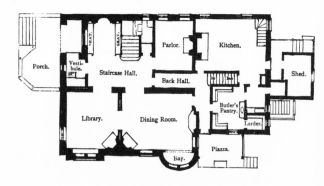

136 *and* 137. Metcalfe House, Buffalo, New York, by McKim, Mead, and White. 1883-84. Exterior and plan. (Sheldon)

38 *and* 139. Charles J. Osborn House, Mamaroneck, New York, by McKim, Mead, and White.
884-85. *Above*, entrance. *Below left*, plan.

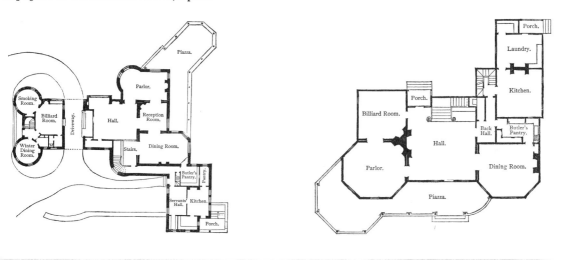

40 *and* 141. Charles T. Cook House, Elberon, New Jersey, by McKim, Mead and White.
885. Exterior and, *above right*, plan. (Sheldon)

142 *and* 143. Misses Appleton House, Lenox, Massachusetts, by McKim, Mead, and White. Exterior and plan. 1883-84. (Sheldon)

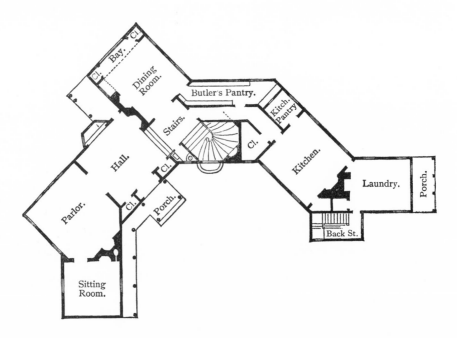

155. Frank Lloyd Wright House, 428 Forest Avenue, Oak Park, Illinois, by Frank Lloyd Wright. 1889. (Photo courtesy of H.-R. Hitchcock)

156. W. Chandler House, Tuxedo Park, New York, by Bruce Price. 1885-86. (*Architecture*, 1900) Published as a perspective rendering in *Building*, 1886.

157. Frank Lloyd Wright House. Living room. (Hitchcock, *In the Nature of Materials*)

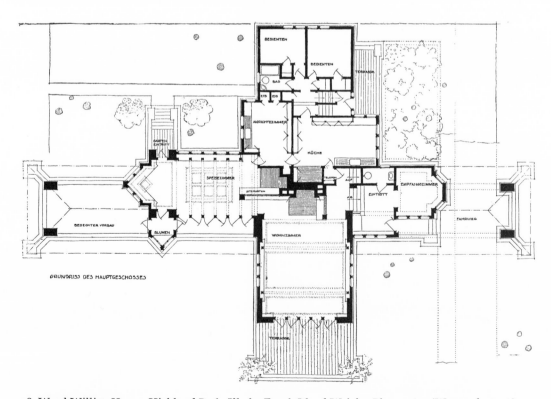

158. Ward Willitts House, Highland Park, Ill., by Frank Lloyd Wright. Plan. 1902 (Wasmuth, 1911)

59. D. D. Martin House, Buffalo, New York. Living room. 1904. By Frank Lloyd Wright. (Wasmuth, 1911)

60a) . Ward Willitts House. (Hitchcock, *In the Nature of Materials*)

160b). Ward Willitts House. Detail. (Wasmuth, 1911)

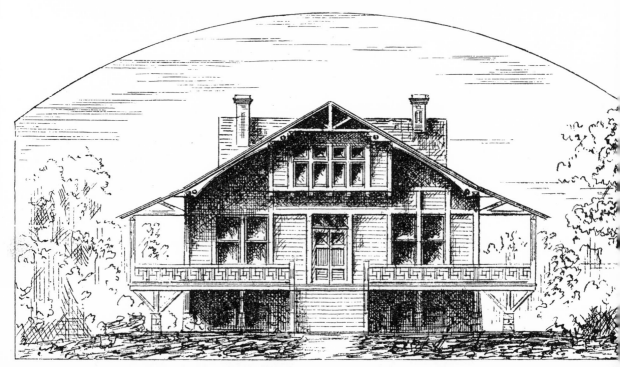

161. "Planter's House." (E. C. Gardner's *Illustrated Homes*, 1875)

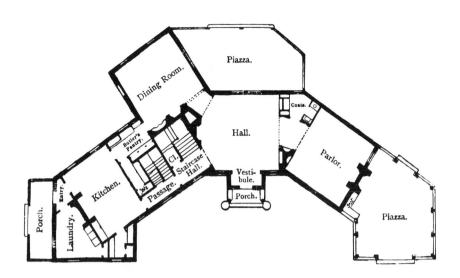

144 and 145. "Wave Crest," John Cowdin House, Far Rockaway, Long Island, by McKim, Mead, and White. c. 1885. Exterior and plan. (Sheldon)

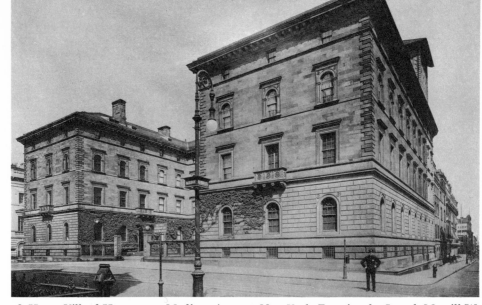

146. Henry Villard Houses, 521 Madison Avenue, New York, Exteriors by Joseph Morrill Wells for McKim, Mead, and White. 1883. (*Monograph*)

147 *and* 148. Commodore William Edgar House, Newport, R.I., by McKim, Mead, and White. 1885-86. Exterior and plan. (Sheldon)

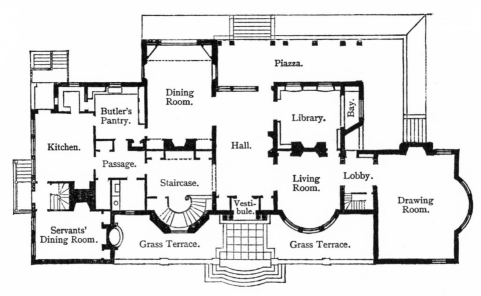

149 *and* 150. H. A. C. Taylor House, Newport, R.I., by McKim, Mead, and White. 1885-86. Exterior and plan. (Sheldon)

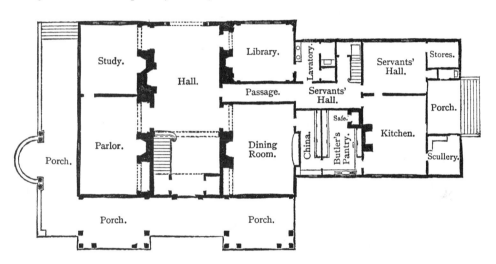

151 *and* 152. George D. Howe House, Manchester-by-the-Sea, Massachusetts, by Arthur Little. *c.* 1886. Exterior and plan. (Sheldon)

153. William Low House, Bristol, R.I., by McKim, Mead, and White. Sea side. 1887. (Wayne Andrews)

154. Atwater-Ciampolini House, Whitney Avenue and Edwards Street, New Haven, Connecticut, by Babb, Cook, and Willard. 1890-91. (Mrs. Charles Wakeman)

cacy, the temperate, telling use of detail; so desirable in architectural composition.[9]

And they go on to say: "This 'Old Colonial' style, based on the Classic Orders, is particularly well adapted to domestic work. . . . A decided preference for the American Classic examples of the eighteenth and early nineteenth century is doubtless manifest in those specimens of our own work which we venture to publish." [10]

The attitude of mind into which Stevens and Cobb fall thus participates in what Geoffrey Scott was to call "The Ethical Fallacy," which Pugin had developed early in the Gothic revival. Even allowing for this, however, an antiquarian or academic imitation of the past had not been central to the most original aspects of developing romantic theory, as I have tried to show elsewhere.[11] It was not the attitude of the original cottage architects of the early 80's, nor was it the attitude of Stevens himself until after 1885. Possibly Cobb's Emersonian idealism tended to confuse Stevens' more instinctive design after the former joined the firm in 1886. Both Stevens and Cobb would have vehemently denied that their eventual movement toward a near-Palladian position was also caused by the attraction of monumental forms, which Cobb at least loathed. It might be possible to show that this was indeed the case.[12] Yet in the movement toward order—although it was eventually made antiquarian and academic by colonial Palladianism—there was nothing itself necessarily academic or restricting. A similar movement toward discipline in design was taking place in the work of Richardson himself.[13] In Stevens' work, too, in the middle 80's, the movement toward order was manifest.

Only three houses and one project by Stevens need be considered in this

9. *Ibid.,* p. 23.

10. *Ibid.,* p. 24. It must be remembered that Stevens and Cobb were writing in 1889, by which time the academic reaction was well under way.

11. Pugin's love for the middle ages insisted upon the use of Gothic forms, partly because of their moral nature as expressing the good society. See especially, A. Welby Pugin, *Contrasts: or, a parallel between the noble edifices of the middle ages and the corresponding buildings of the present day; showing the present decay of taste,* London, 1836. However, the insistence upon the social basis of architecture was basic for new growth, as was also Pugin's maxim: "Architectural skill consists in embodying and expressing the structure required; and not in disguising it with borrowed features." Kenneth Clark, *The Gothic Revival* (New York, 1929), ch. 7; *Pugin,* pp. 152–91. I have discussed the American corollaries to this elsewhere, as, e.g., "Romantic Rationalism," *passim.* Also, Geoffrey Scott, *The Architecture of Humanism* (London, 1914), ch. 5, pp. 121–64.

12. See my discussion of Joseph Morrill Wells, Ch. 8, pp. 147–8.

13. See Ch. 6, pp. 91–8.

connection. The first of these is Stevens' own house (Fig. 86), built at Portland, Maine, in 1883.[14] This house is a comparatively contained block, freely,
if not too imaginatively, planned. The first story is of brick, of which the
bricks "protrude here and there at random."[15] A deep gambrel roof contains
the second story. Two dormers protruding from the second floor are pulled
back into the roof slope and a loggia between them is similarly controlled
by the plane of the roof. As in the early Emerson houses of the late 70's, in
which the roof became a plastic entity uniting the volumes of the house, so
here the roof goes a step further toward drawing all subsidiary volumes under
the dominance of one main volume. The house becomes one sculptural unit,
three-dimensional but contained. The varied equilibriums of the cottage
style are resolved into a single unity, and while there is still an indication of
the movement of various spaces within the main volume, they are all eventually drawn in under one sheltering roof.

Stevens' masterpiece in this kind of design—one which resembles rather
closely such gambrel-roofed structures as the early 18th-century additions to
the Fairbanks House at Dedham (Fig. 30)—is the James Hopkins Smith
House at Falmouth Foreside, near Portland, Maine, built in 1885 (Figs.
87, 88).[16] This house is a more sweeping and coherent version of Stevens' own
house. It has the added advantage of having been built as a summer cottage,
making possible in plan the elimination of vestibules and entrance halls. The
rough stone first story of the house and the piers and archway of the piazza in
the same material are especially fine. Sheldon says of these stones that they
"had lain for a century and a half in a farm wall, where, it is said, they were
originally piled up by slaves. Covered with gray moss and lichens, their color
effect was beautiful; and, in order to preserve this unique beauty, they have
been laid with their old faces exposed. The upper portion of the house is
shingled, and stained a warm, grayish brown."[17]

The plan of the Smith House is extremely important. Entrance is directly
into a large hall which serves as a general living area. The large fireplace has
a built-in seat, beside the stairs to the bedroms above. Opening widely off
the hall is a small parlor which fulfills the function of a small and intimate

14. *Am. Arch., 16,* Dec. 20, 1884. This is the first Stevens project published in the *American Architect* (see n. 2 above). Stevens, pls. 7, 8. One is referred to this book for other houses
and projects by Stevens not discussed here, including semi-Palladian work, done after 1886,
and his powerful alterations for the Poland Springs House, a summer hotel.

15. Stevens, pl. 8.

16. This house is the *pièce de résistance* in Sheldon, *1,* 177–80. Strangely enough, it is
not in Stevens' own book. For the Fairbanks House at Dedham see Ch. 4, p. 69.

17. Sheldon, *1,* 177. One wonders what Cobb would have thought of using material prepared by slaves. See p. 116, above.

sitting area. Both these rooms open with full height French windows onto the deep piazza. Behind the hall fireplace the dining room connects with the kitchen through a china closet. Here is open planning compactly organized, with the mass of the hall fireplace forming a plastic pivot around which the space swings, while the parlor fireplace pulls away from the main space to give meaning to its own special sitting area away from circulation. The feeling of extension to the outdoors is also very developed. In the unified mass of the exterior the gambrel roof is beautifully related to the deep void of the covered piazza. The porch penetrates the volume of the house itself, so that interior and exterior are not merely closely related but actually inter-woven in a serene extension of space which is continuous and clear. There may be a "classic" equilibrium here, and Sheldon himself, in one of his flashes of percipience, recognized this fact. He says,

> The architect of Mr. Smith's house . . . has struck out for himself, with due regard for the spirit and meaning of classic works, but without subservience to their details. He desires, also, that the comparatively small cost of the building should be emphasized. One rarely sees so much breadth, so much roominess and so much solidity obtained with so small an outlay of money. Effect has been sought by strength of mass and sim-plicity of form.[18]

"Strength of mass and simplicity of form" are also characteristic of Stevens' C. A. Brown House, Delano Park, near Portland, 1885–86.[19] Powerful gables

18. *Ibid.*, p. 179. (The Smith House cost $7,000.) In another connection Sheldon states (*1*, 183–4):

> Throughout the entire range of ancient classic work in architecture, the leading prin-ciple—the principle which vitalizes and is pervasive—is that every plan must be in harmony with the needs of the building for which that plan was designed [and of American cottage architecture in the 80's]. . . . in this respect they are justly entitled to be called classic. For it is always to be borne in mind that at many important points there is a wide divergence between the classic and the academic; and that progress in architecture is possible only insofar as the burden of academic conventionalism is re-moved from the artist's back. The life of art is freedom, and the characteristic of the new Renaissance of American architecture, with an exposition of which this volume is concerned, is the absolute emancipation of the architect from the shackles of the Academy; and the relegation of his sphere of operations to the broad realm of freedom —a freedom which is Greek, to be sure, because at the same time it is natural, in the highest and best sense of the word.

That Sheldon applies this statement to a fantastic, *retardataire,* pictorially Gothicizing castle in stone (the Isaac Clothier House, in Wynnewood, Pa., by Addison Hutton) robs it of some of its effect.

19. Published as drawings in Stevens and Cobb, pls. 21, 22.

slope down over the deep void of the porch (Fig. 89). Stevens here carefully puts together stone, varied shingles, and precise, white-painted sill and window details. There is a strong structural sense and a decisive visual impact (Fig. 90). The house begins to take on that archetypal intensity toward which one feels the deepest yearnings of its period—however confused by semantic complexity—to have been directed.

Another design by Stevens, indicative of important later developments, was a project called "A House by the Sea," (Figs. 91, 92) apparently never built.[20] Most significant in this project was its emphasis of the horizontal, both in space and in massing. The plan is a long thin rectangle, with the long axis further extended by covered piazzas. Only the staircase and the kitchen break out of the rectangle on one side. The wide stairwell opens up the volume of the house vertically in a way which makes the dominant horizontals of the floor levels read clearly as planes in space. A feature of the main bedroom upstairs is a window alcove behind the fireplace mass. Upon the exterior of the house the shingled second story projects slightly beyond the stone below it, in a shadow line which further emphasizes the horizontal. Similarly, the roof over the bedrooms in the crossed gable to the left of the entrance projects decisively across and contains the loggia between the indented window bays of the bedrooms themselves. The void of the extended piazza to the right is also contained within the main volume of the house by the serene sweep of the roof line from ridge line to porch piers. There is not only a decisive unity of various elements but also a sense of horizontal plane above horizontal plane and of continuity along the horizontal both in interior space and exterior massing. Even the stripping which connects the windows of the main gable is directed toward enhancing this effect.

The desire for horizontal continuity was not unique with Stevens. It is to be seen also in the Lyman C. Joseph House at Newport by Clarence S. Luce of Boston (Figs. 93, 94). The Joseph House, finished in 1883, is earlier than the Stevens project.[21] The continuous eave line of the gambrel roof and its extension over the piazza creates a long, clear horizontal above the stone first story and encloses the bay window projection of the staircase landing. This is another house pierced by a driveway. The inclusion of the stable in the mass of the house increases the horizontal extension of the whole, and the

20. *Am. Arch., 18*, Sept. 12, 1885. Stevens, pls. 38, 39. Another house by Stevens not to be confused with his Smith House near Falmouth (n. 16) is "Bellefield," the Henry St. John Smith House, Cape Elizabeth, near Portland, Maine. Bellefield was originally a medium-sized summer cottage, with a fireplace and stair arrangement showing some resemblances to that of the James Hopkins Smith House. Bellefield was expanded later by extensive additions, Boston *Architectural Review, 11* (1904), 72-3.

21. Sheldon, *1*, 46.

62. Chestnut Hill, Pennsylvania. Venturi House. 1962. Venturi and Rauch (cf. Fig. 155)

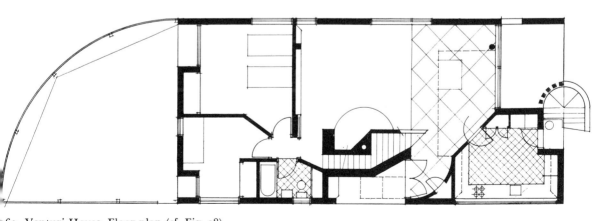

63. Venturi House. Floor plan (cf. Fig. 98)

similar conceptions (though not always the practice) of Sullivan and of
Wright. The philosophical system which Stevens and Cobb develop from
these premises must be considered to owe something to William Ralph
Emerson, whom they choose as the righteous architect. A further relationship
with the philosophy of Ralph Waldo Emerson, referred to in Stevens' and
Cobb's encomium, may also be implied. Certainly the architecture of William Ralph Emerson, in the very looseness, naturalness, and informality of
its organization, can remind one of the older Emerson who renounced rule,
embraced nature, and had a vision of free society based upon love and the
acceptance of life. The strain of American thought which the older Emerson
represents owes much to the whole international romantic movement and is
clearly evidenced in the midcentury romantic rationalist architectural theory
underlying the American stick style. It may thus have been prolonged in the
work of the younger Emerson and of the other cottage architects of the early
80's.[7] Stevens and Cobb sum up the whole attitude when they state:

> Let us not be over-disturbed, then, by flings at the temporary character
> of much American architecture. Indeed it is of far more importance that
> during our own day and generation we live wholesomely together in
> brotherly love and something like community of comforts, than that we
> build splendid, long-enduring monuments to catch the wonder of com-
> ing generations. We may bequeath them better things than these splen-
> dors: the virtue that gleams God-like from the eyes of a living people
> excels infinitely the glory of carved and emblazoned piles of insensate
> masonry and timber, evolved at sad sacrifice of human health and hap-
> piness. And though, in the beneficent process of taking the corrupt souls
> of society and making them holy, we should be compelled to strike an

romantic rationalists—from Pugin to Morris and Webb in England, and from Downing
through Wheeler, Cleveland, and the others to E. C. Gardner in America. Sullivan began
to state his philosophy as early as 1885 and 1886 in "Characteristics and Tendencies of
American Architecture," a paper read before the Western Association of Architects, St.
Louis, 1885, printed in *Builder's Weekly Reporter,* London, 1885, and in "Inspiration,"
also read before the Western Association of Architects, Chicago, Nov. 19, 1886, published
by *Inland Architect Press,* Chicago, 1886. The first culmination of this thinking comes with
"Kindergarten Chats," *Interstate Architect and Builder,* 2, No. 51; 52 issues from Feb. 16,
1901, to Feb. 8, 1902. These were published in book form, 1934, latest edition, *Kindergarten
Chats (Revised 1918) and Other Writings,* New York, Wittenborn Schultz, 1947. See also
Morrison, *Louis Sullivan,* pp. 229–61, 306–17. Wright's philosophy derives from that of
Sullivan as well as more directly from midcentury Gothic revival sources. See *Autobiography,
passim.* See also my Conclusion, below.

7. William Ralph Emerson, as noted earlier, was from a western branch of the family.
See n. 5 above.

average of wholesome, air-swept wooden huts for everybody—which however is far from needful—we should then be preparing a better heritage for posterity than we now prepare through our ill advised process of finding cities brick and leaving them marble.[8]

If Stevens and Cobb sum up in their theory many of the basic premises of the shingled cottage style, they also indicate what might be called a classic stage in its development, namely a desire for unity, order, and discipline which should formalize and, as it were, objectify the picturesque. Writing in 1889, they had already, in this desire, fallen into some of the pitfalls in their own reasoning. If society must be democratic and righteous, then the best architecture must have been created when society was most righteous, and such architecture should serve as models for new work:

> And it is worthy of note that wherever the democratic spirit was earliest developed and most marked, there the work done by our Carpenter-Architects of the Colonial and early National times exhibits most of pure beauty. In and about Philadelphia, and along the New England coast from Plymouth to Portland; throughout that territory where the protest against black slavery rang out long before the protest against tyrannies of the Crown; there, especially, we find the genuine refinement and deli-

8. Stevens, p. 25. When Stevens and Cobb judge work of the past, they base their criticism almost entirely upon social grounds (p. 21):

> Neither is there much else than warning for us in those vast, ornate structures, bequeathed by that breed of tyrants whose sins were visited upon the best monarch of their line in the wrath and woe of the French revolution. Equally serviceable as warning is a large part of the Renaissance work in Italy; work at the portals of which swarm specimens of the breed of beggars evolved in the process of its erection. In truth there is little to commend in any of the Renaissance architecture of continental Europe; architecture inspired by an admiration of tyrants for the works accomplished by their arche-types in the splendid, corrupt days of Old Rome.

This point of view is exactly analogous to that of Sullivan concerning "feudalism." See n. 6. For a significant contrast see Ch. 6, n. 65. Stevens and Cobb (pp. 14–15) also attack the philosophy behind such structures as McKim, Mead, and White's Algonquin Club, New York, 1888, as socially unhealthy. They proudly state (pl. 6) their own philosophy—and one which it must be repeated was at the heart of the whole inventive American cottage development—in connection with a small house of their own. They state:

> This simple cottage at Island Point, Vt., cost $2,300 complete. It exhibits the most primitive elements of architectural design. Such an authority as James Ferguson, D.C.L., F.R.S., M.R.A.S., F.R.I.B.A., might classify it as a specimen of 'mere building,' not architecture: but in our own terminology the word 'architecture' comprises in its meaning even so primitive a structure as this.

single vertical of the stable tower further stresses the basic horizontality of
the main mass. The interior space is interesting, with a boudoir tucked behind the parlor fireplace, but the two sets of doors on either side of the fireplace impede real flow between the two rooms. The plan also is more comcom-
plicated and less axially ordered than that of Stevens' project. The single unified volume indicated by the massing of the house is not fulfilled by the interior space.[22]

A sense of axial discipline, of spatial interpenetration, and of horizontal
continuity is even more marked in the work of Wilson Eyre, Jr., of Philadelphia.[23] Eyre fits into the development of the shingle style of the early 80's in
a very odd way. First of all, his houses were rarely shingled completely. Secondly, while the work of the early 80's discussed above had been all more or
less positively original, Eyre's work always remained at least superficially
Shavian. Eyre often used half-timber, which in most of the mature building
of the early 80's was a temporarily forgotten eclecticism. Eyre's Charles A.
Newhall House (Figs. 95, 96)—built, like much of his work, at Chestnut Hill,
in the heart of the Main Line near Philadelphia—makes use of much decorative half-timbering, and of a pictorial tower. However, Eyre's abstract rectangles, created with stripping and windows, turn the wall into a thin and
articulated panel. Its delicate scale indicates that there may have been Japanese, as well as Shavian, influences at work in Eyre's design. The interior of
the Newhall House makes use of a variety of spatial effects and stresses the
horizontal ceiling plane. The lower gallery around the hall, which then rises
two stories, should also be noted.[24]

22. Sheldon felt this house to be both "original" and "colonial." *Ibid.*, p. 46.

23. Wilson Eyre was born in 1858 in Florence, Italy, and died in 1944. He went to school
at Newport; Lenoxville, Canada; Woburn, Mass.; and M.I.T. From 1878 to 1881 he worked
with the architect James P. Sims in New York. In 1881 he began practice in Philadelphia,
where his main work was accomplished, although he also erected important buildings in
Louisiana (Newcombe Memorial, New Orleans) and Detroit. He was a member of the A.I.A.
(*Herringshaw's National Library of American Biography; Who's Who*, 1944).

24. Sheldon, *1*, 99–101. The design, says Sheldon, is "modified Flemish." However: "The
rooms around the gallery are a few steps above it, the reason being . . . to make the gallery
lower than it otherwise would have been. . . . Notice also the stair which is three-quarters
closed off from the hall and which "starts straight, turns to the right to a full landing, thence
to the left, and finally lands on the south side of the gallery" (*ibid.*, p. 100). In other words,
movement upstairs is broken and discontinuous; one mounts a few steps at a time. Concerning Eyre's work, it is unfortunate that the scope of this study does not allow a consideration of his city building, which is comparable to the best of that being done in England
at this period by the Queen Anne architects there. See Dudley Habron, "Edward Godwin,"
Architectural Review, 98 (1945), 48–52. Mention should be made of such buildings as the
City Trust Safe Deposit and Surety Company and the Doherty Tailors of 1887, both in

Eyre's Charles A. Potter House, also at Chestnut Hill (Figs. 97, 98), appears
from its entrance front very Queen Anne and Shavian.[25] The lower story is
of brick and the upper not of shingles but of authentic tiles. This expensive
commodity was evidently well within the reach of Chestnut Hill. There is a
Shavian seat under a flat window arch. The whole looks English but fairly
crude. The gables are disorganized and the second story porch at the right
corner is especially awkward. Yet the interior of this house is entirely different. It is one long but subtly varied rectangle of space, with only the kitchen
off the main axis. Each room receives light from at least two opposite sides,
and on the garden front a large covered piazza extends the length of the house
and beyond. The ceilings are fairly low, and the flat, simple moldings over
the doors increase a sense of actual spatial flow from room to room, uniting
the volumes. Since the fenestration is almost continuous and since the door
from the hall opens widely onto the piazza, there is a further sense of spatial
flow to the outside. The porch itself, through a continuation of the main
roof, is united with the main volume of the house, as in the Stevens project.
Eyre's concern with horizontal continuity further extends to his treatment
of the staircase, which might easily break through and rupture the insistent
horizontal. Sheldon notes: "the newel posts of the stairs are carried up to
the ceiling with brackets thrown in between them, the idea being to give an
effect of continuity of design." [26] What happens here is that the movement of
the stairs becomes framed within dominant members which subordinate its
vertical to the continuous ceiling plane. In a sense this is decisively different
from the spatial aesthetic of most of the developed shingle style—which was
one of variety and change of level opposing dramatically rising stairs to open
hall. With Eyre, the stairs are rigidly controlled. They become less a special
feature which cascades "like a mountain torrent" into the hall and more an
element, carefully contained, whose very movement is a foil to set off the
dominant horizontality of the whole space.[27] The trend in Eyre toward a
continuous horizontal which includes the subordination of the stairs must
be considered an important prefiguration of future developments, notably
in the work of Wright. It represents an intensification of the consciousness of
space and a channeling of that consciousness into a study of the continuity
of the dominant horizontal plane low overhead.[28]

Philadelphia. In these Eyre combines calculated asymmetries, which recall Mackintosh,
with a peculiarly fluid ornament related to that of Morris, Richardson, St. Gaudens, White,
and the later Art Nouveau. Moreover, in its interlaces it recalls the ornament of Sullivan
as developed during the same period.

25. Sheldon, *1*, 48–50.
26. *Ibid.*, p. 49.
27. See the first part of n. 24 above.

Eyre's development of continuity in design reached solutions surpassing those of the Potter House. A sketch for a proposed country house at Downington, Pennsylvania (Fig. 99), published in the *American Architect* in 1883, shows an advance in skill.[29] Here the space was again extended horizontally along one axis with a double fireplace between the hall and dining room and the living room fireplace pushed close up to a bay window—a delicate adjustment of rhythms within a unifying continuity of direction. A large piazza again covers the back of the house and extends along the side. The staircase slips up from one side of the hall and appears again to be framed by its newels. The exterior is somewhat more coherent than that of the Potter House, and the dominantly horizontal character of the interior space is better expressed. Again half-timbering appears, as well as a Palladian window, but the continuous strip of casement windows on the second story is expressive of a similar continuity in interior volumes.

Eyre's masterpiece in country house design during this period was the Richard L. Ashurst House, Overbrook, Pennsylvania, *ca.* 1885 (Figs. 100, 101).[30] This house is a culmination of all the tendencies noted in Eyre's work. The plan of the living area extends along one axis and flows out to the sheltered and contained space of a piazza, which is made an integral visual extension of the interior living space itself. Within this there is also a continuity, a discipline of axis again subtly varied by the inglenook of the dining room and the corner bay of the drawing room. The stairs also flow upward very subtly, without disturbing the horizontal serenity of the whole. One enters slightly below the level of the staircase landing, descends three steps to the hall, turns left to mount the stairs, and comes back up three steps, turns left

28. Wright, whose preoccupation with the continuous horizontal ceiling plane is well known, once remarked (September, 1948, when a certain staircase was mentioned as 'beautiful"), "Who ever saw a beautiful staircase?" The principle at work here is the same as in Eyre's, containing, screening, and breaking the flights of his stairs. In Wright's work as well, when stairs appear they are contained, as in the new, small houses; or, as in the earlier houses where economic conditions allowed, they glide to the second level a few steps at a time. Their mission is always to change level without interrupting the horizontal continuities of the space and the consequent expansion of the whole. It should be noted further that Voysey, in the 90's, also tended to screen his stairs, as did Mackintosh. See Thomas Howarth, *Charles Rennie Mackintosh and the Modern Movement* (New York, 1953), pl. 29. [In 1970: On the other hand, plans like that of the Potter House were to inspire a new development in the opposite direction during the second half of the twentieth century, when not their continuity but their free accommodation of different functions, as seen in diagonal wall planes, narrowing stairs, and so on, were directly to influence the beginnings of Robert Venturi's design. Cf. Venturi, *Complexity and Contradiction in Architecture* (New York, 1966), pp. 117–21, and my Figs. 162, 163.]

29. *Am. Arch., 13,* March 10, 1883.

30. Sheldon, *1,* 93–7.

up five more to reach the landing and then turns again out of sight of the hall. The whole complex is contained by the newel posts. Its entire point is to make the rise of the stairs almost imperceptible, a gradual, partially screened flow. The exterior massing of the Ashurst House fully expresses the dominant horizontality of its interior space. The foundations are stone; the first story is shingled, and the projecting second story is of pebble dash plaster, integrally tinted a warm beige and with delicate half-timbering. Indeed the half-timber is so inoffensive here, so flat and gently scaled, that were it not for the occasional curved diagonals which obviously hope to recall medieval diagonal braces, one might believe that Eyre was seeking to express the actual stud skeleton inside. Certainly the wall is treated as a thin skin, constructed with a thin frame and functioning primarily as a shell for interior space. The long strip of casement windows, continuing around the corner, expresses not only the volume of space inside but also the insistent rhythm of the structural stud. The overhang of the second story contains beneath it such a projecting feature as the corner bay window of the drawing room, emphasizing the horizontal spread of the house. The first story is very low, and the overhang, which rides just above one's head, forces the scale. Passing underneath it, as where it projects above the entrance, one is forced into an awareness of its horizontal extension. The casual, easy scale of most of the cottage architecture of the 80's has been intensified. The effect of the building becomes emphatically more insistent. In this way it achieves a powerful subjective reality. It not merely receives the individual but forms him.[31]

That this sense of extended horizontal plane and intensified, "positive" scale evident in Eyre's work becomes later a basic component in the work of Wright does not need extended discussion here.[32] It represents, however

31. Sheldon was well aware of all this (p. 95): "The main gable heavily overhangs the first story, producing very dark shadows. . . . Indeed, the heavy overhangs and the lowness of the structure, together with its length and the number of its gables, are the principal features of all of Mr. Eyre's suburban cottage work." Sheldon, however, ascribes (p. 96) this lowness to a love of Tudor architecture, probably as did Eyre himself: " 'The sweet low level lines of the Tudor house' . . . appeal powerfully to Mr. Eyre's taste. . . . All the main lines of the building, that is to say, the lines that characterize its style, are horizontal." One other feature of the Ashurst House should be mentioned, namely the stone shelf, the top of the actual structural base of the house itself, which runs around the first floor under the windows. "It will be noticed that the object of carrying the stone-work of the outside to the sill-height of the windows, was to form a shelf inside the house in the dining-room, hall, and parlor, which serves the purpose of a ledge all around" (loc. cit.). This device has been used recently by Marcel Breuer, not only in the Geller House, Long Island, 1946, but also in a house at Williamstown, Mass., 1948 (Architectural Record, Feb., 1949).

32. Wright has explained this process: "Believing in no other scale than the human

—as Wright's work later represents in a much more complicated way—the pulling together of the free architecture of the 80's into a stronger and more coherent order. It simplifies, unifies, and intensifies. It reveals, especially in plan and in space, the development of an integrated, disciplined design.

That the ebullient Bruce Price should also have created such free but disciplined plans in the early 80's is perhaps astonishing. One need not be concerned here with his Roosevelt Cottage at Oyster Bay, L.I. (1881–82), a typical and undistinguished shingled cottage, nor with his projected Bay-Window Parlor Car for the Pennsylvania Railroad, 1886. One should perhaps note his excellent and many-windowed Queen Anne city residence for Dr. C. G. Thomas (Fig. 102), 600 Madison Avenue, New York (1885). This house is actually a rather close adaptation of the 16th-century House of Diane de Poitiers, at Rouen. It reveals again the important influences exerted during the early 80's, especially upon city houses, by the so-called François Premier, combining, as this did, medieval skeletal construction with Renaissance detail and the beginnings of Renaissance geometric control.[33]

Price's "Seacroft," near Seabright, New Jersey (built while Price was in partnership with George A. Freeman), is important in the question of an organic spatial discipline.[34] The massing is as loose as that of "The Craigs," but the plan is clear and ordered (Fig. 103). One enters into a stair hall, beyond which, on a cross axis, is the living hall with parlor and dining room. These are surrounded by a piazza, so that in plan one is reminded of Wright's large living areas, on a cross axis to the entrance and opening to a terrace, which appear in such of Wright's early houses as the Hickox House of 1900.[35] One is also reminded of some of Jefferson's plan studies of similar spatial volumes with polygonal ends.[36] The parlor of Seacroft is, in reality, a separate volume, closed off by doors from the living hall, and the resemblances to Wright's work are thus only superficial here. Yet the presence of the cross axis is significant. A similar remote resemblance to the later planning of Wright may be seen in Price's George F. Baker House, also at Seabright, New

---

being I broadened the mass out all I possibly could to bring it down into spaciousness." *Autobiography* (ed. 1943), p. 141.

33. Roosevelt Cottage, Oyster Bay, L.I.: *Am. Arch.*, 11, Jan. 28, 1882; A Bay-Window Parlor Car for the Penna. R.R.: *18,* Aug. 15, 1885; Dr. C. G. Thomas House, 600 Madison Ave., N.Y.: *19,* Mar. 13, 1886. The House of Diane de Poitiers was destroyed during the Second World War. Cf. *Lost Treasures of Europe,* ed. Henry LaFarge (New York, 1946), p. 29, fig. 262.

34. *Am. Arch., 12,* Jan. 6, 1883.

35. Hitchcock, *In the Nature of Materials,* figs. 53, 54.

36. See Fiske Kimball, *Thomas Jefferson, Architect* (Boston, 1916), fig. 108 *bis.*

Jersey (Figs. 104, 105), built a year or two after Seacroft.[37] The dining room, library, and parlor, opening into each other on axis and communicating with a piazza, recall Wright's similar axial unity of living space. At any rate, Price's spatial order in the Baker House is simple, unified, and decisive. The massing also expresses its interior spatial unity better than that of Seacroft. Of red brick below, tiles above, and with a heavy tile roof, the house is a pronouncedly horizontal mass, extended by its porte-cochère. This heavy, solemn house has a kind of "classic"—or even archaic—poise and a monumental gravity. It shares this quality, also, with Wright's later work.[38]

Most advanced of all Price's houses of these years—and probably representing the true high point of his career—are the cottages he began to build in 1885, for Pierre Lorillard's residential development at Tuxedo Park, New York, founded in that year. Because this was a commuting community, intended especially for wealthy, younger couples, the houses were comparatively small.[39] From their compactness of design they derive much of their historical importance: like Wright's later houses, they exploited to the full the possibilities of shingle style open planning and of clear geometric order. Pierre Lorillard's own cottage (Figs. 106, 107), one of the group, has a plan which may owe something of its order to Palladian colonial inspirations.[40] A recessed entrance loggia under a stone arch opens into a central hall with parlor and den on one side and dining room and butler's pantry on the other. The kitchen is downstairs in a basement, as in almost all of these houses. The interior space and the exterior massing, however, are articulated by the

37. Sheldon, *1*, 77–80.

38. Any of Wright's buildings can serve as an example of this. Each element presses down with a specific density of its own. The whole is stable, contained. This is profoundly true even of the two Taliesins, which appear most to ramble. An apprentice of Wright's once remarked (September, 1948) upon the "playfulness" of some of Wright's elements. This is probably incorrect. Wright never "plays," although, especially in his own homes, he may experiment widely with a variety of structural and plastically decorative devices. It is impossible to observe any one of his buildings without feeling its essential gravity. In this, of course, they are quite different from the loose and casual adjustments of many of the shingled cottages of the early 80's. See especially my discussion of Emerson's work of the 80's, Ch. 6, above.

39. The houses here have been referred to as "honeymoon cottages," set up for comparatively simple living, if as always in this period, with servants. This fact has certainly something to do with the spatial eliminations and simplifications which take place in the houses, as well as with the general compactness; but the decisiveness of the order is Price's own. He planned the entire community as well.

40. Sheldon, *2*, 41. Lorillard's whole interest in Tuxedo Park is sociologically important. In 1885 he sold his "Breakers," Newport, by Peabody and Stearns, to Vanderbilt and set about organizing what was intended to be a simpler suburban community.

great fireplace masses which rise on either side of the entrance loggia and by the play of void and solid arising therefrom. Such play of oppositions reminds one of Ledoux.[41] Although the arrangement of elements is perhaps rigidly symmetrical, it is very strong, and in the Lorillard House it is extended by the second story balconies which jut out over the side verandas. In this kind of extension it differs from Ledoux's more sharply differentiated and compartmented forms. Set decisively upon the flat pedestal of its terrace, the house knits vertical masses with horizontal voids in a way which causes the elements to interlock, interpenetrate, and project beyond each other. About the massing of the house there is a sense of being "inside-out," as if interior volumes and exterior spaces also in a way interpenetrated each other. The mixture of stone with brick is perhaps not happy, although necessary in order to articulate the chimneys and the entrance arch. On the whole, the design is clear, coherent, and vibrating with archaic directness.

Similar qualities are found in Price's William Kent House on Tower Hill, Tuxedo Park, another of this group.[42] Here again the clear, abstract shape of the house is set upon the platform of a terrace, this time of stone (Figs. 108, 109). The elements are simple and strong. The dominant form is a powerful gable end, recalling both late medieval town house and Japanese farmhouse prototypes. Indeed, Price seems to have accomplished here the plastic revelation of those architectural archetypes toward which his age had been tending: the massive platform, the precise posts, the solemn gable. Even the half-timbered woodwork is so obviously decorative in intention as to create an abstract pattern of considerable force. The simplicity of the massing is a straightforward expression of the plan. The parlor extends on a cross axis from the hall and dining room; porch, den, and pantry extend behind. There is a simple flow of space in plan from hall to parlor to dining room; and if the various fireplaces were all pulled together into one mass in the center, the plan would be extremely close to that of such houses by Wright as the Ross House or the Ward Willitts House, both of 1902.[43] Once more, aspects of Jefferson's planning are recalled: for example, the crossed axes

41. As discussed by the late Emil Kaufmann in his inspired analysis of Ledoux's design. Many of his comments concerning Ledoux's "revolutionary" classicism might be extended to the similarly inventive "classic" order of Price. See Emil Kaufmann, "Three Revolutionary Architects, Boullée, Ledoux and Lequeu," *Trans. American Philosophical Society*, n.s. *42*, Pt. 3 (1952), 476–547. Also, Kaufmann, *Von Ledoux bis Le Corbusier; Ursprung und Entwicklung der autonome Architektur*, Vienna and Leipzig, 1933.

42. Sheldon, 2, 45.

43. Charles S. Ross House, South Shore Road, Delavan Lake, Wis., 1902. Hitchcock, *In the Nature of Materials*, fig. 78. Ward Willitts House, Highland Park, Ill., 1902, *ibid.*, figs. 73–6.

of space around central fireplace masses in his first plan for Monticello.[44] Again the word "classic" comes to mind, coupled with a sense of archaic forces. The crossing of axes in the Price plan is so decisive, and the shape arrived at thereby is so set as a contained object upon the pedestal of its terrace, that the whole takes on a classic finality, simplicity, and completeness. For all its natural materials and romantic intent, this house is an abstract object placed in a natural setting which it complements but with which it by no means mingles. This quality was also to become characteristic of the work of Wright,[45] and the crossed-axes plan, allowing in space both order and complexity, and in massing both control and variety, thus becomes a primary tool for the amalgamation of invention with order. The Kent House thus marks a kind of climax in the shingle style.

The cottages of Price represent, therefore, a simplification and clear ordering of all the plan and spatial elements of the cottage architecture of the early 80's. The plan of the Travis C. Van Buren House at Tuxedo Park (Fig. 110) may serve as our final illustration of the fact.[46] Again set upon a terrace,

44. See Kimball, fig. 5, and Clay Lancaster, "Jefferson's Architectural Indebtedness to Robert Morris," *Journal of the Society of Architectural Historians, 10* (1951), 3–10, fig. 1. For a sensitive and acute discussion of Jefferson's own personal reliance upon Palladian and classic forms see Karl Lehmann, *Thomas Jefferson, American Humanist,* New York, 1942.

45. Mention has already been made of Wright's practice of setting his houses upon a firm pedestal (Ch. 6, n. 9) and of the contained discipline of his design (n. 38). However much the house evokes, complements, or re-creates its site, it remains decisively itself, always apart, in its geometrical disciplines always asserting itself strongly as a work of man— in close harmony with nature, but not nature itself. A glance at the plan of Taliesin West, for example, can show the classic decision of the plan (Hitchcock, *In the Nature of Materials,* fig. 353). The axes are strong, the energies of the plan are abstract energies strictly ordered. The house can evoke its site closely without becoming "rustic," can spread freely without falling to pieces, precisely because its geometries are abstract, pure, concretely manmade, and its own. This subtle relationship between Wright's houses and the nature which they embrace but do not imitate can perhaps best be grasped in his own phrase as to what a house should be: "Dignified as a tree in the midst of nature but a child of the spirit of man." *Autobiography,* p. 147.

46. Sheldon, 2, 38. Various other buildings by Price at Tuxedo were reproduced by Russell Sturgis, "The Works of Bruce Price," including a Japanese tea pavilion. Before we leave Price it should be noted that he built also on the West Coast during this period, including the W. H. Howard House, San Francisco, California. *Am. Arch., 20,* Dec. 25, 1886. This house is described in Bruce Price, *A Large Country House,* New York, 1887. It should also be noted in this connection that there was much shingle style building in some of the resort areas and fashionable suburbs in the West at this period. The fact, however, lies somewhat outside the range of our investigation into developments taking place at the heart of the style, which was in the East. Another notable example of western work was a hotel at Los Angeles, California, by Frank E. Zerrahn of Boston, drawings for which appeared in the *Am. Arch., 15,* May 3, 1884.

it consists of one large living hall on axis from the entrance and a small dining room and parlor on the cross axis. The space is articulated more economically than in the other cottages by central fireplace masses, a method which Wright was to use. The shapes are varied, but the strong spatial directions, extended by porches, control and harmonize the mass.[47]

Thus by 1885 a real order was growing, not imposed by codified canons but developing creatively from a variety of spatial experiments. Founded upon a sense of materials, space, and creative structural techniques which was essentially inventive and original, the developing classic equilibrium of the cottage architecture had nothing to do with "classicism" itself, in the usual meaning of the word. The order of the inventive architecture toward 1885 had no necessary relationship to Palladian precedent or academic rule. Its own new order, still tentative and capable of growth toward more advanced solutions, had nothing in it necessarily arbitrary or stifling.[48] After 1885, however, the developing order of the free style came in general under the dominance of a different kind of order: imposed, shallow, often substituting antiquarianism for invention and scholarship for experiment. It is not the purpose of this book to discuss the outcome of such imposition in any detail; but in order to make clear the process whereby free cottage architecture came to maturity and was then turned toward a kind of academicism, one must consider the career of the young firm of McKim, Mead, and White to the critical date of 1887.

47. Now, however, Samuel Graybill's doctoral dissertation has turned up Mayan influences on Price's work at Tuxedo. The connection seems to have been made through Pierre Lorillard, Price's client. Lorillard had just financed excavations in the Usumacinta area, and the results had been published in D. Charnay, *Les Anciennes Villes du Nouveau Monde*, Paris, 1885. The relationship between Price's richly textured, mansarded, and platformed cottages and Charnay's renderings of similar Mayan forms seems an obvious one, and it would appear to offer the best explanation for the very special quality of Price's work for Lorillard—never again to be equalled in his career. Cf. Samuel Huiet Graybill, Jr., "Bruce Price, American Architect," unpublished doctoral dissertation, Yale University, June 1957.

48. These characteristics were detected in the architecture of Detroit during this period by B. L. Pickens. He notes what he calls a "post-Victorian" movement toward geometrical simplicity and "compact and interrelated interior spaces." He publishes also a later house by Wilson Eyre, the Freer House, 1890. B. L. Pickens, "Treasure Hunting at Detroit," *Architectural Review, 96* (1944), 169–76.

8. McKim, Mead, and White.
Originality, Order, and
Academic Reaction, 1880–87

In the present consideration of the cottage architecture of McKim, Mead, and White during the early 80's, it will not be possible to discuss all their country houses. Their popularity grew steadily from 1880 on, and by 1885 it more than rivaled that of McKim's and White's master, Richardson. Their production was enormous. It is listed in detail in Moore's biography of McKim.[1] The importance of cottage and country house architecture in the growth of their general popularity can also be seen from Moore's list. In many instances it reveals how a client was first brought to the firm through the alteration of an old, or the building of a new, country house and then went on to order town houses, office buildings, clubs, and so on.[2] As their cottage architecture was important in a business sense it also carried, as with the other architects we have considered, the most lively and original aspects of their design. It is important, therefore, to understand the characteristics and development of their country, suburban, and resort building during this period. Yet these very buildings have for the most part been ignored by their biographers, since in general they have not been considered monumental

1. Moore, *McKim*, appendix 3, pp. 338–48: list of work from 1880 to 1910 inclusive. A peculiarity of Moore's list is that he gives only the terminal date of a commission.

2. Their work for Robert and Ogden Goelet is an excellent example of this. The firm's first work for this family was Robert Goelet's Southside, at Newport, R.I., 1882–83. Then followed New York buildings at 9 West 17th St., 1886; Broadway and 20th Sts., 1887; 5th Ave. and 37th St., 1890; 5th Ave. and 16th St., 1890; The Hotel Imperial, 1891, with two additions, 1894 and 1896; more work at 5th Ave. and 37th St., 1892; 8th Ave. and 135th St., 1897; and last of all, completing the circuit, the family Mausoleum, Woodlawn, N.Y., 1900. In this list all dates are terminal. (Moore, p. 341.)

enough to deserve extended analysis.[3] The existence of this belief is additional evidence of the direction which McKim, Mead, and White's architecture eventually took: toward the monumental and the academic. In the early
80's, however, their cottage architecture was of high quality and originality.
Even then, the trends which led eventually to later academic classicism may
already be detected in it. To McKim, Mead and White was given the largest
opportunity, and what they made of it was of utmost importance for the
future of American architecture.

The first work in the 1880's which should be considered is the Newport
Casino, 1879-81.[4] This building was the first of three important country

3. Moore devotes only half a page to the country houses of this period. His comment
(p. 47) is characteristic: "During these years the firm was employed largely with country
and city houses planned to minister to and also to stimulate the taste of people of stabilized
wealth. . . . The list of clients reads like a social directory—Tiffany, Higginson, Goelet,
Auchincloss, James Gordon Bennett, Coleman, Skinner, Tuckerman, and Fargo, are some
of the names." Charles Baldwin, *Stanford White*, echoes Moore in a description of the
clients, but as is usual with Baldwin he is more intelligently critical than Moore and less
pompous (p. 120): "They went after their share of such business as offered, and secured
more than their share—as a list of their clients will prove. It reads like the social register:
Charles L. Tiffany, James J. Higginson, Robert Goelet." Baldwin, moreover, quoted
(pp. 120-1) the following statement from Lewis Mumford which appeared in the latter's
pamphlet, *Architecture* (1926):

> The great problem of the architect is to mold the essential structural form in such a
> way as to perform all the purpose for which the building exists. It must fit its site,
> harmonize with or stand out from its neighbours, fulfill its own function as a shelter,
> a work-place, or a play-place, and give a special pleasure to every one who passes it
> or enters it. . . . H. H. Richardson, for instance, in the middle of the 'eighties [*sic*],
> had developed a type of cottage, using stained and unstained shingles, with long, steep
> roofs, wide windows, and ample bays, which was admirably suited to the domestic
> needs of the day. The best of Richardson's cottages, and those of the same quality at
> first built by his pupil, White, were fine adaptations to the climate of our Atlantic
> seaboard, and our modern mode of life. They mellowed into the landscape year by
> year, and their greens, yellows, crimsons, blues, and russet browns became as native to
> the land as the goldenrod, asters and sumach. These houses were thoroughly domestic;
> they were modern; they belonged to the scene; they were traditional in their use of
> materials and fresh and vigorous in their working out of new forms. In short, they
> answered satisfactorily all the practical and esthetic problems that could confront an
> architect in the years between 1880 and 1890.

4. Sheldon, *1*, 67-70. Sheldon (p. 68) calls this "an extremely beautiful adaptation of
Early and Modern English." The cost (p. 70) was "about one hundred and twenty-five
thousand dollars, without the grounds." The work was undertaken at the instigation of
James Gordon Bennett, for whom White later built the Herald Building in New York in
the form of the Consiglio at Verona (Moore, pp. 47, 338; Baldwin, pp. 218-20). The New-

clubs done by the firm during this period, the others being the casinos at Short Hills and Narragansett Pier.[5] The Newport Casino is planned to enclose a large open court (Fig. 111). The site on Bellevue Avenue is in the heart of Newport, making it necessary to enclose as a court whatever area was to be used for outdoor entertainment. As such the plan is supremely logical. A main block across the street front contains various shops whose rent assisted in the maintenance of the building. A central entrance passes between the shops to the enclosed court. To the left, in the court, are a cafe and a restaurant, and on the right is a long piazza. The whole is joined at the end by a semicircular sweep of piazza containing a fountain.

One should note that the street front of the building is bilaterally symmetrical (Fig. 112). The piers between the shops, and the arched central entrance, are of fine thin roman brick. Across these piers, corbeled slightly forward over them, rides the long, gabled upper story, with its surface patterned subtly in variously cut shingles. These shingles were stained a deep warm brown. The void of the second story balcony, over which the gable front is hollowed and screened by a Palladian motif, is flanked by the double side gables in an exactly symmetrical balance not only of masses but of solids and voids. It is apparent that this façade was studied in elevation, and while it manipulates a series of changes of planes and of light, it is basically frontal in conception. For all its symmetry and order, the façade is by no means static or academic. Indeed its restricted city site would have made a plastic picturesque massing seem out of scale and restless.[6]

The interior court was under no such restriction. It is treated freely, with the fat, bulging tower above the committee room (Fig. 113) forming a contrasting element with the general horizontal extension of the rest of the building. The surrounding piazzas are handled very lightly (Figs. 114, 115). The skeleton of the construction creates open airy volumes which are shadowed by White's spindle work screens. The differentiation in scale here between the framing members and the grilled panels between them recalls

port Casino is discussed in Downing and Scully, pp. 149–50, but its importance demands that it be mentioned here. Regrettably, it was damaged by a hurricane in 1954.

5. These are also in Sheldon, which indicates the important position these club houses held in the cottage style. They were in a sense the social nucleus around which the private residences may be said to revolve. Short Hills: Sheldon, *1*, 115–18; Narragansett: *1*, 5–7.

6. One is reminded of the exaggerated picturesqueness of the stick style in the early 70's as it attempted to assert itself in rapidly crowding cities. For a building of the 80's, made up of Queen Anne and cottage style elements, which also attempted with disastrous results to assert itself in the city, see the present Knights of Columbus Club, 436 Orange Street, New Haven, Conn. This was originally the Clarence C. Hooker House; architect, if any, unknown. Dana, "Pictorial New Haven," *40*, 19.

Japanese wooden architecture—with the post, the *kamoi*, and the *ramma*—and reveals McKim, Mead, and White's important amalgamation of influences from that source with indigenous American framing habits. Both interweave structural elements—as in the stick style—and so organize them as to cause the interweaving of spaces.[7] The screens at the Casino have been unjustly criticized as complicated and frivolous. The spindle work creates partially transparent lattices through which the light constantly changes. Their effect is like that of some of the 20th-century constructivist experiments with transparent spatial screens and with light.[8] The architecture opens up in a loose arrangement of pierced and articulated elements, around which the space constantly changes and through which the light breaks up, recombines, and creates continually shifting patterns. The spatial volumes also smoothly interpenetrate and flow.

The Casino at Newport is a remarkable building. It combines a sense of order by no means academic with a variety of experiments in picturesque massing and spatial articulation. Moreover, it combines Japanese and American stick-style sensitivities with that sweep of design which is typical of the shingle style.

The Short Hills Casino of 1882–83 (Fig. 116), by McKim, Mead, and White, does not approach the quality of that of Newport. There is a certain confusion in intent here. A desire for picturesque features tends to obscure the real simplicity of the building as a whole. This simple structure has only a large recreation hall and stage and a few subsidiary rooms, but the attempt at decorative complexity considerably confuses the design. The entrance, with its shell motif decoration, pushes awkwardly out beyond the gable. Another example is the fantastic rounded tower with its gabled top all askew. Similarly, the semi-Japanese lattice decoration of the main gable has considerably less point than the spindled screens with space behind them in the Newport building. Yet the Short Hills Casino is not without a certain charm. The interior space is unified and open, the scale is delicate, and the building opposes the frivolous abandon of its tower to the firm brick pedestal upon which it sits. Certainly as a summer clubhouse it is a lighthearted and perhaps appropriately irresponsible pastiche of the picturesque.[9]

7. Japanese influence, as noted earlier, now nears its culmination, with "lattice of lathwork," "open-work fascia," a variety of shingle work, and articulated framing members with open spaces between. *Am. Arch., I* (1876), 26–7, 136: See Ch. 2, n. 4.

8. Cf. Laszlo Moholy-Nagy, *The New Vision*, 1928; 3d ed., New York, 1946. *Idem, Vision in Motion*, New York, 1947.

9. Sheldon (*I*, 116) calls this building "modern English with no traces of Norman and but few of colonial." See n. 4 above.

A much greater building, and one of the finest of the 80's, was the casino at Narragansett Pier (Figs. 117, 118), conceived and begun as early as 1881 but not finished until 1884.[10] Its plan was an admirably sweeping extension along a freely broken axis. The open cafe spans the shore road, and the rest of the building stretched out behind it: kitchens, billiard room, palm room, dressing rooms, and theater. The towers and archway across the road form a Richardsonian mass of stone. Over this mass the roof seems almost to float, supported only by widely spaced stone columns. The continuous open volumes above contrast with the solid geometry of the mass below. Over the whole a high towered roof—covered with rough shingles, sprinkled with dormers, and capped by an open pavilion—served as a foil to the long, continuous horizontal elements which stretched out behind. In this building the shapes vary both in plan and massing; and the materials vary with a sense of the structural qualities of each—the mass of the rough stone, the thin lightness of wood frame covered with shingles. The masses are solid, the voids are clear, the final horizontal extension total and serene. In its way the Narragansett Casino may have been a finer building than that at Newport; and yet it is somehow less characteristic of McKim, Mead, and White. Although the ebulliency peculiar to White is apparent, the whole sense of the structure recalls Richardson.[11]

For a building which exhibits qualities more peculiar to McKim, Mead, and White at their original best one must turn back to the Victor Newcomb House at Elberon, New Jersey (1880–81).[12] The exterior (Fig. 119) is a patchwork of elements which seem derived from various features of the Newport Casino: the gables, bulging towers, and varieties of shingles. Although they are not expressed on the exterior, the main areas of the plan are magnificent (Fig. 120). The handling of the interior space completely develops the openness and flow apparent in plan (Fig. 121). Appleton's publication had this to say: "The general exterior plan [sic] of this beautiful villa is that of the Casino, at Newport, and the architects not having felt themselves cramped for space, the visitor receives a corresponding impression of freedom and roominess, especially in the extraordinarily spacious hall, and experiences a fine pleasure in drawing a long breath." [13] This hall is paneled in vertical

10. Moore's dating method here (p. 344) causes trouble, since he lists only 1884. This is also the only date listed in the *Monograph of the Work of McKim, Mead and White*, New York, 1915. The building, however, was commissioned and begun in 1881.

11. Moore (p. 47) calls it, not without a deprecatory sneer, "quite in the Richardson manner." The extended portion of the structure later burned, and the debris was further dilapidated by the hurricane of 1938. Only the portion by the road still stands.

12. Sheldon, 2, 95.

13. Appleton's *Artistic Homes*, 2, Pt. 1, 1. Appleton includes two plates showing the hall of this house.

wood siding, with battens, up to door height, where a strip molding passes around the wall. This molding is continuous above the doorway openings (Fig. 121). It is a decorative and nonstructural derivation from the Japanese *kamoi,* the bracing beam below which the screens slide in a Japanese interior (Fig. 124). The space between molding and ceiling in the Newcomb House is filled by a latticework screen, derived from the Japanese *ramma;* this creates a continuous flow of space, partially screened, between the hall and the other rooms, as well as a constant sense of scale. The Japanese use of the continuous beam or molding with open work above had been clearly described in the *American Architect* in 1876:

> From the level of the top of the screen to the ceiling is a fixed frame or upper partition; and a slot in the bottom of this receives the upper ends of the screens, which, being slipped into the slot, can be lifted enough to clear the rail at the foot, and allow the lower edges to slip into the groove. . . . Thus at any moment any partition can be taken down, and two or more rooms, or the whole house, be thrown into one large apartment, broken only by the posts which marked the corners of the rooms. Doors and windows, as we use them, there are none. . . . The frames or partition-tops over the screens are plastered in the poorer houses; but in the better are filled with wood carved, often very richly, in open work.[14]

As a concession to American living McKim, Mead, and White eliminate here the movable screens, but they are obviously experimenting with the continuous frame and open work to give an impression of movability and spatial continuity. The windows in their bays reach to the ceiling, and where the molding, perhaps unfortunately slightly arched, passes across the bays, the screens again appear between it and the ceiling. The large and simple fireplace is the same height as the continuous molding, further increasing the sense of scale and of spatial flow through the wide opening beside it. The elegantly rectangular floor pattern, probably derived from the Japanese mat and looking much like 20th-century De Stijl work, also functions to enforce scale and spatial direction. In all this appears again that feeling for flowing, expansive, partially screened spaces which were noted in the piazzas of the Newport Casino. The materials are simple, although the "costly articles of bric-a-brac and vertue" which fill the room may strike, for modern viewers, a surrealist note of unlikelihood and surprise.[15]

14. *Am. Arch., 1* (1876), 26–7. Other works discussing the open work fascia (ramma) and continuous molding or beam (kamoi) began to be published at this time, notably Christopher Dresser, *Japan, Its Architecture, Art and Art Manufactures,* 4th ed., London, 1882. See also Morse, *Japanese Homes,* figs. 121–3, 129.

15. The phrase, "costly articles, etc." is Appleton's (2, Pt. 1, 30). Appleton, like Sheldon,

The architecture itself is straightforward and decisively interwoven. The ceiling overhead, emphasized by the subtly varied exposed timbers—which are crisscrossed in patterns a little like a Japanese mat system—slides visually through from room to room; the continuity of human scale is kept by the molding. The spaces do not merely open widely into each other, they actually penetrate each other; and the whole space thereby expands horizontally with absolute, not relative, continuity. While the total space thus expands, each unit of space continues to keep its own individuality through the passage of molding and screen. Consequently, space is at once integrated and articulated. This spatial concept, representing a creative assimilation of Japanese influences, appears as a basic principle in the work of Wright; indeed it has been erroneously believed that Wright was the first to achieve it in America.[16]

Another structure of similar quality by McKim, Mead, and White is the Cyrus McCormick House, built at Richfield Springs, New York, in 1881–82.[17] This house (Fig. 122) combines the Newport Casino characteristics of frontal, symmetrically conceived order (Newport façade) with spatial articulation and invention (Newport piazzas). The McCormick House encloses an irregular and open plan within one gable of roof, pierced by high chimneys. The upper front is decorated by plaster panels symmetrically disposed around a central window with a high and sinuously curved pediment. The strong, gabled volume of the house is intersected and bitten deeply into by the horizontal voids of overhangs and porches. The horizontal plane of the porch roof repeats in the horizontal overhang which shadows the second story, and both sweep around the corner into octagonal porches which become full pavilions. These turn the corner of the house, intersect the main gabled volume with their open voids, and deepen the composition. The whole rich system is given stability by the striking extended wall, or podium, upon which it rests. This clean, abstract base makes a solid foil, both to the ground below and to the basketry above. Simulated bamboo porch posts are arranged, as on the second story of the corner piazza, so that they appear to penetrate the horizontal

had as a prime motive the flattering of the taste of his patrons. One is reminded that his book was printed in 500 copies only, for its subscribers. See above, Ch. 6, n. 38. Note should be taken of the cane summer chairs in the Newcomb hall, which are lively, sculpturally expressive pieces of 19th-century furniture. One is reminded of the use Le Corbusier made of such a chair in his own apartment, 1933. See *Œuvres, 2,* 144–53. Le Corbusier consciously seeks the surrealist effect.

16. See Hitchcock, *In the Nature of Materials:* Frank Lloyd Wright House, Oak Park, Ill., 1889, pl. 13. Wilson Eyre, a few years after the Newcomb House, was to work toward a somewhat similar horizontal continuity and an articulation of spaces. See Ch. 7, pp. 121–4.

17. Moore, p. 343.

members. These basket-like penetrations in space are further enhanced by the restrained latticework of the porches, which forms elliptical voids at the right end of the porch.

As in the piazzas of the Newport Casino one senses an experiment in the screening of space and the manipulation of light. Once more the delicacy, articulation, and spatial interpenetrations of the McCormick House recall important aspects of 20th-century constructivist experiments. Textural experiment as well, coupled with a genuinely free exuberance, is seen also in the rough plaster panels filled with shells, bits of glass, and assorted debris. These by no means take over the architecture, but they enhance its vitality. If lush, these details are by no means despicable. The critical attitude toward White's ornament should be loosely analogous to that accorded Louis Sullivan's. If White's ornament is perhaps more specifically semi-Japanese and less broadly based upon a total architectural philosophy than was Sullivan's, it is at this period not unarchitectural or antiarchitectural. Its use, as in the spindles and lattice of the screens or the textures of the plaster panels, was, like Sullivan's, truly experimental and related to broad concepts of the definition of surfaces through contrasts of light.

The McCormick House, it must be admitted, is peculiarly McKim, Mead, and White's own. Its lightness of scale and its creative combination of gable front, porch pavilions, and structural and textural vitality form the basis for their best cottage building in the early 80's. For much of this vitality credit must probably be given to Stanford White. The playfulness was his, as was the feeling for screened and interpenetrating spaces and for domestic scale. These elements appear clearly in White's dining room which was added to Kingscote, at Newport, a remodeling done in 1880–81.[18] Here the continuous plate rail of the dining room, approximately six feet, ten inches above the floor, creates a horizontal continuity of positive scale (Fig. 123). It passes across the beautifully detailed glass block walls flanking the fireplace, across the fireplace itself, and knits the space of the room together, in a definition not by planes of wall but by an interwoven basketry of skeletal elements. Here again there is much of the Japanese (Fig. 124) and much of the later Wright. Similarly striking in their interwoven spatial unity are the interiors of the Mrs. Samuel Tilton House, Newport, 1881–82 (Fig. 125).[19] These in-

18. Kingscote, Bowery, Newport. The dining room is purely White's. See Hitchcock, *Rhode Island Architecture*, pl. 63. Kingscote, by Richard Upjohn, was built in 1841. Downing and Scully, pp. 122–4, 138, 150; pls. 160, 161, 200.

19. Moore, p. 346. Other rooms in this house, published in Downing and Scully (pl. 202), are equally distinguished and use delicately scaled details partly colonial, partly Japanese, and wholly proto-Art Nouveau.

teriors at Kingscote and the Tilton House represent the integration of colonial, Queen Anne, Japanese, and stick-style traditions into an intensely scaled,
new, and coherent kind of architectural space.

Of the houses of the firm of McKim, Mead, and White during the next
few years, "Southside," the Robert Goelet House at Newport, 1882–83, is
one of the more important, although its exterior massing at least is not particularly coherent.[20] The later addition of dormers has not improved the
sea side, and the front toward the land is a little heavy and out of scale. Once
again, the entrance front is symmetrical. The color of the shingles is peculiarly
warm, and from the main gable of the sea side they actually do flow to the
roof. White's plaster panels also, especially as seen in summer, when the
shrubbery surrounding the house is luxuriant and in bloom, add an appropriate textural warmth. Significantly, there is little relation between the two
elevations. They might be for different houses.[21] The plan, however, is very
open and spatially inventive (Fig. 127). The high brick fireplace, its breast
covered with paneling, which is again delicately scaled, intersects at second
story level with an open gallery (Fig. 128). The high space of the hall opens
wide to the veranda, and the vertical fireplace pulls the whole space into a
relationship with the volume of the second floor. Movement to the gallery is
by a staircase passing behind it. The turned balusters of the stair and the gallery rails play off against each other as screens in space.[22]

20. Hitchcock, *Rhode Island Architecture,* pl. 61. Sheldon, *1,* 7–10.

21. Sheldon states (pp. 7–8):

> The rear of the house, fronting directly on the ocean, has an immense octagonal bay-
> window opening from the dining-room, continuing up from the second story, and
> terminating in *loggias* in the third story, with an octagonal roof. . . . Much success
> has been obtained by the architects, Messrs. McKim, Mead and White, in giving to
> each elevation attractive and strong traits of its own.

The photograph reproduced by Sheldon gives a better idea of the quality of the sea front
than more recent photographs, made after the additional dormers appeared. There is still
something of the beautiful voiding of the mass by porches and loggias which was so strong
a characteristic of the McCormick design.

22. Sheldon (p. 9) says of the hall:

> the spectator is at once attracted and delighted by the magnitude and beauty of the
> main hall, which is forty-four feet long, thirty feet wide, and twenty-four feet high, and
> the fireplace is large enough for a man to walk into. A gallery, supported on a series
> of columns and open arches, extends around the second story, and the ceiling shows the
> open timber-work. . . . The fireplace is faced up with brick instead of marble, in order
> to show the construction of the chimney.

The Bell House, also of 1882–83 and at Newport, is less spatially ambitious than Southside but perhaps a better house (Figs. 129–31).[23] One enters through a vestibule into a great hall. To the right is a reception room and to the left a study tucked in near the hall fireplace, which is placed in an inglenook. The tremendous fireplace has an extended hearth running from the study wall to the great stairs. Beside the inglenook a post supports a transverse beam. Behind its span the stair well rises. From the stair landing a huge window, flooded in the afternoon by the western sun, lights the hall. Off the central space of the hall, drawing and dining rooms open widely and connect with the piazza through French doors. Thus the interior space is one of continuity through interwoven areas. Varieties of space and light blend together into an ample harmony. The exterior blends similar variety and order. The light shingled mass of the upper stories—the balloon frame sheathed and expressed as closed box—is deeply penetrated by the balancing voids of projecting piazzas. These have a post structure using a variation of the simulated bamboo posts which were seen on the McCormick House.[24]

Appleton (2, Pt. 1, 81–2) states of this open hall that it

> lets in the breezes of the ocean with force enough to make the gas-jets flicker . . . extensive and beautiful balcony effects of the second story . . . the magnitude of the fireplace . . . the visitor . . . can get from the center of the hall, just in front of the fireplace, one of the most extensive views to be found within any private house in this country.

Another beautiful interior by White is the living hall of the J. Coleman Drayton House in Boston, a remodeling. Here again appear balconies, and delicately scaled paneling. The rather oriental and beautifully rectilinear decoration of the fireplace—again the Japanese touch—is also noteworthy. *Ibid.,* p. 1.

23. Hitchcock, *Rhode Island Architecture,* pl. 62. Sheldon, 1, 23–7. Sheldon (p. 23) calls the Bell House "of a modernized colonial style." He devotes two pages (24–5) to an attempt to describe the hall of this house.

> The finish is in oak. . . . Immediately around the fireplace is an extensive space of tiling, and a row of marble seats runs between the staircase and Mr. Bell's room study. . . . Opposite the staircase, eight feet wide, appears an open transom, supported on carved brackets . . . and in front of the staircase a series of doors into the drawing-room can be rolled back, thus making the entrance-opening sixteen feet wide and eight feet high. . . . A beautiful and much-carved screen, with panels of wood, separates the staircase from the fireplace, while over the fireplace the ceiling is lowered somewhat, being eight feet four inches, instead of ten feet and a half, as in the main hall, in order to give a comfortable cozy look to the recess.

Here is another of White's most successful interiors.

24. Hitchcock (*Rhode Island,* pl. 62) states: "The delicacy of detail of White's best early

The Bell and the McCormick Houses are certainly masterpieces of the shingle style, as are the interiors of Kingscote and the Tilton House. All are touched by the specific individuality of McKim, Mead, and White during the early 80's. A much less distinguished work, but one which indicates a good, general level of design, is the Samuel Colman House at Newport, 1883.[25] Its plan is less imaginatively free than that of the Bell House, and the axial juxtaposition of library, dining room, and smoking room is slightly stiff, although indicative of an attempt toward spatial order (Figs. 132, 133). The interior space has the advantage of White's delicate scale and real talent in decorative design, but the space as a whole tends to boxiness. The exterior massing shows a fairly coherent adjustment of the voids of verandas and the shingles of walls under one gambrel roof.

The Colman House may be taken to represent a norm in McKim, Mead, and White's free design during this period. It is neither a masterpiece nor a conspicuous failure. Nevertheless, the firm by this time was a large and busy office and it could hardly be expected that all their designs should attain even to this norm.[26] If disciplined freedom formed their best houses, in several

work is well illustrated by the bamboo-like porch columns." One should also note that these columns closely resemble those drawn by Viollet-le-Duc for his Chinese house (Fat Fau's house) in the first part of his "Habitations of Man in All Ages," published in *Am. Arch., 1* (1876), 68–70. See above, Ch. 3, n. 2.

25. Sheldon, *1*, 87–92. He states (p. 87):

> Mr. Samuel Colman, the landscape painter, is one of the few artists in this country who has been able to express his ideas of beauty in a home; and the old colonial villa which he built a few years ago in Newport is as notable a structure of the kind as can be found anywhere, being both externally and internally a distinct contribution to the new Renaissance of American architecture.

Concerning the colonial nature of this house, Appleton (2, Pt. 1, 71) makes a statement more significant concerning the nature of the relationship of McKim, Mead, and White's general design of this period, the colonial style, and client taste: "The general style of architecture is colonial, in harmony with the spirit of the old residences of the place, although Mr. Colman, perhaps, would have preferred the effect of an old English house; but the architects . . . have preserved their independence in elaborating the scheme, greatly modifying the pure colonial style."

26. Moore, of course, depicts the office as a paradise of high ideal and noble effort. Nevertheless, between the lines a sense of the truth emerges, namely that the commissions were numerous, the draughtsmen many, and in general all the problems of the modern big business architectural office were pulling constantly at the design. Moore states: "Two features marked the office of McKim, Mead, and White: first, the struggle to obtain perfection; and, second, the training of younger men, not so much in technical skill as in the underlying principles of architecture." Chapter 6, "The Quest of Beauty in the Eighteen Eighties," p. 55. It becomes apparent that in this typical welter of practice the real driving

houses the two qualities were apparently unable to work together toward a coherent solution. Examples of this are the Cresson and Metcalfe Houses of 1883–84, the first at Narragansett Pier and the second at Buffalo.[27]

The plan of the Cresson House (Figs. 134, 135) is fairly open but mediocre. Yet it shows, like the Colman House, a step toward axial symmetry in plan which is not without significance. The massing of the house is a fantastic combination of an absurdly high gable with peculiar dormers of which the conical roofs are pulled up into spikes. The twisted posts of the loggia in the gable face are unusually coarse for the period. The Metcalfe House is somewhat less inspired (Figs. 136, 137). The interior space is tight: broken up and dark. The exterior reveals a jangled combination of shingles, tiles, brick, and stone, all oozing jaggedly into each other. The circular opening in the lattice work of the porch is a burlesque of the ellipses of the McCormick House, and in the change of shape it loses point and vitality.

In their free design, therefore, the popular young firm sometimes created, as in the Metcalfe and Cresson Houses, works which were often well below the general level of design of the period. Since, however, the commissions came in rapidly and with that urgency which comes from rich clients, there can never have been time to study each project in adequate detail or with the necessary unity of attention.[28] The firm's best brand of disciplined but picturesque design must have put a continual tax upon powers of invention and integration. Each house had to be an individual structure, studied in its environment, worked out with maximum unity within the freedom of the method itself. In a large office with three designing partners and numerous assistants, among whose number was the talented but difficult Joseph Morrill Wells,[29] this can only have been a harried process. Under such circumstances

---

pressure could not be "the struggle to attain perfection" but the necessity to attain a formula. This was to become the critical weakness of the big office, now typical of American architectural practice. Hitchcock (*Richardson*, pp. 286–9) discusses the same characteristic in Richardson's office: "Only a few architects in America, all cranks, have known how to protect their artistic integrity." The reference implicit here to Wright's methods of self-protection is obvious but important. If the move toward academicism in the later 80's was tied up with architectural practice as a big business—which it certainly was—then Wright's constant rejection of all that and his insistence upon the creation of his own milieux fall, like many of his other often peculiar characteristics, into a coherent and important pattern of continuing architectural life. This is further discussed in the Conclusion below, Ch. 9.

27. Metcalfe House, Buffalo: Sheldon, 2, 95; Cresson House, Narragansett Pier: *ibid.*, p. 179.

28. One is referred again to Moore's list, which speaks for itself. See also n. 26 above.

29. See n. 46 below.

it would not have been surprising if the firm had occasionally wished for some formula of design whereby a general level of quality could be presumably maintained without the continual tensions and hazards associated with free picturesque design. Thus, by about 1884, certain more overt eclecticisms began to appear in the work of the firm.

A house such as that for Charles J. Osborn at Mamaroneck, New York, 1884–85, is really a large chateau (Figs. 138, 139).[30] Although the space of its two-storied entrance hall, entered from the drive piercing the house, is magnificent, there is too much of it and it is rather grandiloquent. Even more than in the Goelet hall, the great volume is not only a spatial center but also a baronial evocation. For all its occasionally beautiful handling of materials and their intersections with each other, the house as a whole is representational.[31] The exaggeratedly conical roofs of its stone towers are meant to recall Normandy, and the client is meant to feel himself a baron.[32] For all this the house is sensitively adjusted to its site. The rough stone of its towers opposes the lithic masses of the shore. The void of its piazza pushes out above the rocks of the point. Nevertheless the powers of its mimicry tend somewhat to supersede its purely formal power.

That such representationalism on the part of the firm was not confined to the Osborn House can be seen by a consideration of the Charles T. Cook

30. Sheldon, *1*, 1–5. He states (p. 1): "Mr. Osborn transformed the appearance of the entire region by constructing what might be called an immense modern feudal castle."

31. Other examples of this moment in McKim, Mead, and White's design are to be seen in Newport, R.I., as in the Glover House and Gordon King House, both 1887–88. See Downing and Scully, p. 157 and pl. 214.

32. Nevertheless, the interior space of this house was certainly magnificent:

the main hall . . . has two stories, and is of unusual size, being twenty-five by thirty-one feet long, and twenty-five feet high. Very important is the mantel-piece, two stories high, the fireplace so large that you could almost drive a horse in, and the single flue enormous. The dimensions of the fire-opening are—width six feet; height, six feet; depth, two feet four. . . . To the left of the fireplace a wide seat, with casement-windows opening out on the Sound, and near it an ornamental niche, constitutes a striking feature.

Sheldon, *1*, 4. It should be noted further that high brick fireplaces such as those in the Goelet and Osborn Houses—which owe their ultimate inspiration to the medieval fireplaces reproduced by Viollet-le-Duc in his *Dictionnaire raisonné* and to those which appeared in the fireplace studies carried on by the *American Architect* in the early 80's (See above and p. 64)—remain also a feature of Wright's work, becoming even more numerous in later years. Examples are those in the Willey House, 1934, and the Manson House, 1941. See *Architectural Forum*, Jan., 1938, for Willey House and *In the Nature of Materials*, fig. 400, for Manson House.

House, at Elberon, New Jersey, 1885 (Figs. 140, 141).[33] Sheldon, after quoting Holly's remarks on the Queen Anne in 1878, says that this style is now
"practically obsolete," and that the Cook House is "of a modified Norman
style, with colonial features." [34] Sheldon speaks here more truly than he
knows, since in the Cook House much of the originality of the free cottage
style has indeed become "obsolete." The plan is still free, with a large and
well-lighted hall, but there is somewhat less open flow to the other rooms.
More significantly, the house, built entirely of wood frame covered with
shingles, less immediately expresses its flexible wooden structure than it
flaunts some peculiarly Norman features. The high conical roofs of the projecting bays, for example, sacrifice that expressive continuity of roof flow, so
characteristic of the shingle style, in order to stand forth decisively as Norman
towers. As the towers become evocative rather than technically expressive
elements, the whole house sacrifices the continuous surface, expressive of
interior volumes, in order to stiffen and make angular all its changes of plane.
This angularity is arbitrarily arrived at. It is not controlled by large spatial
directions. Consequently, the walls tend to break up into panels, pasted over,
as above the dining-room window, with "colonial features." This is not to
say that the Cook House is totally inexpressive of interior volumes or of
spatial order in general, but it does represent a step in that direction. It also
signifies a step away from creative technique and original expression toward
representation and eclecticism.

McKim's long-standing antiquarian interest in colonial architecture, identified—as already noted—with 18th-century semi-Palladian design, became by
the mid 80's an even more important factor in the work of the firm.[35] One
should recall his Moses Taylor House of 1876–77 at Elberon (Fig. 26). As evidence of this the firm produced, in 1883–84, a house in Lenox, Massachusetts,
which was recognizably colonial in all its exterior surface and details, if not
in plan and interior volumes. This was the "Homestead" (Figs. 142, 143), a
residence for the Misses Appleton. (McKim was to marry Julia Appleton in
1885.) [36] Considering his intimate relation to the family, it is reasonable to
suppose that McKim himself was largely responsible for the design of the
house, although the ornamental frieze under the roof was certainly White's.

33. Sheldon, *1*, 57–60.

34. *Ibid.*, p. 58.

35. McKim's restoration work in Newport in the early and middle 70's will be remembered, as well as his other work "among the antiquities" at that time, referred to earlier. See
Ch. 2, n. 17.

36. Sheldon, *1*, 61–5. Julia Appleton, McKim's second wife, died in 1887 after only a
year and a half of married life. Moore, pp. 51–4.

The fact that the house was decorated with old mantels and woodwork taken from authentic 18th-century houses, suggests that McKim was intent on building a house specifically antiquarian, if not rigidly academic, in design.[37] Such an antiquarian intention might identify the Homestead as a partial reversion from the original synthesis achieved by the architects of the early 80's.[38] In purely formal terms the rejection of shingles has the effect of turning the walls into painted panels, decorated like stage flats with richly ornamental but cardboard-like Renaissance motifs. The shingles disappear, but the old mid-century sense of the skeletonized wall is not reasserted. In these developments the scale changes. It loses the direct relationship to structural unit of the stick style and the intense adjustment to human height of the shingle style. It assumes instead the more abstract and elegant proportional relationships of a Renaissance sensibility. Each wall plane becomes an elegantly abstract two-dimensional panel upon which motifs may be applied: the large Georgian window, the Ionic portico, the semi-Renaissance frieze.[39] Yet the Homestead is by

37. Sheldon was wildly enthusiastic over this house: "Undoubtedly the private residence in Lenox, Massachusetts, which of late has caused most discussion and awakened greatest interest is that of Miss Julia Appleton." Interest would seem to have been twofold, first in regard to the partial encirclement of the elm tree and secondly because of the overtly colonial nature of the house: "There are only two stories, and the sides are clapboarded instead of shingled, while the general treatment is unquestionably Old Colonial with not the faintest vestige of Queen Anne or Early English. . . . The color of the exterior is a creamy brown" (p. 61). There are many bits from old houses used in the Appleton House, as in the small sitting room, where there is "an old Colonial mantel, which was found in an out-of-the-way place and transferred bodily to this bright apartment, chiefly because its moldings are fine and delicate—like those of most of the Old Colonial work" (p. 65). It should be noted that the delicacy of White's scale undoubtedly derived in part from his creative vision of the qualities of Georgian work. However, as here where a mantel not White's but authentically 18th-century is used, a step is taken backward from the original creativity of White toward a more antiquarian and academic position. Sheldon, who had not yet seen the H. A. C. Taylor House at Newport when he wrote in 1886 of the Appleton House, says (p. 65): "Miss Appleton's house is doubtless the most important example of the Old Colonial revival in the new American Renaissance of Architecture."

38. See especially the final discussion of the general attitude toward colonial in 1883—as something capable of creative inspiration but not to be copied (Above, Ch. 4, *passim*). McKim in the Appleton House certainly turned away from the influence of White—which in its own painterly way had been responsible for much of the original experiment in the firm's cottages of the early 80's—to his own always more antiquarian and academic tendencies. See n. 35 above. Again it will be remembered that the Moses Taylor House at Elberon, done by McKim alone in 1877, had, significantly enough, features of colonialism in common with the Appleton House. See Hitchcock, "Frank Lloyd Wright and the 'Academic Tradition,'" p. 51.

39. Hitchcock (*ibid.*, p. 51) calls this of "a peculiar hybrid 'Queen-Anne-Adam' character."

no means an academic house. Its plan is an organization of richly knit diagonals, strongly and unconventionally changing direction in order partially to
enclose an entrance court around a large elm tree. Its relation to the site is
worked out with extreme sensitivity. The strong breaking of its axes in order
to conform to—and by their abstract decisiveness to enhance—the nature of
its site reminds one of later plans by Wright.[40]

Consequently, if the Homestead tends toward a classicistic and antiquarian
formula of design, it by no means attains one. It remains an original house
with these primary and very positive characteristics: a new kind of axially
broken and strongly ordered plan, space, and massing, and a tendency to
lose at once the scale and the easy continuity of most of the cottage style.
These characteristics are important because they mark a general shift in
sensitivity. They all reappear strongly in McKim, Mead, and White's "Wave
Crest" at Far Rockaway, Long Island, built for John Cowdin around 1885
(Figs. 144, 145).[41]

The plan of the Cowdin House is a more developed but less sensitively handled organization of diagonal axes than is that of the Appleton House. Plan
directions are translated into a strong organization of diagonally interwoven
spatial areas. As the spaces interlock, strictly controlled by a directional geometry, one is forcibly reminded of Wright's much later hexagonal organiza-
tions. Moreover, the Cowdin House continues neither the clapboards nor most
of the Renaissance detail of the Appleton House. It does use an Ionic entrance
porch, and, perhaps because of proportions desired in this porch—although it
does seem tacked on—the stone first story appears too high and the shingled
upper story too squeezed. An over-all stiffness and rigidity mark the massing.
The scale is heavier than was usual in the shingle style. The house becomes
more stolid, static, and heavy-handed. The walls, while still shingled, are more
clearly planar, like the later walls of Wright. An important shift in sensitivity
has taken place, and the integral discipline and order achieved by Stevens,
Eyre, and Price is, in the Cowdin House, even more fully developed by Mc-
Kim, Mead, and White. The solutions of the Cowdin House also became a
kind of type for much later building. For instance, the Hayes Q. Trowbridge
House at 100 Edgehill Terrace, New Haven, Connecticut, of 1908, is a typical
case of diagonally axial planning around an entrance court, with strict ordering and heavier scale.[42] The type reminds one not so much of work done later

40. See especially the Paul R. Hanna House, Palo Alto, Cal., 1937. Hitchcock, *In the
Nature of Materials,* figs. 347, 348, 351. See also Ch. 7, n. 45.

41. Sheldon, 2, 123.

42. Dana, *44,* 81.

by Wright himself as of many of the houses designed by other members of the
Second Chicago School, such as Purcell and Elmslie, and Walter Burley
Griffin.[43]

This double movement—on the one hand toward disciplined order, on the
other hand toward representational eclecticism—reached by 1885 a kind of
synthesis in McKim, Mead, and White's design, a synthesis which was to be
partly creative and partly academic and which was eventually to find its
vocabulary in Renaissance forms. It has been shown that the Appleton
House, begun in 1883, while partially antiquarian in intention was by no
means academic and had no academic progeny. Indeed, its effect, as in the
Cowdin House, was toward creative spatial control and clear planes of
wall.[44] Yet in the same year as the Appleton House a building appeared which
was strictly academic in intention: the Villard Houses on Madison Avenue,
New York, 1883.

It is well known how Stanford White, having enjoyed a great success with
his semi-Queen Anne and semimedieval Tiffany House, in construction in
1883, had also drawn up the plans and elevations for the Villard Houses,
using Richardsonian rock-faced masonry.[45] White was then called out of town

43. The note on the Trowbridge House which appeared in the *New Haven Saturday
Chronicle,* May 24, 1913, is perhaps interesting as revealing how confused the whole process
which had formulated this architecture in the 80's had become by 1913, although we may
observe elements of truth in it. "While the style has much of the Elizabethan feeling it has
been so freely treated as to give it a very marked character and individuality of its own." A
further point in connection with this house—and its mirroring as a general phenomenon of
the freer architecture, a loss of scale through too great a height of the ground story—is again
the fact that Wright, working through the early 20th century in his Prairie Houses, was constantly concerned with keeping the ceilings low, the scale down. Here again is a comprehensible Wrightian reaction against a specific loss of design sense in his own time. At the
same time he mirrors the general development in a greater heaviness of elements, a turn away
from delicacy, as seen in the Trowbridge House or the Cowdin House and in any of Wright's
houses. Wright's followers often lost that scale which Wright usually maintained. See the
Conclusion below, Ch. 9.

44. Only the colonial details exercised a confusing influence. The Georgian abstract
panels of decorated wall and the academic entrance and window motifs tended to throw
off the scale.

45. It should be mentioned that the interiors in an apartment which was done by Lewis
C. Tiffany for himself—on East 26th Street, *not* the Tiffany House by White, which was on
Madison Avenue at 72nd Street—are extraordinarily interesting. Delicate in scale, they
have at once a vaguely eclectic oriental feeling, as well as a certain affinity with Japanese
prints. The light bookcase over the mantel in the library recalls considerably later Art
Nouveau work in England, such as that by Voysey, Mackintosh, and Baillie Scott, as well
as such Viennese Art Nouveau interiors as those by Hoffmann. Appleton (*1*, Pt. 1), pls. 1–6.
For Mackintosh see Howarth, *passim.* For Voysey and Hoffmann see Nikolaus Pevsner,

on a trip to New Mexico, and the project was turned over to Joseph Morrill
Wells for completion.[46] Wells was an extraordinarily gifted draughtsman, almost a designing partner in the office. Indeed, he was eventually offered a
position as a member of the firm but refused it.[47] His personality has been
discussed at length by Moore and Baldwin, and among the encomiums certain salient facts appear. He was a Bostonian and a descendant of Samuel
Adams. Although of this distinguished family, he was in reduced circumstances and had never gone to college. He was difficult to deal with, sometimes biting in speech. It is quite clear that he inspired his employers and his
friends with an affection not unmixed with terror. He was that kind of dedicated and yet somehow pathetic personality who establishes moral ascend-
ancy over his more relaxed associates and who makes them ashamed of their
urbanity, relaxation, and success.[48] It is perhaps inevitable that such a man,
born as it were to a kind of privilege but never granted it, should have been
enamored of the abstract elegance of Renaissance architecture in its more
coldly correct and nobly ordered phases. When he took over the Villard
commission he exacted permission to retain only the plan and to treat the
exterior in a manner based upon the "High Renaissance palaces of Rome." [49]
Although his intention to use a light-colored stone was thwarted by Villard,
the houses otherwise stand as Wells designed them (Fig. 146). Their exterior
details, especially around the windows, copy as closely as possible those of the
Cancelleria, believed at that time to have been the work of Bramante.[50] The

---

Pioneers of the Modern Movement, New York, 1937. For Baillie Scott see *Architectural
Review, 98* (1945), lv–lvi. Additional material on Baillie Scott and Hoffmann is also to be
found in C. Howard Walker, "L'Art Nouveau," Boston *Architectural Review, 11* (1904),
13–20. Lewis C. Tiffany, in his interior decoration as well as in his glass and metal work,
consequently emerges as an extraordinarily important personality in the creation of Art
Nouveau.

46. Moore, pp. 47–8. Wells had joined the firm earlier than Stanford White, and Hitchcock thinks that he received influences from Russell Sturgis and George Fletcher Babb. It
is also apparent that after his death in 1889 the quality of the firm's work may be felt to
have declined considerably. Hitchcock, *Richardson,* pp. 296–7.

47. The story is that he said he would not "sign his name to so much damned bad work."
Baldwin, p. 359.

48. This becomes quite clear from the tone of Mead's comments concerning Wells
(Moore, p. 42) as well as from Baldwin's biographical anecdotes, pp. 357–68. The portrait
of Wells which Baldwin reproduces—one painted in two hours by Wells' friend, Thomas
Dewing—is strangely heartbreaking.

49. Baldwin, p. 358. Hitchcock, *Richardson,* p. 297.

50. This is not without significance, since it is improbable that at this moment Wells
would have based a design—or McKim accepted one—upon a monument believed to have
been by a lesser man. It is perhaps not without point that McKim was regarded as the

Villard Houses are strong, controlled geometric cubes in the best Renaissance manner. This is their positive aspect. At the same time they were consciously and pointedly unoriginal, and they represented the apotheosis of the "adapted" over the invented, of archaeological exactitude over intrinsic growth. More than this, in their design method they were book architecture: flat, two-dimensional, antiplastic—essentially academic paper work.[51] Yet as urban architecture they have to the most intense degree those qualities which Wells intended them to have: a monumental calm, a bitter dignity. Solemn, withdrawn, and proud, they represented the tragic refuge of Joseph Morrill Wells; and they expressed the hard core of his integrity as he wished to believe it to be. They were his personal archetype of order.

It will not be possible here to trace the growth of a Renaissance or semi-classic type of design in the general work of McKim, Mead, and White and through them in American architecture as a whole.[52] Notice should be taken, though, of the Commodore William Edgar House at Newport, 1885–86 (Figs. 147, 148), where a stricter Georgian classicism began to invade their cottage architecture itself.[53] Unlike the Appleton House, in which the plan was still open and dynamic and where the new axial discipline was a supple and creative one, the Edgar House presents an interior space beginning to break up into boxes, losing something of flow while it searches for positive order. The central hall is arbitrarily tight in shape, and the subsidiary elements are quite symmetrically arranged. In both plan and elevation asymmetrical elements are introduced. Although these still freely express the varying functions

"Bramante" of the firm. (White was looked upon as the Benvenuto Cellini). Moore, p. 57. That the Cancelleria, 1485–98, is now known almost definitely not to have been done by Bramante turns the whole business into one of those barbed jokes which history occasionally produces.

51. Wells' source for the Villard Houses was the hard line engraving of the French academician Letarouilly, pupil of Percier, whose *Édifices de Rome moderne* had appeared in three Atlas volumes, Paris, 1840, 1848, 1857. See Hitchcock, "Frank Lloyd Wright and the 'Academic Tradition,'" pp. 52–3.

52. This has been done by Hitchcock in the article cited above, n. 51. If McKim, Mead, and White's own view of their rise is desired, one is again referred to Moore, Baldwin, and the monograph of 1915. Mention should be made of their house at 21 East 30th Street, New York, which is classic in feeling without being academic or unoriginal and which Hitchcock has compared to Wright's Charnley House of 1892. *Ibid.*, pl. 16. A more integral and structurally inclusive movement toward volumetric clarity and urban dignity would seem to be taking place in American architecture at the present time, in the work of Mies Van der Rohe, Philip Johnson, Louis I. Kahn, and others. See my "Archetype and Order in Recent American Architecture," *Art in America* (December, 1954), pp. 250–61.

53. Sheldon, 2, 28; Downing and Scully, pp. 156–7; pl. 212.

of the different areas, they appear forced and out of place in relation to the whole. The varying shapes of the projecting bays of the exterior, as well as the variety of window sizes and placement, are examples in point. They are not integrated elements in a free organism but awkward elements in a rigid composition. The void of the porch over the drawing room is a welcome foil to the smooth solid brick of the service wing, but nothing unites the whole, and the scale again is uncertain. The point which may be grasped from this house is that a rigid, volumetrically fixed method was beginning to dominate McKim, Mead, and White's design.

The fine, thin Roman brick of the Edgar House perhaps excludes it from the general class of house designs in wood which had long been predominant in America.[54] Nevertheless, the classicizing tendencies apparent in the Edgar House came to an early and full fruition in the H. A. C. Taylor House (Figs. 149, 150), a wood frame structure built at Newport in 1885–86.[55] (The Taylor House was torn down in 1952, an unhappy end for one of the most important and distinguished monuments in the history of American architecture.) Here for the first time the symmetrical and abstract order apparent upon the exterior of the Villard Houses and of some importance in the Edgar House took full charge of both plan and elevation. Moreover, this order was purposely antiquarian. It allowed for the first time an intentionally Palladian-colonial system to take over the plan, which closely resembles such 18th-century plans with transverse halls as that of the Chase House, Annapolis, 1769–71.[56] The principle of plan order, at a decisive moment in the American development, thus became associated with 18th-century adaptation.

There was an axial central hall in the Taylor House, with two rooms on either side. The service wing occupied an ell symmetrically disposed on a cross axis. Although the doors from the rooms of the living area into the hall slid into the wall and were fairly wide, and although there was a narrow com-

54. Roman brick, introduced into America by McKim, Mead, and White, was much used by Wright in his early houses. Note especially the Winslow House of 1893. *In the Nature of Materials*, pls. 25, 27, 28. In this house, as in others by Wright, the influence of the Edgar House is very apparent. Brick was also used to form an absolutely smooth and unbroken façade in Wright's Morris Store, San Francisco, California, 1948.

55. Sheldon, 2, pp. 9–11: "Mr. Taylor has the benefit of a very simple straightforward, and commodious design; and the covering of clapboards, without shingles, except on the roof, is a novelty, in the presence of so many examples of the modern shingled treatment" (p. 9). Sheldon (p. 10) notes how all the interior finishing is "in the Old Colonial style." Significantly enough, as an unconscious comment upon the interior space he gives no description of vistas or of movement, as he had in the Goelet House, for instance, but instead describes the first floor methodically and briefly, room by room. See also Downing and Scully, pp. 156–8; pl. 213.

56. Cf. Kimball, *Domestic Architecture*, fig. 46.

municating door between library and parlor, each room was nevertheless a separate cube of space, rectilinear, and clear in its own volume. Certainly a principle of order in plan was clearly stated in the Taylor House, and this principle was to have a positive effect upon later invention, as in the work of Wright. Yet the academic precedent upon which McKim, Mead, and White here based that order was to exert a dominant effect upon most later domestic design.[57]

The exterior of the Taylor House, like American 18th-century architecture itself, imitated semi-Palladian forms in wood. The intrinsically wooden character of the American cottage development since the 1840's now tended to disappear. The thin walls became painted stage flats, partly screened by elegantly detailed, columned porches. Again there was a certain rather piquant ambiguity in scale, as the relationship of entrance door to window above it makes amply clear. The walls now expressed neither continuity of surface, as in the shingle style, nor the skeleton as in the stick style. Instead they were related to each other as slightly differentiated planes in advance or recess. Their color—light yellow, trimmed with white—broke with the darker, richer tones of the cottage development.[58]

Obviously the Taylor House had many positive qualities. It was a calm, quiet, abstract form. The order of a clear spatial geometry was substituted for the often tumultuous spatial effects of shingle architecture. This order, coming directly from the Taylor House, was to be of profound importance in the formation of Frank Lloyd Wright's design.[59] The restfulness of the Taylor House must have seemed to many like balm to the spirit after the frequent "excesses" of the shingle style.[60] It seemed to create a clear intellectual and psychological repose. Yet this might possibly be interpreted as partly a lotus eater's peace, based not merely upon simple form but also upon

57. A different kind of order in the middle 80's has been shown in the work of Richardson, Stevens, Eyre, and Price. The order of the Taylor House could in other hands serve to enhance and reinforce design discipline, unrelated to academicism of approach. Reference may be made to Wright's Blossom House, 1892. Hitchcock, *In the Nature of Materials*, pls. 19, 20. The exterior of this house is so similar to that of the H. A. C. Taylor House that it can only have been adapted from it. Certainly the Taylor House was available to Wright, in Sheldon. Hitchcock, "Frank Lloyd Wright and the 'Academic Tradition,'" p. 60. This temporary experiment seems to illustrate how Wright absorbed the discipline inherent in the whole development toward "classic" order of the middle 80's but soon renounced the academicism. Unlike the architects who became permanent antiquarians, Wright was fortified, not destroyed, by the movement toward order of his time.

58. See my discussion of Downing's color, "Romantic Rationalism," pp. 126–7.

59. See n. 57 above.

60. This is undoubtedly why Sheldon (2, 9, 11) felt moved to call the Taylor House "simple, straightforward" and "not showy." See n. 55 above.

antiquarian expedient. The Taylor House must therefore be understood as having had two diverging effects upon later development: one toward order *per se,* the other toward academicism and eclecticism. In this it relates not so much to the early colonial revival as it does to such consciously academic adaptations as the Villard Houses. To call its Palladian colonialism American, as its advocates later did, is probably to apply a misnomer so far as intrinsically American design is concerned. Its "Georgian" forms were to become primarily a suitable vehicle for the kind of academic work which was shortly to be disseminated throughout America by the Beaux-Arts schools. Thus, its brand of "colonial" became what might be called an American Beaux-Arts vernacular, a kind of design where the principles of the école might be applied to a general run of American domestic building and where correctness and antiquarianism could substitute a suburban prestige for the inventions of an earlier day.[61]

Probably most serious of all was the fact that the Taylor House and its descendants made antiquarianism respectable and originality suspect. To this can be linked also a general loss of design principle, both in large things and small. One has arrived at the curious world of Joy Wheeler Dow. Eighteen years later, for example, Dow criticized the Taylor House because it was not correctly colonial enough, condemning especially the large glass areas and the ornament, and stating:

> Such modern obtrusion would be relegated to their draughtsman who has set up in business for himself, and to whom they might direct the poorer-class client seeking a low-priced plan. Experience alone has taught these architects that the closer the adaptation up to a certain point, the greater the success. I do not believe that they ever think of expressing history in executing their designs. Certainly, they do not look upon their

61. The kind of decay in sensitivity which this house and its innumerable descendants brought to American architecture can be seen at its nadir in the average "Builder's Colonial" of the present day. A cube of space is divided arbitrarily into separate spaces. The question involves not merely economics but a loss of awareness of space and movement. Nor is order as such long retained; pure expediencies become the dominant factor in design. See "The Cape Cod Cottage—A Design Analysis," Pt. 1: *Architectural Forum,* Feb., 1949; Pt. 2: Mar., 1949. The usually white paint must also be traced back to this monument, which demonstrates the renunciation of the rich colors of the free style. The loss of sensibility to the expressive possibilities of materials in general can be seen perhaps nowhere more clearly than in the fact that today, when relief is desired from the colonial box, the builder turns to quaint "ranch house" types which demonstrate none of that capacity to deal successfully with asymmetrical forms which was to be found in the shingled work of the 80's. The ability to think in terms of conceived form rather than of advertised fashion seems weak among builders and clients alike.

profession as eleemosynary to make the world a more beautiful world, a kindlier world, a happier world for mankind generally. The chances are they are still figuring very closely with American cunning and expediency for commercial martinets, whose favor means the largest commissions.[62]

Dow also referred to earlier American invention in domestic architecture as "The Reign of Terror." [63] He himself stated very clearly the attitudes of the eclectic architects of the early 20th century. For example:

> Invention belongs to science. Happily, in the field of art, everything was planted, arranged and cultivated for us ages ago, so that we have only to wander as children, in an enchanted garden that our days are not half long enough to encompass.[64]

For the earnest idealisms of an earlier generation Dow thus substitutes an unpleasant mixture of cynicism and sentimentality. Insisting upon "adaptation" of the "traditional," he and his eclectic colleagues appear to have rejected some of the most potent aspects of their own tradition.

In general, the larger future of domestic design in the east after 1887 was charted by the Taylor House. Arthur Little's House for George D. Howe at Manchester-by-the-Sea (Figs. 151, 152), dated immediately after the Taylor House, certainly shows influence from it, especially in plan.[65] Any flow of space was blocked.

McKim, Mead, and White built yet another shingled house which has been much admired—and which was at once a climax and a kind of conclusion— the Low House at Bristol, Rhode Island, 1887 (Fig. 153).[66] This is rigidly frontal, if large and simple in conception. It has a truly classic unity without classicizing detail. Again it attacks the classic problem of the pediment or gable, and the great roof slope defines the mass with majesty and calm, while the windows are banked in grouped bays, contained by horizontal overhangs. From the plan it would appear that McKim was attempting to create order by means of crossed axes—a little like Price's houses and much like the

62. Dow, *American Renaissance*, pp. 130–1.

63. *Ibid.*, pp. 108–18.

64. *Ibid.*, p. 149.

65. Sheldon, 2, 141–3. It will be recalled that Little always had particularly colonial tendencies. His book, *Early New England Interiors*, appeared as early as 1878. Furthermore, his Shingleside was a large salt box, and all his detail was colonial. Yet with all this he combined a sense of spatial volumes. It is typical of a real lapse into academicism that such should disappear.

66. Hitchcock, *Rhode Island*, pl. 67.

later plans of Wright. Also, as later with Wright, McKim originally intended to use a broad terrace as a base for the gable shape of the house, but this feature was eliminated because of excessive cost. In general, the Low House, however ample and powerful, must be seen as a kind of arbitrary final effort, the swan song of McKim's shingle design, and so far as articulation and the expression of wooden pavilion is concerned it compares badly, I think, with the Cyrus McCormick House (Fig. 122). Its archaically powerful gable of wood, like some prototypal form from the beginnings of design, was almost immediately to be abandoned for the more conventionally conceived columns and pediments of McKim, Mead, and White's later buildings.

Perhaps midway in conception between the McCormick and Low houses is the Atwater-Ciampolini House on Whitney Avenue, New Haven, Connecticut (Fig. 154), built in 1890 by the New York firm of Babb, Cook, and Willard.[67] Here the simple gable shape with its continuous horizontals in the window bands and the voids of the porches extends more subtly but with less expansive power than in the Low House. A feeling for the continuity of interior volumes gives meaning to and articulates the exterior mass. The Atwater-Ciampolini and Low Houses show how the sense of control which had developed by the middle 80's did not necessarily entail academic precedent or antiquarian detail. They could have demonstrated to their own time how classic order had nothing intrinsically to do with classicistic archaeology in design. Babb, Cook, and Willard never built another such house, nor, after 1887, did McKim, Mead, and White, who were from then on fully embarked upon their renowned academic career.

While McKim, Mead, and White were to build other interesting and important houses, such as the E. D. Morgan House at Newport, 1888–91,[68] they were never again to strike out consistently in domestic architecture into what by any stretch of the imagination could be called the unknown. Much of their later work may be felt to have had considerable quality, but it is possible that a decisive opportunity for American culture was lost because con-

67. Babb, Cook, and Willard's De Vinne Press building, Lafayette Street, New York, 1885, should also be mentioned in this connection. A simple block with a gable roof, it is a masterpiece of what we might call the "free classic" urban architecture of the middle 80's. It is very similar in conception not only to Babb, Cook, and Willard's Atwater House of 1890 but also to McKim, Mead, and White's Low House of 1887. Hitchcock, "Frank Lloyd Wright and the 'Academic Tradition,'" p. 52. Since Babb and Wells were close friends— and furthermore since Wells used the De Vinne Press as a model for the Judge Building, 5th Avenue and 16th Street, New York, built in 1890—it is reasonable to assume a strong influence from Babb in the Low House as well.

68. Downing and Scully, p. 158; pl. 214. Moore lists the Morgan House as of 1891. However, the building was apparently almost complete as early as 1888.

fidence in invention failed those to whom the opportunity was presented. Given the background of 19th-century theory which we have discussed, it was probably inevitable that the architects involved should have settled for types in place of the archetypes which they sought. They perceived the critical moment of discipline, integration, and order, but in the end they seem to have mistaken its nature, to have seized the shadow and let the substance go. In this way creative discipline was itself deprecated. Adapted evocations of past disciplines were called to the support of a culture apparently unwilling any longer to sustain its own—or unaware of the possibility of sustaining them. By the 1890's cultural invention and new growth may thus be felt to have passed from the eastern architects, but the whole development of American domestic architecture, including its classic moment of the 1880's, was to be absorbed and extended in the suburbs of Chicago.

9. Conclusion: Frank Lloyd Wright

Between 1840 and 1875 the architects and theorists of the stick style of the midcentury had laid a broad philosophical and technical platform for future architectural growth. They had based it upon a feeling for the land, endowed it with the expression of wooden frame techniques, and thereby translated not only the picturesque but also the ethical principles of the Gothic revival into peculiarly practical American terms. Into this had come, in the 1870's, a new sense of space and surface continuity, first developed in America by Richardson and later widely disseminated after an assimilation of influences from the American colonial and the English Queen Anne. By the early 80's a free shingle style had developed: it moved more and more toward cohesion and order in design. It sought for basic forms, for the essential elements of architectural expression. Yet the poignant evocation of past ages was integral in Queen Anne and, especially for Americans, in colonial enthusiasms. From it arose the danger of unoriginal antiquarianism. This, reinforced by a newly growing academic attitude toward design, had produced by 1885 the H. A. C. Taylor House, the first and possibly the best of a long line of Palladian, colonial, and eclectic monuments.

It will not be possible here to discuss the events which took place after 1885 in American domestic architecture. Such might properly be the subject of another volume. Certain lines of future development should, however, be indicated. First of all, in the decades after 1885, the colonial revival became more specifically antiquarian, academic, and unoriginal.[1] Second, allied

1. An excellent indication of this trend is the fact that in Feb., 1886, the *American Architect* began a series of measured drawings of "Old Colonial Work," consisting mostly of details of moldings, etc., all archaeological in intention rather than re-creative or picturesque. *Am. Arch., 19,* Feb. 6, 1886. These were drawn by Frank E. Wallis and were eventually collected and published by William Rotch Ware, who, it will be remembered,

to this and reinforcing its eclectic academicism, came a preoccupation by the late 8o's with public monumentality and great size, even in suburban architecture. This preoccupation would seem to have arisen from the more class-conscious pretensions of the end of the century, and it was destructive to the more democratic orientation of the earlier suburbs.[2] Whatever qualities the architecture so inspired may have possessed,[3] it still struck what was eventually a deathblow to the shingle style. Like the whole domestic development in wood, the shingle style was basically antimonumental in materials, techniques, and point of view. In low cost and great quantity its intent was democratic. Third, by the 9o's the growing power of the schools, based primarily upon the "projet" philosophy and the eclectically classicizing forms of the late 19th-century École des Beaux-Arts, militated toward an eclectic, unoriginal, and pretentious kind of design.[4] Coupled with this trend was the continued growth of the large architectural office, where deep thought became of necessity ever more subservient to the day-by-day expediencies of business practice. The loss of a sense of basic needs, real tradition, and cultural daring which these factors entailed may be regarded as bringing about the partial collapse of the native development in American domestic architecture. Yet it did not by any means subdue it entirely. The shingle style, for instance, continued for some time much as it had developed by 1885. Many excellent houses were built not only in the late 8o's but also in the 9o's and the early 20th century.[5] However, cut off as they became from what were the

_____

had been the first editor of the *American Architect*. William Rotch Ware, *The Georgian Period*, New York, 1898.

2. Richard Morris Hunt's "Ochre Court," Newport, 1888–91, is an excellent example of this. See Downing and Scully, pp. 159–60; pls. 216, 217. It is at once "archaeological French Late Gothic" and tremendous in size. Compared with the Bell House or even the Goelet House of the early 8o's, it may be felt to have left "reality" behind. Even more striking is Hunt's "Breakers," Newport, 1892–95. *Ibid.*, pp. 147–8, 160–1; pls. 196, 218–22. Also, Hitchcock, *Rhode Island*, pls. 65, 68.

3. Some contemporary critics feel that it had a good deal of quality. For a statement of this position see Christopher Tunnard, *The City of Man* (New York, 1953), *passim*.

4. The schools may really be said to have come into their own in 1895, by which time McKim, Burnham, and others had succeeded in establishing the American Academy in Rome. See Moore, pp. 128–81. Also important in this, later, was the financial assistance of J. P. Morgan. *Ibid.*, pp. 171–81.

5. A characteristic of this later development was that for some time architects who worked in the most rigidly academic style in public buildings and town houses were capable of building freer shingled houses in the country, where, in a sense, they could relax. Among many, one example is a house at Lake George, New York, by Guy Lowell of Boston, who built Georgian mansions in Cambridge and Boston. For the Lake George House see the Boston *Architectural Review, 11* (1904), 46–8.

main architectural movements of the time, these houses eventually became more and more self-consciously countrified, "rustic," exemplifying a slow disintegration of earlier vitality. Unlike the houses of the early 80's, they no longer carried the important aspects of new growth.

To the last phase of an earlier cottage style belong the houses built by Greene and Greene in California in the late 90's and early 20th century, as well as the streets upon streets of "California Bungalows" which copied them in Pasadena and elsewhere.[6] Exciting as the work of Greene and Greene often is, in the sensitive exploitation of wood techniques—especially in its exploration of plank and beam construction—it still represents the end of a long line of development, not the beginning of a new. Yet it has come to life once more in the hands of the modern generation of California architects. Its influence can be strongly felt at the present time in the work of men such as Joseph Esherick and Harwell Harris.[7]

Note should be taken that both Greene and Greene, around 1900, and Harris, in the 1940's, designed with a sensitivity which recalls that of the old stick style, especially in the total articulation of structural members and

6. The California bungalow type of the 1900's is a builder's adaptation of Greene and Greene's work to smaller residences, disseminated by a variety of small "bungalow books" in the early 20th century. Examples of such work can be seen at 389 and 390 North Parkway and 460 Ellsworth Avenue, New Haven, Connecticut. The best of the bungalow books is Henry L. Wilson's *The Bungalow Book, a short sketch of the evolution of the bungalow from its primitive crudeness to its present state of artistic beauty and cosy convenience,* 4th ed. Los Angeles, 1908. These books and the thousands of cottages built from their designs represented the last gasp of the shingle-style tradition of open planning and sensitivity to materials as a general vernacular. On the West Coast this tradition was finally destroyed by the California mission style, an eclectic pastiche after Spanish Colonial prototypes which came to prominence with the San Diego Exposition of 1914. This coincided with the San Francisco Exposition of the same year. These expositions completed the movement toward popular eclecticism which the Chicago World's Fair of 1893 began. The architect most influential in Spanish colonial work on the West Coast and to whom the major responsibility for the destruction of the more creative tradition must be assigned was Bertram Goodhue, *beau idéal* of 20th-century Beaux-Arts eclecticism.

7. Greene and Greene's planning grows directly out of that of the early 80's but represents no real advance over it. Their use of materials—rough wood, cedar shakes, and cobblestones—also grows out of the use of natural materials of the shingle style but in a sense exaggerates it, insisting obsessively upon the total articulation of each element. Also significant in their work is a strong oriental influence, the apotheosis of that insistent relationship with Japanese framing and spatial techniques which had been important since the 70's. See Jean Murray Bangs (Mrs. Harwell Hamilton Harris), "Greene and Greene," *Architectural Forum, 89* (1948), 80-9. This contains a short discussion of Greene and Greene's work and some photographs. Miss Bangs' projected book on Greene and Greene and Maybeck has now been awaited for many years.

their multiplication. Thus articulated, the work of Greene and Greene—
and sometimes that of Harris when most similar to theirs—often lacks the
continuity and sweep which were achieved in the fully developed shingle
style. The positive quality which emerges is that of the skeletal pavilion.

In a sense the ultimate development of the last and "crafty" phase of the
cottage style around 1910 was to be found in the "Craftsman Homes" and
furniture of the early 20th century, propaganda for which was carried on
most extensively by Gustav Stickley.[8]

The seeds of future growth apparently lay neither in the eclectic reaction
against the free domestic style of the 80's nor in the more and more unrealistic attempt to prolong it without renewed disciplines and restudied objectives. Instead, the main power of growth which lay within the developments in 19th-century American domestic architecture would seem to have
entered into the work of Frank Lloyd Wright, and secondarily into that of
other members of the Second Chicago School.[9] Indeed, one of the important
aspects of the development which has been traced is that it makes Wright's
work more explicable, not only by fitting Wright into his historical sequence
but also by heightening visual awareness of the factors which entered into
the formation of his design. Again, it will by no means be possible to discuss
Wright's early work in detail. Certain aspects of it have already been pointed
out in passing. It should now be necessary only to indicate how the different
threads of the earlier development united in his design.

Wright's introduction to domestic building came in 1887 in the office of an
architect who was at that time a practitioner of the free shingle style, namely
Joseph Lyman Silsbee, who had come to Chicago from Syracuse in 1885.[10]
From him Wright got a sense of picturesque shingled design at the moment
when it was beginning to move toward a certain order. Drawings by Wright

8. Gustav Stickley, *Craftsman Homes,* New York, 1909. Also, *idem, More Craftsman
Homes,* New York, 1912. These must be taken as evidence of a preoccupation with dying
handicrafts which was probably as architecturally escapist and unrealistic as was the too great
lack of concern with basic techniques to be found in the Beaux-Arts schools of the period.
Stickley owes a certain debt to Greene and Greene and published photographs of their
work. See *Craftsman Homes,* pp. 104, 106–8.

9. Hugh Garden, George Maher, Mary Mahoney, Walter Burley Griffin, Purcell and
Elmslie, Theodore von Holst, and others. The work of this group was published in *Inland
Architect and Builder,* Chicago, to 1908, and after that date in *Western Architect.* It tends
to fall apart and lose direction by the time of the first World War.

10. Silsbee was of an old Salem, Mass., family. Through his wife he was allied with several
Rhode Island families and visited there often, both before and after he moved to Chicago
in 1885. His work was never very distinguished, but he may be considered as the architect
who brought the mature shingle style to Chicago. See Wright, *Autobiography,* pp. 67–74.
Hitchcock, *In the Nature of Materials,* pp. 3–6; pls. 1, 2.

of houses designed by Silsbee appeared in the *Inland Architect* in 1888.[11] After leaving Silsbee and joining the firm of Adler and Sullivan, Wright built his own house at Oak Park in 1889 (Fig. 155). A shingled structure, set upon a terrace, and with a gabled roof, it relates visually to McKim, Mead, and White's Low House of 1887, to Stephens' gabled houses, and most of all to the houses which Bruce Price built at Tuxedo Park, 1885–86. These of course were published in Sheldon, which was available to Wright (Figs. 108–10). Moreover, Wright's house—with its terrace, its strong gable, and its window arrangement—is a very close adaptation of Price's W. Chandler Cottage, also at Tuxedo Park and of 1885–86 (Fig. 156). This was published in the periodical *Building* in 1886 and was therefore also available to Wright.[12] Wright, at the beginning of his career, was thus seeking direct inspiration from the masters of the developed shingle style, and especially from Bruce Price. He seems to have seized especially upon the essential forms toward which Price and the others had developed, beginning as here, with the decisive and archetypal gable. Hence the articulated and interwoven spaces of Wright's house continue the spatial order of the cottages of the early 80's. Wright also further assimilates Japanese influences (Fig. 157; see also Figs. 121, 123–5, 130).[13] Wright's tie with the shingle style is thus well established and need not be dwelt upon in any greater detail.

In one of the first houses by Wright where all the elements of his design reached their early maturity, we can now single out those aspects which had been important in the earlier development. Perhaps the best example is the Ward W. Willitts House, Highland Park, Illinois, 1902.[14] In plan (Fig. 158) it exhibits the characteristic openness of the shingle style. In the crossed axes of the plan, articulated by the central fireplace mass, appear that classic coher-

11. These were the J. L. Cochrane House, published in *Inland Architect and Builder*, *11*, No. 3 (1888), and Row houses for William Waller, *ibid.*, No. 6. *Inland Architect* began publication in Feb., 1883.

12. A plan and two perspectives were published, one of the latter being of the side elevation used by Wright for his façade. *Building, A Journal of Architecture, 5*, September 18, 1886. I am indebted for this reference to Samuel Graybill, whose doctoral dissertation on the work of Bruce Price is now nearing completion at Yale University. Price's "delineator" was Fred Wright, a peculiar coincidence. The Chandler House was later published in 1900 (*Architecture, 1*, May, 1900).

13. Hitchcock, *In the Nature of Materials*, pls. 11–13. It will be recalled that a similar continuity of spatial flow, achieved by the use of the Japanese continuous soffit, had already been achieved by McKim, Mead, and White as early as 1881, in the Newcomb House, Elberon, New Jersey. See also White's dining room in Kingscote, 1880–81; the interiors of the Tilton House, 1881–82; and the Bell House, 1882–83.

14. Hitchcock, *op. cit.*, pls. 73–6. Hitchcock calls this "the first masterpiece among the Prairie Houses."

ence of interwoven volumes toward which the shingle style had been moving. One need only compare it to the plan of Bruce Price's Kent House of 1885–86 (Fig. 109). Wright had obviously studied the possibilities for spatial variety combined with strong geometric order which Price's crossed-axial planning possessed.

As in the shingle style, the interior space of the Willitts House extends out into porches, here clearly developed as continuous extensions of the interior space. In order to see how Wright developed with a grander sweep the spatial interweaving and continuity of the shingle style, one should compare the interior of Wright's Martin House, Buffalo, 1904 (Fig. 159),[15] with the interiors of McKim, Mead, and White's Newcomb, Tilton, and Bell Houses (Figs. 121, 125, 130). Classic decisiveness and unity of plan, space, and building fabric are also fully expressed upon the exterior of the Ward Willitts House (Fig. 160). The house sits firmly upon its base. The masses interweave cleanly, and while they extend widely into space with an expressive continuity of plane which is new and Wright's own, their whole movement is nevertheless abstract, ordered, and "classic." Again, direct Japanese influences are also clearly apparent.[16]

Thus, if Wright absorbed the free shingle style of the early 80's in most of its elements, he also assimilated the design discipline of its classic moment and developed it more powerfully than did any of the architects who saw discipline only in the academic rules of the schools.[17]

The freedom of the shingle style and the discipline of a truly classic moment are consequently both present in Wright's design. Finally—and the fact is of interest in relation to the continuing dislike for Wright's work which exists among eclectically "colonial" architects—those qualities which architects valued in the early days of the colonial revival in the 70's are important factors in Wright's houses: the great fireplaces, the low ceilings, the sense at once of shelter and of horizontally extended space.[18] One may say, therefore, that Wright absorbed not only the developed shingle style and the

15. Cf. *Frank Lloyd Wright. Ausgeführte Bauten* (Berlin, 1911), p. 50. This was the second of the important publications by the German publisher Ernst Wasmuth. The first, using only drawings, was entitled *Ausgeführte Bauten und Entwürfe von Frank Lloyd Wright*, Berlin, 1910.

16. As from the Japanese "Hōōden" at the Chicago Columbian Exposition, 1893. See Clay Lancaster, "Japanese Buildings in the United States before 1900: Their Influence upon American Domestic Architecture," *Art Bulletin*, 35 (1953), 217–24; pl. 9. See also D. T. Tselos, "Exotic Influences in the Architecture of Frank Lloyd Wright," *Magazine of Art*, 46 (1953), 160–9.

17. Wright's relationship to the academic design of the early 90's is best discussed in Hitchcock, "Frank Lloyd Wright and the 'Academic Tradition,'" pp. 46–63 and *passim*.

18. As discussed in Chs. 2, 3, and 4, above. Of his deep fireplaces Wright (*Autobiography*,

academic reaction against it but also the formal principles of the colonial revival at its most creative.

If Wright combined all this, he also reached farther back into the heart of the American development. Basic to the growth of his design was a sense of the timber skeleton and of the pavilion which it creates. A glance at the exterior of the Willitts House shows how that continuity of window which had been important in the shingle style is articulated here by an expression of the wooden framing. In this it is much like E. C. Gardner's "Planter's House" of 1875 (Fig. 161).[19] Always across the long horizontal spreads of Wright's window bands comes the insistent rhythm of the vertical stud. This is inherited both from the stick style and from its related Japanese elements, which are expressed even more explicitly in Wright's design. However, in line with the movement toward continuity of surface which was so important in the shingle style is Wright's insistence, mirrored in his work, that if a sense of the skeleton is basic to design in wood, the expression of an over-all plastic continuity is nevertheless more important than the expression of the skeleton itself. He states: "Plasticity may be seen in the expressive flesh-covering of the skeleton as contrasted with the articulation of the skeleton itself. . . . In my work the idea of plasticity may now be seen as the element of continuity." [20]

Even more important for Wright's early development than the formal nature of the midcentury stick style was his direct link with the principles upon which that style was founded. Just as it had developed in America the social, ethical, and structural principles of the Gothic revival, so Wright's contact with those same principles was immediate and direct. He says of himself in 1887:

> From the library of All Souls I got two books you would never expect to find there. Owen Jones' "Grammar of Ornament" and Viollet-le-Duc's "Habitations of Man in All Ages." I had read his "Dictionnaire," the "Raisonné," at home, got from the Madison city library.
>
> I believed the "Raisonné" was the only really sensible book on archi-

---

p. 141) has this to say: "So the *integral* fireplace became an important part of the building itself in the houses I was allowed to build out there on the prairie. . . . It comforted me to see the fire burning deep in the solid masonry of the house itself. A feeling that came to stay." The low ceilings were also a feature of Japanese architecture, as discussed by Morse in 1886, p. 108.

19. The relationship is one of families of sensibility, structural expression, and intent. Although the Willitts House is orchestrated through Wright's own sweeping design power, the sense of "organic" life which it projects has its roots in that same feeling for the structural skeleton as a plastic element which is also basic in the Gardner design. Again, there are insistent Japanese evocations in both. Gardner, *Illustrated Homes*, p. 170.

20. *Autobiography*, p. 146.

tecture in the world. I got copies of it for my sons, later. That book was enough to keep, in spite of architects, one's faith alive in architecture.

The Owen Jones was a reprint but good enough. I read the "propositions" and felt the first five were dead right.[21]

Of equal importance are the indications in Wright's own career of the sociological significance of domestic architecture in America. Behind the whole development of free design ran the insistent belief that man must live as a free human being, in close contact with nature, in order to realize his own potentialities. The early stick style, for example, was not only part of an international movement toward the suburban and the picturesque; it was also an expression of confident and still semiagrarian, semi-Jeffersonian America, and it went to pieces in post-Civil War industrialized society. The colonial and Queen Anne revival and the shingle style then emerged in reaction against the industrialized world, and its architects attempted to create a new cottage and suburban refuge. Wright, of course, has always completely accepted the premise that the industrialized city is evil and that human beings can live fully only in rural surroundings. His "Broadacre City" of the 1930's represents in his work a culmination of these Jeffersonian, agrarian enthusiasms. In Broadacre City the suburban orientation of the 19th-century

21. *Ibid.*, p. 75. With the importance of Viollet-le-Duc's *Habitations* and *Dictionnaire* one is already familiar. See Ch. 3, above. Owen Jones' *The Grammar of Ornament* (London, 1856) is less well known but was important in Wright's development. Wright introduced it to Sullivan through his tracings from it when he applied for a job with Adler and Sullivan in 1887. *Autobiography*, pp. 91–2. It is perhaps not coincidental that Owen Jones' book contains examples of Celtic interlaces and that the interlaced forms so characteristic of Sullivan's mature ornament do not appear in it to any extent until after this time. Since Wright found Owen Jones' first five propositions "dead right" it might be well to quote them here, since they reveal a mixture of the social, structural, and ethical thought of the Gothic revival with that basic feeling for the repose of classic form which becomes important in Wright's own work. Jones (p. 5) asserts:

1. The Decorative Arts arise from, and should properly be attendant upon, Architecture. 2. Architecture is the material expression of the wants, the faculties, and the sentiments, of the age in which it is created. Style in Architecture is the peculiar form that expression takes under the influence of climate and materials at command. 3. As Architecture, so all works of Decorative Arts, should possess fitness, proportion, harmony, the result of all which is repose. 4. True beauty results from that repose which the mind feels when the eye, the intellect, and the affections, are satisfied from the absence of any want. 5. Construction should never be decorated. Decoration should never be purposely constructed. That which is beautiful is true; that which is true must be beautiful.

domestic development is forcibly projected into the city planning problems of the 20th.[22]

Wright also absorbed from Sullivan a broad, rather Whitmanesque concept of democracy as essential for architectural growth in America, and their personal beliefs seem related to the specifically Populist agrarian-radicalism which was powerful in Chicago in the early 90's. Consequently, when the academic reaction brought to Chicago the classicism which had been embraced by the financial magnates of the day, and which to Sullivan meant a relapse from democracy into "feudalism," it was probably inevitable that Sullivan, dependent upon monumental projects for his commissions, should have become embittered and self-destructive. But Wright was deeply entrenched in what was at that time the idealistically radical and agrarian-minded suburb of Oak Park. Finding scores of clients who were still ready and anxious to support original experiment, he was able to continue the development of the domestic tradition and to grow toward the fulfillment of his own genius. Into the primarily domestic program thus open to him Wright directed his and Sullivan's will for sculptural, massive, ceremonial forms. The traditional interweaving of elements—as in the domestic development and in Sullivan's skyscraper façades as well—became combined with visual weight and an intensely "classic" order. Out of these elements grew, beyond all question, a profoundly monumental expression. America consequently produced her most original monuments where one after all might have expected to find them: in the homes of individual men.

So the 19th-century suburb, as a milieu of architectural growth, nurtured Wright during his formative years; and he built its final memorials. Similarly, when around 1910 the psychological atmosphere in Chicago became less idealistically agrarian-radical and more receptive to "eastern" ideas, Wright felt forced to flee the area and create his own milieu at Taliesin. Those around Wright who did not flee eventually sank back into various aspects of the conformist and eclectic stream or else froze into an academic repetition of their earlier design.

Since that time Wright has lived continuously in an environment created by himself—an environment which strives always, and sometimes apparently absurdly, to keep alive that sense of union with the land which had been at the root of the intrinsically American domestic development since the time of Andrew Jackson Downing.

Not all of Wright's work can be explained by the domestic architectural tradition of the later 19th century, nor can it be understood solely through a

22. Cf. Frank Lloyd Wright, *An Organic Architecture, the Architecture of Democracy* (London, 1939), *passim.*

discussion of his uses of it. Nevertheless, the tradition fused in him, and through him it formed one of the bases for the modern architecture of the 20th century.[23] One must conclude that in Wright's work the creative traditions of the 19th century still live and have given rise to the new.

Wright's career forces us to return a double answer to the critical question concerning what happened to American invention in domestic architecture during the later 80's. On the one hand it subsided in the East, eventually marking an important cultural break, a temporary exhaustion of experiment. On the other hand Wright picked up and continued the tradition of invention and sustained the architectural program of the single family house as its vehicle. But more than this, he seems to have accomplished the extraordinary feat of constantly redirecting the inheritance of his tradition into new disciplines and fresh sources of inspiration.

The history of the shingle style, therefore, reveals certain characteristics of rupture, discontinuity, and reaction at a significant moment in American culture. It also asserts continuity and the ability to sustain experiment as well. Most of all, the shingle style itself—in its earnest mixture of motives, its quickly fired vitality, and its impatient search for the roots of experience in a newly industrialized world—seems a most poignantly 19th-century and American phenomenon. It can serve as a useful memory for us all.

Indeed, the gentle principles of spatial accommodation and vernacular order on which it was based were to take a new lease on life during the second half of the twentieth century (Figs. 98, 155, 162, 163).

23. Wright's influence, through the Wasmuth publications of 1910 and 1911, was apparently direct and formative upon the Dutch De Stijl group and Gropius in the 'teens and through them upon the Bauhaus and Mies Van der Rohe in the 20's. Cf. n. 15 above. Later, in the 20's and early 30's, Wright in turn was influenced by the European architects. Elsewhere I have briefly attempted to point out this double relationship. See "Frank Lloyd Wright vs. the International Style," *Art News,* 53 (March, 1954), 32 ff. For the objections of several critics to this thesis, and my reply, see *op. cit.* (September, 1954), pp. 48–9.

Bibliographical Note

The bibliography for this study has been treated in some detail throughout the notes and need not be listed in its entirety here, but certain aspects of it deserve further consideration.

Hitchcock's bibliography is still the main tool for a study of the literature of 19th-century architecture (Henry-Russell Hitchcock, Jr., *American Architectural Books. A list of books, portfolios, and pamphlets on architecture and related subjects published in America before 1895*, 3d ed. Minneapolis, 1946). This invaluable work, remarkably complete within its prescribed limits, should one day be expanded by being brought further along in time and by the inclusion of important articles. Roos' bibliography is also useful. It could be amplified and its few and minor errors corrected (Frank J. Roos, Jr., *Writings on Early American Architecture, an annotated list of books and articles on architecture constructed before 1860 in the eastern half of the United States*, Columbus, 1943).

Less systematic than these bibliographies but full of valuable material which still awaits the analysis of historians are the various compilations of newspaper clippings, maps, and photographs which are often to be found in local libraries and historical societies. An example is Arnold Guyot Dana, "Pictorial New Haven, Old and New. Its homes, institutions, activities, etc. Disclosing changes that present problems," 145 volumes. Pt. 1: "Maps of New Haven, 1641–1879"; Pt. 2: "General Historical Matter, Text and Pictures"; Pt. 3: "Chiefly Houses and Noteworthy Occupants." New Haven Historical Society. Such collections are often the only sources for real estate maps of the period and for records of house building and ownership.

For the stick style of the period 1840–76 the pattern books are the most important source. I have endeavored to assess them and the importance of the development carried by them in my article "Romantic Rationalism and the Expression of Structure in Wood. Downing, Wheeler, Gardner, and the 'Stick Style,' " *Art Bulletin, 35* (1953), 121–42. The direction indicated by

the pattern books can then be tested against actual buildings in specific locali-
ties. I have attempted to do this in "The Stick Style" in Antoinette F. Downing and Vincent J. Scully, Jr., *The Architectural Heritage of Newport, Rhode
Island,* Cambridge, Mass., 1952. The most important pattern books are listed
below. They are chronological, with variations to indicate the order in which
they might be most efficiently used. Less important examples have been
omitted and a few of the earlier English books have been included.

LATE ENGLISH PICTURESQUE

Humphry Repton, *Fragments of the Theory and Practise of Landscape Garden-
ing,* London, 1816.
J. B. Papworth, *Rural Residences,* London, 1818.
P. F. Robinson, *Rural Architecture,* London, 1823.
Thomas F. Hunt, *Architettura Campestre . . . in the Modern or Italian Style,*
London, 1827.
John Claudius Loudon, *Encyclopaedia of Cottage, Farm and Villa Architecture
and Furniture,* London, 1833; 2d ed. 1835.
Francis Goodwin, *Domestic Architecture,* London, 1834.
S. H. Brooks, *Designs for Cottage and Villa Architecture,* London [1839?].

FIRST PHASE OF THE STICK STYLE

Alexander Jackson Davis, *Rural Residences,* New York, 1837.
Andrew Jackson Downing, *A Treatise of the Theory and Practise of Landscape
Gardening Adapted to North America—with remarks on rural architecture,*
New York and London, 1841 (16 issues of 8 eds. to 1879).
——— *Cottage Residences; or a series of designs for rural cottages and cottage
villas. And their gardens and grounds,* New York and London, 1842 (13
issues to 1887).
——— *The Architecture of Country Houses, including designs for cottages, farm
houses and villas, with remarks on interiors, furniture, and the best modes
of warming and ventilating,* New York, 1850 (9 issues to 1866).
George Wightwick, *Hints to Young Architects . . . with additional notes and
hints to persons about building in this country,* by A. J. Downing, 1st Amer.
ed. New York, 1847.
John Warren Ritch, *The American Architect,* New York, 1847.
William Brown (of Lowell), *The Carpenter's Assistant,* Worcester, 1848 (6 issues
to 1856; 5th ed. Boston, 1853).
Gervase Wheeler, *Rural Homes, or sketches of houses suited to American country
life, with original plans, designs, etc.,* New York, 1851 (9 issues through
1868).

—— *Homes for the People in Suburb and Country, etc.,* New York, 1855 (6 issues through 1868).

SECOND PHASE OF THE STICK STYLE

Samuel Sloan, *The Model Architect,* 2 vols. Philadelphia, 1852.

Lewis Falley Allen, *Rural Architecture,* New York, 1852 (8 issues to 1865).

Orson Squire Fowler, *A Home for All; or, the gravel wall and octagon mode of building,* New York, 1848.

John Bullock, *The American Cottage Builder: a series of designs, plans, and specifications from $200 to $20,000. For homes for the people,* New York, 1854; "new revised ed." 1854.

Henry William Cleaveland, William Backus, and Samuel D. Backus, *Village and Farm Cottages,* New York, 1856 (4 issues to 1869).

William E. Bell, *Carpentry Made Easy; or, the science and art of framing on a new and improved system. With specific instructions for building balloon frames,* Philadelphia, 1858 (9 issues to 1894).

Calvert Vaux, *Villas and Cottages,* New York, 1857.

Samuel Sloan, *Sloan's Constructive Architecture,* Philadelphia, 1859 (3 issues to 1873).

THIRD PHASE OF THE STICK STYLE

Henry Hudson Holly, *Holly's Country Seats,* New York, 1863.

George Evertson Woodward, *Woodward's Country Homes,* New York, 1865 (8 issues to some time after 1870; last two n.d.).

—— *Woodward's National Architect,* New York, 1868 (95 issues in various forms to 1877).

Amos Jackson Bicknell, *Detail, Cottage and Constructive Architecture,* New York, 1873 (7 eds. to 1886).

—— *Specimen Book of One Hundred Architectural Designs,* New York, 1878.

Gilbert Bostwick Croff, *Progressive American Architecture,* New York, 1875.

E. C. Gardner, *Homes and How to Make Them,* Boston, 1874.

—— *Illustrated Homes: a series of papers describing real houses and real people,* Boston, 1875.

—— *The House that Jill Built,* New York, 1882.

Later pattern books, published after 1876, illustrate the movement toward Queen Anne design, the decadence of the pattern book itself as the most important carrier of development, and the last phase of pattern book activity in California during the early 20th century. Presenting "colonial," "Old English," California bungalow, and craftsman types, they reveal the disintegration into its several components of the synthesis which the shingle style had achieved in the 80's. A few of the most typical among many examples are (chronologically):

Henry Hudson Holly, "Modern Dwellings. Their Construction, Decoration and Furniture," Pt. 1 *Harper's*, 52 (1876), 855–67.
—— *Modern Dwellings in Town and Country, Adapted to American Wants and Climate,* New York, 1878.
A. F. Oakey, *Building a Home,* New York, 1881.
George Shoppell, *How to Build a House,* New York [1883?]
—— *Modern Houses, Beautiful Homes,* New York, 1887.
George Palliser, *Palliser's New Cottage Homes and Details,* New York, 1887.
C. Francis Osborne, *Notes on the Art of House Planning,* New York, 1888.
Louis H. Gibson, *Convenient Houses with Fifty Plans for the Housekeeper,* New York, 1889.
William Martin Johnson, *Inside of One Hundred Homes,* New York, 1904.
Modern Dwellings with Constructive Details, New York, David William Co., 1907.
The Bungalow Book. A short sketch of the evolution of the bungalow from its primitive crudeness to its present state of artistic beauty and cosy convenience, 4th ed. Los Angeles, Henry L. Wilson, 1908.
Detached Dwellings, Country and Suburban, New York, Swetland, 1909.
William L. Price and Frank S. Guild, *Model Houses for Little Money,* New York, 1910.
Henry H. Saylor, ed., *Distinctive Homes of Moderate Cost, being a collection of country and suburban homes in good taste,* New York, 1910.
Detached Dwellings, Country and Suburban, published by the *American Architect,* New York, 1911.
Gustav Stickley, *Craftsman Homes,* New York, 1909.
—— *More Craftsman Homes,* New York, 1912.

The growth of colonial revival attitudes in the 1870's is discussed in my Ch. 2 above. References to the popular articles and books of travel and description which reflected and supported this development are made chronologically in the footnotes to that chapter and will not, therefore, be listed here.

The periodicals which are the most important sources for a study of the attitudes and designs of the architects after 1876 should, however, be listed. Note should be taken of the fact that no specifically architectural periodical was able to sustain itself in America before 1876, with the solitary exception of the *American Builder.* This was the spokesman for the vernacular builder and was hostile to architects as such. Early publications which were intended specifically for architects, such as the *American Architect,* are useful for the shingle style in their published designs and in their direct statements of contemporary opinion. Later reviews, such as the *Architectural Record,* reveal different attitudes and also, as time goes on, become important for this study as they publish retrospective articles and the obituaries of shingle-style architects. The following listing is alphabetical:

American Architect and Building News, Boston and New York, Jan., 1876–Dec., 1908.

American Builder, Chicago and New York, March, 1868–May, 1895 (to 1873 as *American Builder and Journal of Art;* to 1879 as *American Builder, a Journal of Industrial Art;* to 1895 as *Builder and Woodworker*).

Architectural Record, New York, 1891–.

Architectural Review, Boston, 1891–1910.

——— London, 1896–.

Architectural Review and American Builder's Journal, Philadelphia, 1868–70 (Jan. to Dec., 1868, separate numbers as *Sloan's Architectural Review and Builder's Journal*).

Architectural Sketch Book (Portfolio Club), Boston, 1873–76.

Architecture, New York, 1900–36.

Architecture and Building, New York, 1882–1932. See below, *Building, a Journal of Architecture.*

Art Journal (American ed. of London *Art Journal*), New York, 1875–87.

Builder; an illustrated weekly magazine for the architect, engineer, archaeologist, constructor, sanitary reformer and art-lover, London, 1842–.

Building, a journal of architecture, 1886–87. Continuous publication, with different titles: *Building, an architectural monthly,* 1882–85; *Building, a journal of architecture* 1886–87; *Building, an architectural weekly,* 1888–89; *Architecture and Building,* 1890–99; *Architecture and Building, a magazine devoted to contemporary architectural construction,* 1900–.

Building News and Engineering Journal, London, 1854–1926.

Harper's Magazine, New York, 1850– (between 1850–1900 called *Harper's New Monthly Magazine*).

Inland Architect and Builder (Western Association of Architects), Chicago, Feb., 1883–Dec., 1908.

New Path (Society for the Advancement of Truth in Art), May, 1863–Dec., 1865. Suspended Jan., 1864–Dec., 1865.

New York Sketch Book of Architecture, New York, 1874–76.

North American Review, Boston and New York, 1815–1939/40.

Western Architect, Minneapolis and Chicago, 1901–31.

For the shingle style itself the two most important books of the period which have as yet come to light are certainly George William Sheldon's *Artistic Country Seats: types of recent American villas and cottage architecture, with instances of country club-houses*, 2 vols in 5 pts. (50 illus., 50 pls., 500 copies), New York, 1886–87; and Appleton's publication of interior views and descriptions: *Artistic Houses, being a series of interior views of a number of the most beautiful and celebrated homes in the United States, with a description of the art treasures contained therein*, 2 vols. in 4 (500 copies), New York, D. Appleton, 1883–84. Other books of the period which are also of use in understanding sources, methods, and designs of the shingle-style architects include, listed alphabetically by author:

Nathan Henry Chamberlain, *A Paper on New England Architecture*, Boston, 1858.

Christopher Dresser, *Japan, Its Architecture, Art and Art Manufactures*, 4th ed. London, 1882.

Charles Wyllys Elliott, *The Book of American Interiors*, Boston, 1876.

Examples of Architecture (selected from the *Sketch Book*, Boston, 1880; some of the plates from both the Boston and New York *Sketch Books*).

Homes in City and Country (articles by Russell Sturgis, John W. Root, Bruce Price, Donald G. Mitchell, Samuel Parsons, Jr., and W. W. Linn), New York, 1893.

Robert Kerr, *The English Gentleman's House, or, how to plan English residences*, London, 1864; 2d ed. 1865.

Arthur Little, *Early New England Interiors*, Boston, 1878.

Edward Sylvester Morse, *Japanese Homes and Their Surroundings . . . illustrations by the author*, Boston, 1886.

Bruce Price, *A Large Country House*, New York, 1887.

Montgomery Schuyler, *American Architecture*, New York, 1892.

Richard Norman Shaw, *Architectural Sketches from the Continent*, London, 1858; 2d ed. 1872.

———— *Sketches for Cottages and Other Buildings* (drawings by Maurice B. Adams), London, 1878.

John Calvin Stevens and Albert Winslow Cobb, *Examples of American Domestic Architecture*, New York, 1889.

Richard M. Upjohn, "Colonial Architecture of New York and the New England States," *Proceedings of the Third Annual Convention of the American Institute of Architects* (Nov. 17, 1869), 47–51.

Mrs. Schuyler Van Rensselaer, *Henry Hobson Richardson and His Works, with a portrait and illustrations of the architect's designs*, Boston and New York, 1888 (500 copies).

Frank Edwin Wallis, *Old Colonial Architecture and Furniture*, Boston, ca. 1887.

———— *American Architecture, Decoration and Furniture of the 18th Century,* Boston, 1896.

William Rotch Ware, *The Georgian Period,* New York, 1898.

Edwin Whitefield, *The Homes of Our Forefathers in Boston, Old England and Boston, New England,* Boston, 1889.

———— *The Homes of our Forefathers . . . in Massachusetts,* Boston, 1879.

———— *The Homes of our Forefathers in Maine, New Hampshire and Vermont,* Boston, 1886.

———— *The Homes of our Forefathers in Rhode Island and Connecticut,* Boston, 1882.

W. M. Woollett, *Old Homes Made New,* New York, 1878.

To the above list should be added at least the following exceptionally important articles, a few of the many which appeared in the *American Architect* during the period:

"Archaeology and American Architecture," *Am. Arch. and Building News, 4* (Oct. 5, 1878), pp. 114–15.

Alexander F. Oakey, "The Possibility of a New Style in Architecture," *Am. Arch. and Building News, 3* (Jan. 19, 1878), 22.

Robert Swain Peabody, "Georgian Homes of New England," Pt. 1: *Am. Arch. and Building News, 2* (Oct. 20, 1877), 338–9; Pt. 2, *3* (Jan. 26, 1878), 54–5.

"Practise of American Architects and Builders during the Colonial Period and the First Fifty Years of Our Independence," *Am. Arch. and Building News, 10* (1881), 71–4, 83–5.

See also Russell Sturgis, "The Works of Bruce Price," *Supplement to the Architectural Record, 9,* No. 5 (June, 1889), 1–65.

No history of the shingle style has hitherto been written, nor has it previously been properly evaluated in relation to the history of American architecture as a whole. At first the reasons for this omission lay in the academic reaction against the shingle style itself. The short articles upon domestic architectural history which began to appear in the early 20th century were generally superficial. See, e.g., Robert S. Andrews, "The Changing Styles of Country Houses," Boston *Architectural Review, 11* (1904), 1–4. Thus the first histories of American architecture were in varying degrees contemptuous of the whole period between 1840 and *ca.* 1886 (Joy Wheeler Dow, *The American Renaissance,* New York, 1904). The broader attitudes of Montgomery Schuyler and Russell Sturgis, published generally through articles in the *Architectural Record* and elsewhere were not influential enough to overcome this widespread contempt for 19th-century invention, nor did either of these critics concern himself at any length with developments in wood. Moreover, F. R. Vögel, writing in 1910 a history of American domestic architecture, was considerably less thorough and perceptive than was his predecessor, Muthesius, who had written on the domestic architecture of England. Vögel's book failed to present the American development adequately or convincingly (F. R. Vögel, *Das Amerikanische Haus,* Berlin, 1910; Herman Muthesius, *Das Englische Haus,* Berlin, 1908). By 1910 Wright's work was being published on the Continent. Its power and originality apparently had the effect upon Europeans of making interest in its antecedents seem superfluous. The *Übermensch* myth which Wright fostered thus had the result—one which extended into later progressive criticism—of obscuring the actually more impressive reality of his relation to his past (*Ausgeführte Bauten und Entwürfe von Frank Lloyd Wright,* Berlin, Ernst Wasmuth, 1910; *Frank Lloyd Wright. Ausgeführte Bauten,* Berlin, Ernst Wasmuth, 1911).

Wright's work was thus taken to be untraditional or antitraditional, and "tradition" as such seemed to be continued in America only by the eclectic architects of the early 20th century. So in the general histories of American architecture which began to appear in the 1920's the shingle style and its antecedents in the American tradition were given inadequate consideration. The emphasis was upon the "renaissance" of earlier "tradition" achieved by McKim, Mead, and White and their followers (Talbot Hamlin, *The American Spirit in Architecture,* New Haven, 1926; Thomas C. Tallmadge, *The Story of Architecture in America,* New York, 1927; Sidney Fiske Kimball, *American Architecture,* New York, 1928).

The major studies of individual architects to appear during this period were also concerned primarily with the later work of the eclectics (*A Monograph of the Work of McKim, Mead and White, 1879–1915,* New York, Architectural Books Publishing Company, 1915; Charles Moore, *Daniel H. Burnham, Architect, Planner of Cities,* New York, 1921; *idem, The Life and Times of Charles Follen McKim,* Boston, 1929; C. H. Reilly, *McKim, Mead and White,* New York, 1924; and Charles Baldwin, *Stanford White,* New York, 1931).

Yet already other critics were insisting upon the importance of earlier, more original phases in American design. Lewis Mumford was a pioneer of this movement (*Sticks and Stones,* New York, 1924; *Architecture,* Chicago, 1926). In the latter short work Mumford included a eulogy (though not a study) of the shingle style, and this was quoted by Baldwin in his biography of Stanford White, as noted earlier.

By the 1930's historians began to concern themselves more seriously with 19th-century developments. Henry-Russell Hitchcock, after his work in European modern architecture, turned to the American past (Henry-Russell Hitchcock, Jr., *The Architecture of H. H. Richardson and His Times*, New York, 1936). In this work Hitchcock referred favorably to the shingled houses of the 80's and called them "Suburban Richardsonian." He was able to go on with a further consideration of the quality of 19th-century architecture as a whole in his *Rhode Island Architecture*, Providence, 1939. In line with this new direction, Talbot Hamlin organized in 1941 an exhibition at Columbia of "A Century of Summer Resort Architecture in the United States." Out of this exhibition grew a short and rather inaccurate article by R. H. Newton. This illustrated some midcentury and shingle style houses and referred to a few architects, but it failed adequately to characterize, to describe, or to evaluate the nature of the development which had taken place. Wright's work, presumably including that of his early years, was bracketed with that of Oud and Gropius as being of the "International Style." There was no hint of his connection with an American past: Roger Hale Newton, "Our Summer Resort Architecture—An American Phenomenon and Social Document," *Art Quarterly* (Autumn, 1941), 297–318.

Hitchcock's indispensable book on Wright appeared in 1942. This work noted the relationship of Wright's early domestic design to that of his first employer, Silsbee. It did not delve, however, into the general background of domestic design or into the work of other architects (Henry-Russell Hitchcock, Jr., *In the Nature of Materials. The buildings of Frank Lloyd Wright, 1887–1941*, New York, 1941).

In 1944 Hitchcock published an important article which attempted to analyze the nature of the "classic" reaction of the 80's and 90's and Wright's relationship to it: "Frank Lloyd Wright and the 'Academic Tradition,'" *Journal of the Warburg and Courtauld Institutes*, 7 (1944), 46–63.

In 1943 Giedion's *Space, Time and Architecture* was published. This book asserted that Wright's work had indeed grown out of earlier developments in America. Yet it partly obscured the nature of those developments and of Wright's relation to them. While referring to a number of characteristics as being specifically "American," it ignored the actual history of 19th-century events (Siegfried Giedion, *Space, Time and Architecture*, Cambridge, 1943). Following the rather mechanistic determinism which was one aspect of Giedion's approach, some later discussions of American tradition have tended to concentrate upon technological and "functional" problems and to dismiss

19th-century phenomena which could not be explained in those terms (James Marston Fitch, *American Building, the forces that shape it,* New York, 1948; John A. Kouwenhoeven, *Made in America. The arts in modern civilization,* New York, 1948).

European observers have generally accepted this materialistic view of American invention. Bruno Zevi has been the most vocal exception. He has reacted against the Giedionesque approach and has insisted upon the spatially inventive and "organic" qualities of Wright's and earlier American work. Zevi's information concerning actual developments in America, especially of the pre-Wright period, is, however, rather restricted (Bruno Zevi, *Towards an Organic Architecture,* London, 1949; *idem, Storia dell'Architettura Moderna,* Torino, 1950).

Recent articles have added considerably to our knowledge of certain aspects of the later 19th century and its sources of inspiration: Clay Lancaster, "Oriental Forms in American Architecture, 1800–1870," *Art Bulletin, 29* (1947), 183–93; *idem,* "Japanese Buildings in the United States before 1900; Their Influence upon American Domestic Architecture," *Art Bulletin, 35* (1953), 217–24; B. L. Pickens, "Treasure Hunting at Detroit," *Architectural Review, 96* (1944), 169–76; D. T. Tselos, "Exotic Influences in the Architecture of Frank Lloyd Wright," *Magazine of Art, 46* (1953), 160–9.

My sections of Mrs. Downing's and my book on Newport were written in 1949 but not published until 1952. Although probably weakened by what seems to me now a sometimes excessively polemical tone, they attempted to treat the domestic architecture of the later 19th century as a coherent development (Antoinette A. Downing and Vincent J. Scully, Jr., *The Architectural Heritage of Newport Rhode Island,* Cambridge, Mass., 1952). Various aspects of the problems involved were also treated in my articles in the *Art Bulletin,* June, 1953, and the *Architectural Review,* March, 1954.

————————

As of 1970, comparatively few additions to this bibliography can be made. G. L. Hersey, "J. C. Loudon and Architectural Associationism," *Architectural Review, 144* (August 1968), 89–92, is useful for the backgrounds of the Stick Style, while his "Replication Replicated, or Notes on American Bastardy," *Perspecta, 9/10* (1965), 211–30, is of general collateral interest. Reprinted editions of a number of Downing's books have now appeared, among them several paperbacks with introductions which do not trouble to mention this work: Andrew Jackson Downing, *The Architecture of Country Houses,* with an introduction by George B. Tatum, Da Capo Press (New York, 1968), and *The Architecture of Country Houses,* with an introduction by J. Stewart

Johnson, Dover (New York, 1969). Also: Calvert Vaux, *Villas and Cottages,* with an introduction by Henry Hope Reed, Da Capo Press (New York, 1968). Some of the same texts are treated in James Early, *Romanticism and American Architecture* (New York, 1965), and reprinted in *The Literature of Architecture: The Evolution of Theory and Practice in Nineteenth-Century America,* edited by Don Gifford (New York, 1966). Mrs. Downing's and my book on Newport had a lush revised edition, with new introductions, in 1967, by a publisher who apparently specializes in the science of remaindering (C. N. Potter, New York, 1967).

Apart from the unpublished dissertation by Graybill (see p. 129), the only new contribution to our knowledge of Shingle Style architects is Cynthia Zaitzevsky and Myron Miller, *The Architecture of William Ralph Emerson, 1833–1912* (Cambridge, 1969), an exhibition presented by the Fogg Art Museum in collaboration with the Carpenter Center for the Visual Arts, Harvard University. For later stages of the general movement in domestic architecture, Clay Lancaster, "The American Bungalow," *Art Bulletin, 40* (1958), 239–53, is useful, and for Californian derivations in particular: Stephen W. Jacobs, "California Contemporaries of Wright," *Studies in Western Art: Acts of the Twentieth International Congress of the History of Art, 4, Problems of the Nineteenth and Twentieth Centuries* (Princeton, 1963), 34–63; and Esther McCoy, *Five California Architects* (New York, 1960). Frank Lloyd Wright's debt to the Shingle Style was acknowledged in Grant Manson, *Frank Lloyd Wright to 1910: The First Golden Age* (New York, 1958), and reaffirmed in my *Frank Lloyd Wright* (New York, 1960), and "Frank Lloyd Wright and Twentieth-Century Style," *Studies in Western Art: Acts of the Twentieth International Congress . . . , op. cit.,* 7–21, and in other publications. Frank Lloyd Wright's followers are treated, though with only peripheral reference to the Shingle Style, toward which many of them were in fact much more tenaciously drawn back than he, in H. Allen Brooks, "The Prairie School: The Midwest Contemporaries of Frank Lloyd Wright," *ibid.,* 22–33; and in M. L. Peisch, *The Chicago School of Architecture: Early Followers of Sullivan and Wright* (New York, 1965).

The Stick and Shingle styles entered general studies of modern architecture in Henry-Russell Hitchcock, *Architecture: Nineteenth and Twentieth Centuries* (Harmondsworth and Baltimore, 1958, new eds. 1963, 1968), and in William H. Jordy's nineteenth-century section of *Arts of the United States: A Pictorial Survey,* edited by William H. Pierson, Jr., and Martha Davidson (New York, 1960), and in my *Modern Architecture: The Architecture of Democracy* (New York, 1961), and *American Architecture and Urbanism* (New York, 1969). Recently I was given the opportunity to review their significance in my section "American Houses: Thomas Jefferson to Frank Lloyd Wright," in *The Rise of an American Architecture,* edited with an introduction and exhibition notes (for the Metropolitan Museum of Art) by Edgar Kaufmann, Jr. (New York, 1970), 163–210.

At the present moment the nineteenth-century houses treated here are profoundly affecting the most advanced American architecture in ways I would not have dreamed possible twenty years ago. At that time, it is true, there was a fairly close concordance between my interest in the small, stick-style houses of the 1840s and the generally small-scaled, wooden suburban architecture of the late 1940s. One can guess that architecture and architectural history tend to share similar sensibilities at any given time, as I pointed out in my "Doldrums in the Suburbs," *Journal of the Society of Architectural Historians, 24* (1965), 36–47, and *Perspecta, 9/10* (1965), 281–90; and in "American Architecture, 1945–1969: A Search for Principle between Two Wars," *Journal of the Royal Institute of British Architects, 76* (June 1969), 240–47. During the fifties and early sixties American architecture and architectural history alike came to be moved by a desire for monumental and heroic experiences, evident in the work of any number of architects from Philip Johnson to Louis I. Kahn and, to some extent, in my own preoccupation with Greek temples in landscape. During that period my insistence in this book upon the strength to be found in the vernacular, even consciously democratic, character of the Stick and Shingle styles sometimes seemed a bit naïve to me; but it does not seem so today. The new architects, too, have reacted against the aggressive idealism of the past decades, which now seems the father of so many of our contemporary ills. They, too, are reaching back into vernacular traditions and modest neighborhoods in order to fasten a grip on common humanity and objective reality once again. The most important of those architects, such as Charles Moore and Robert Venturi, have repeatedly acknowledged their debt to the Stick and Shingle styles, and their work is discussed in that connection in my *American Architecture and Urbanism,* noted above (see Figs. 162, 163, added to this edition). Venturi's book, *Complexity and Contradiction in Architecture* (New York, 1966), is still the best source through which to perceive the connection in intention and method between these two American ages— that of the later nineteenth century and our own. In that sense, as with Downing, we start again with a book in our hands.

Most recently, I have tried to assess the debt the present generation of architects owes to the Shingle Style, in my *The Shingle Style Today, or, The Historian's Revenge* (New York, 1974). Venturi still plays a major rôle, and his haunting Trubek and Wislocki houses on Nantucket, of 1971-72, seem at this time to culminate the development. Their debt to Wright and Price in particular, and to the nineteenth-century American vernacular in general, is more direct than ever. A tradition seems to be taking hold.

Index